Social Ties, Resources, and Migrant Labor Contention in Contemporary China

Social Ties, Resources, and Migrant Labor Contention in Contemporary China

From Peasants to Protesters

Jeffrey Becker

LEXINGTON BOOKS
Lanham • Boulder • New York • London

Published by Lexington Books
An imprint of The Rowman & Littlefield Publishing Group, Inc.
4501 Forbes Boulevard, Suite 200, Lanham, Maryland 20706
www.rowman.com

16 Carlisle Street, London W1D 3BT, United Kingdom

British Library Cataloguing in Publication Information Available

Library of Congress Cataloging-in-Publication Data

Becker, Jeffrey.
Social ties, resources, and migrant labor contention in contemporary China : from peasants to protesters / Jeffrey Becker.
pages cm
Includes bibliographical references and index.
ISBN 978-0-7391-9185-9 (cloth : alk. paper) -- ISBN 978-0-7391-9186-6 (electronic) 1. Migrant
labor--China. 2. Working class--China. 3. Demonstrations--China. I. Title.
HD5856.C6B43 2014
331.5'440951--dc23
2014017255

Printed in the United States of America

Contents

List of Figures and Tables

Chapter One

Understanding the Frequency and Form of Chinese Migrant Labor Protests

How have Chinese migrant workers (*nongmingong*) transformed themselves from the "wandering beggars" of the 1980s and 1990s into the "new urban citizens" that we see today: accepted, if still discriminated against, in urban Chinese society? How has this transformation affected the nature of their protests when facing exploitation in the workplace? What new protest options are available to Chinese migrant workers, and when and how do they choose from among these different options?

The answers to these questions have substantial implications for our understanding of China, as well as the comparative study of labor politics and protest in authoritarian regimes more broadly. China has been called the "global epicenter of labor unrest" (Friedman). With over 250 million migrant workers, it is in the midst of one of the largest rural-to-urban migrations in human history; a process affecting economic and political development throughout the country (Lardy 2012).

Many sources point to an increase in the number and types of migrant labor protests, both in the past few years and as a general trend over the last few decades.[1] At an individual level, migrant workers have become increasingly savvy in their dealings with employers. While still bargaining from a highly disadvantageous position, some workers actually succeed in advancing their claims through the use of innovative and creative strategies; taking advantage of cyclical shortages in the labor market to attain higher wages, or employing their knowledge of the labor law, or leveraging their understanding of their industry, to resolve disputes.[2]

1

China's migrant workers are also increasingly willing to bargain collectively through the use of strikes and protests. Although the Chinese government does not provide statistical data on the number of strikes, anecdotal evidence strongly suggests that migrant labor strikes have been generally increasing over the past three decades, with periodic bursts of strike activity.[3] One well publicized burst of strike activity occurred in 2010, when a strike wave in the automobile industry, which began in Nanhai District, Foshan City, Guangdong Province, spread to cities in the Yangtze River Deltas along China's east coast, as well as northern cities such as Tianjin and Dalian ("Recent Worker Actions in China" 2010).

More easily quantifiable has been the growth in use of the legal system, both among migrant workers and labor in China more broadly. In 2000, the total number of labor dispute cases entering the arbitration and court systems was just over 150,000. By 2012, that number had risen almost four-fold to just under 600,000, down from its decade high in 2008, when labor dispute arbitration and court cases rose to almost 700,000 cases nationwide (National Bureau of Statistics 2013).

Developed cities in the eastern third of the country have experienced the greatest share of these protests. According to Zhang Hengshun, the Legal Department Director of the Beijing All China Federation of Trade Unions (ACFTU), migrant labor cases accounted for roughly 70% of the 61,000 labor cases filed in Beijing in 2011, most of which dealt with unpaid wages ("Migrant Workers Make Up 70% of Labor Dispute Cases [Laodong Zhengyi Anjian Nongmingong Zhan Qicheng] 劳动争议案件农民工占七成" 2011). Guangdong Province, the heart of the Pearl River Delta and the destination for roughly 20% of all inter-provincial migration by 2011, was responsible for 16% of all labor arbitration and court cases nationwide that same year (National Bureau of Statistics 2013; National Bureau of Statistics 2012b).

When legal and other appeals fail, migrant workers may resort to violence, and violence as a protest strategy among migrant workers is not uncommon. Between 2011 and 2012, a string of violent clashes took place between migrant workers and police in Zhongshan, Zengcheng, and other cities in Guangdong Province, as workers protested unpaid wages and discriminatory treatment ("Chinese Police Crack Down on Guangdong Protesters" 2012). In addition, the Chinese press has, throughout the past decade, been filled with stories of violent clashes between workers and employers, as well as migrant worker suicides, self-immolations, and other forms of violent protests (Liu 2008; Feng and Lu 2008; Wang and Gao 2007; X. Li 2005; "Requesting Salary Rebuffed: A Nanjing Migrant Worker Has Hand Cut Off [Taoxin Bucheng: Nanjing Yi Nongmingongshou Bei Kanduan]" 2008).

Understanding this process by which peasants become workers and workers become protesters is essential to understanding the future of social movements in other developing states as well. As Vietnam, Bangladesh, Cambodia, and other countries in South and Southeast Asia follow China's path of economic development, opening their markets and relaxing restrictions on internal migration, workers have begun to react in ways very similar to China's migrant workers. Over the past few years, peasant-workers in Vietnam and Cambodia, newly introduced into the cities, have taken to the streets despite state mandated limitations on formal organization, threats of imprisonment, and repression (Montlake 2010; Thul 2010; Al-mahmood 2013; Devnath 2013). Like China's migrant workers, these workers have their roots in the countryside. Also like China's migrants, forces of urbanization are pushing them into the urban labor market, a phenomenon that has had substantial implications for labor relations within those countries.

Much ink has been spilled recently describing China's rural to urban transition (China Development Research Foundation 2013; Hsing 2012; Shen 2013; Miller 2012). Little is known, however, about how an emerging proletariat mobilizes resources for protest under authoritarianism. Existing theories of popular protest, derived from a tradition of scholarship based on research in western democracies, stress the importance of structural transformations and the role of formal organizations (McCarthy and Zald 1977). Yet attempts to organize formally in authoritarian states are often repressed (Opp and Gern 1993, 659). While labor unions in democratic countries serve as useful channels for interest articulation and worker representation, labor unions in authoritarian states are more often mechanisms of control rather than representation.

Previous studies of labor protest under authoritarianism leave a number of important gaps in our understanding. While we know much about the structural difficulties facing labor movements in this context—the limitations on formal organization and the restrictions on the free flow of information for example—less is known about the causal mechanisms that allow actors to overcome those obstacles, and to engage in the level of labor protest that we see in China today.

This book seeks to fill these gaps in our knowledge through an examination of both the historical process of Chinese labor migration over the past three decades, and the current situation of migrant labor protest in China today. Specifically, I develop an argument that first identifies the changes to migrants' environment that have provided new opportunities for protest, and second, examines how workers take advantage of those opportunities, despite the challenge of protesting under authoritarianism.

To summarize, China's move away from state controlled economic production in the early 1980s dramatically remade urban and rural economies, creating a new labor class which did not fit neatly into the traditional worker-peasant dichotomy. As farmers flocked to the cities, the retreat of the state from the workplace, replaced by an unregulated labor market, and provided conditions ripe for labor exploitation.

Conditions for migrant workers began to change in the early 2000s with the Hu Jintao regime's renewed focus on "disadvantaged groups (*ruoshi qunti*)." For migrant workers, this meant relaxing restrictions on their movement, recognizing their status as members of the working class, highlighting their contributions to economic development, and integrating them more closely into the existing labor protection regime. This policy shift had a profound effect on migrants' urban status, providing a new sense of legitimacy and greater legal protections, while increasing their mobility and decreasing state harassment. These changes expanded the space available for migrants to protest their exploitation; changing the environment in which labor protests occurred, increasing the number of protest options available, and modifying their expectations regarding the treatment they should receive at the workplace.

Yet as scholars of popular protest have noted, "changes in a system of institutionalized politics merely afford a potential challenger the opportunity for successful collective action" (McAdam 1999, ix). How have migrant workers taken advantage of these structural changes to engage in the level of protest that we see today?

China's great rural to urban migration dramatically reshaped the country's economy, and migrants' place in it. Simultaneously, this massive migration opened up new opportunities for workers to engage with others outside their traditional social circles. Research in the fields of sociology and social network theory has shown how actors rely on different types of networks to obtain different types of resources (Granovetter 1973; Granovetter 1983, 201). Some of these insights have already been applied to the study of the Chinese student protests in 1989 (Zuo and Benford 1995; Wright 2008) labor protests in other authoritarian regimes (Schock 2005; Ossa and Corduneanu-Huci 2003; Posusney 1997) and more recently, labor protest in China more broadly (Becker 2012; Shi and Cai 2006; Deng and O'Brien 2013).

Building on this scholarship, this book develops an argument that where opportunities for formal organization remain limited, protest can be facilitated through informal ties, which provide both material support and information. Traditional *rural ties* for example; defined here as relationships between family members and hometown associates, have often been a source of stability and material support for migrant workers (Perry 1994). In the chapters that follow, I show how such rural ties can support migrant labor protest by providing material support.

China scholars have long acknowledged that rural ties between family members or hometown associates help migrant workers find employment, housing, and navigate the challenges of urban society (P. Li 1996; Cao 2003). Evidence presented in this book however demonstrates that when seeking to engage in protest activities, information is critical, helping workers to learn new protest options, navigate formal institutions, connect with others sharing similar disputes, and identify additional resources. *Urban ties,* defined in this book as the links that develop between migrants with no prior connections before operating in the cities, serve as critical resources in this process, connecting otherwise disparate groups of workers, and expanding the overall body of knowledge upon which they can draw. Migrant workers with access to urban ties therefore have a more expansive repertoire of possible protest strategies from which they can draw, providing them with a greater capacity to engage in more and more varied types of protest. In contrast, individuals lacking such ties will be limited in their knowledge of possible protest options and strategies, limiting the frequency and forms of protest in which they engage.

THE STRUCTURE OF PROTEST OPPORTUNITIES IN AUTHORITARIAN REGIMES

One important avenue of research on labor protest in post-reform China has focused on changes to the structure of the Chinese economy. Research in this tradition has frequently employed a "structure of political opportunities" framework, derived from the broader social movement literature. Incorporating ideas developed from work on protest in western democracies by theorists such as Peter Esinger, Charles Tilly, and Sydney Tarrow, these models deal primarily with how actors' behavior is influenced by the political context or political structure, in which choices are made (Tarrow 2011, 76–77; Meyer 2004, 128).

This model's flexibility has helped shed light on how opportunities for labor protest have changed over time and across regions, particularly as economic reform and opening (*gaige kaifang*) transformed the nation's economic landscape. In one of the first in-depth, English-language studies to focus exclusively on migrant labor, Dorothy Solinger showed how the introduction of market forces laid the foundation for the creation of the migrant labor class that we see today (Solinger 1999). Looking at labor protest generally, Zhou Xuegang argued that a unified structure of state socialism in post-1989 China created uniformity in workers' responses to grievances (Zhou 1993, 58). As China's regional economies have become more diverse, William Hurst examined how these differences created variations in workers' approach to protest (Hurst 2004).

As a framework, political opportunity structures have also helped China scholars identify how new economic change created motivations for labor protest by exacerbating labor grievances. The uncertainty and volatility accompanying China's integration into the global economy created new problems for the nation's workforce,.as Chinese workers became subject to an increasingly mobile form of international capital (Gallagher 2007a; C. K.-C. Chan 2010). Research by Anita Chan, Ching Kwan Lee, and others has documented this exploitation, as well as workers' responses in the form of violence, strikes, and appeals to the legal system (A. Chan 2001; Lee 2007). Working explicitly in the tradition of James Scott's "moral economy" (Scott 1976) Chen Feng argued that SOE workers' protest are often the result of substance level crises and outrage over corrupt management practices (Chen 2000).

SETTING THE STAGE FOR PROTEST: CHANGES IN THE STRUCTURE OF OPPORTUNITIES FOR MIGRANTS

Structural analyses of China's changing economy and society have much to tell us about the rise in migrant labor protests. The past two decades in China have witnessed a rural to urban migration more extensive than any in modern history. At the PRC's founding in 1949, 11% of the nation's population lived in the cities. Failed economic and social policies such as the Great Leap Forward and the Cultural Revolution slowed urbanization for decades, such that forty-one years later, urban citizens still made up just 20% of the population. Yet over the past two decades, China's urban population has exploded. For the first time in 2011, urban citizens surpassed the rural population, with over 51% (over 690 million) living in cities (National Bureau of Statistics 2012a).

In the early years of economic reforms, migrant workers were considered by urban citizens to be part of a "floating population" (*liudong renkou*). Known as "wandering vagrants" (*mangliu*), they had a reputation for stealing, begging, and generally disrupting a well-functioning urban society (Solinger 1999). This perception, however, is changing. While still discriminated against by government policies restricting access to social welfare benefits and education opportunities for their children, migrants increasingly view themselves not as outsiders or interlopers, but as "new urban citizens" (*xinshimin*); a confident group that has contributed much to China's development.

How did this transformation come about? The introduction of market reforms in the 1980s provided opportunities for peasants to leave the land in search of higher wages in urban areas, while legal labor protections in the early and mid-1990s provided new channels for workers to protest through the courts. The 1995 *National Labor Law*, the first comprehensive labor law in the nation's history, removed many of the differences between workers in the private and the state sector ("Labor Law of the People's Republic of China" 2002; Gallagher and Jiang 2002).[4]

Despite these legal advancements for workers more broadly, migrants' ambiguous classification in the cities, in which they were not considered to be members of the working class, made this system largely inaccessible. Thus, while changes to the structure of migrants' political opportunities created more space for protest activity, access to formal institutions such as labor arbitration or the courts remained limited.

Beginning in 2003 however, the central government began a series of reforms designed to increase migrant inclusion under the umbrella of this emerging labor protection regime. To be sure, implementation of these reforms has been mixed. Migrants still lack access to unemployment benefits and education subsidies enjoyed by their urban counterparts. They still face discrimination in the cities from government actors and society at large. However, these changes were crucial to expanding the space for migrants to protest their exploitation, changing the environment in which labor protests occurred, the dispute options that were available, the subjective understanding of their rights as members of the working class, and their expectations regarding their treatment at the workplace. In the first section of this book, I explore the historical process by which China's migrant workers were transformed from wandering vagrants to new urban citizens, and how this transformation helped create the level of migrant labor protest we see today.

TAKING ADVANTAGE OF OPPORTUNITIES — AGENCY UNDER AUTHORITARIANISM

While structural approaches have done much to improve our understanding of labor protest in China, including migrant labor protest, structural arguments alone cannot explain the variation in protest activity that we see occurring within the same locale. In 2010 alone for example, strikes raged in Honda factories across the Pearl River Delta. Yet in Foxconn, a Taiwanese owned electronics factory employing approximately 420,000 workers in Shenzhen, workers made less than those in the Honda factories, yet strikes were largely absent. Instead, Foxconn was rocked by a rash of worker suicides (J. Chan and Pun 2010). Meanwhile, over 50,000 workers in Shenzhen, a city with a majority migrant population, made appeals to labor arbitration and the courts (J. Chan and Pun 2010). Still many more migrants choose not to act despite suffering significant labor grievances.

This within-region variation suggests the necessity of integrating agent centric variables into our understanding of migrant protest in contemporary China. A greater focus on agency will shed light on *why* some workers within the same region are able to take advantage of emerging opportunities for protest while others are not, *how* those workers choose from among the various protest strategies available, and *when* those choices are made during the process of workers' efforts to resolve their grievances.

Changes to the structure of political opportunities may shed light on new openings for protest, yet taking advantage of these new openings requires actors to locate, mobilize, and utilize resources. This is a key tenant of resource mobilization (RM) theory, an approach to social movements focusing on the actors involved rather than the structures in which they operate (McCarthy, McAdam, and Zald 1996, 3–4). Like political opportunity structure approaches, RM theory also has its roots in the study of protest in liberal, western democracies. For actors in authoritarian regimes however, the challenges workers face when seeking to mobilize resources for protest vary substantially from the western, democratic context in which these ideas were first conceived and applied (Ossa and Corduneanu-Huci 2003). Table 1.1 illustrates these differences.

First, establishing formal organizations for the purpose of protest is not without difficulty in liberal democracies, but the process can be much more challenging under authoritarian regimes, where the state often prohibits independent organizing among politically sensitive groups such as labor. By limiting actors' access to these "coordination goods," authoritarian regimes seek to avoid what scholars have more recently referred to as "the growth trap," the idea that economic growth leads to democratic reform (Bueno de Mesquita and Downs 2005, 77).

Second, civil rights and protections in democracies are more likely to be enforced, while protections for dissenting voices in authoritarian states are restricted, and often ignored in practice. Though exclusionary institutions certainly exist in democracies, U.S. segregation laws throughout the early and mid-20th century are but one example, democratic societies with independent legal and judicial institutions are more likely to provide opportunities for groups to challenge their exclusion (Sarat and Scheingold 2006). In contrast, authoritarian states may provide citizens with legal channels to resolve specific grievances, but the right to formally challenge the exclusion-

Table 1.1. Political Opportunity Structures in Democracies and Authoritarian States

Characteristic Difference	Democracy	Authoritarianism
Opportunities for Formal Organization	Available	Restricted
Institutional Exclusion	Challengeable	Unassailable
Capacity of Legal Institutions	Responsive	Unresponsive
Informational Access	Open	Limited

ary institutions at the heart of those grievances is denied. There is a large body of literature for example, which examines how China has made use of a "rule by law" system to allow citizens to address grievances, while simultaneously denying them the right to demand institutional change (Nathan 2003; O'Brien and Li 2004). For example, Chinese migrant workers are increasingly using the courts to demand redress for unpaid wages, labor injuries, and other benefits, yet the household registration system, the institutional source for many of China's discriminatory labor practices, remains unassailable through legal means.

Third, many authoritarian regimes are experiencing what scholars refer to as "legal systems in transition" (Carothers 2006, 5–7). For China this system has been particularly effective in providing predictability and transparency to the economic sector, helping attract foreign investment and promote growth (Gallagher 2007a). For Chinese migrant workers however, access to such "transitory legal institutions" are restricted; hampered by long delays, financial costs, or significant knowledge requirements for individuals attempting to use this system. Thus, while formal institutional channels are available, their limitations and inefficiencies create problems of access that are more intense than those found in states with more mature legal institutions.

Fourth, constraints on media freedoms and the free flow of information in authoritarian regimes can limit opportunities for action. Kurt Schock for example notes how the use of phone calls, direct mailings, and a free press can help spread knowledge of protest activities in democracies. Yet in authoritarian regimes, similar information flows are constrained (Schock 2005, 28). In addition, Steven Pfaff has demonstrated how low levels of trust in authoritarian societies provide incentives for actors to discount general information sources, relying instead on smaller networks, and thus limiting their access to information (Pfaff 1996).

Faced with these conditions, how do migrant workers in China mobilize the resources necessary for action? There is a growing body of research that demonstrates how informal organizations can help facilitate labor protest under authoritarianism (Ossa and Corduneanu-Huci 2003; Posusney 1997, 151–155). Yet with a handful of notable exceptions (C. K.-C. Chan and Ngai 2009), research on the role of informal organizations among Chinese migrant workers has concentrated not on their capacity to facilitate protest, but on their ability to resolve the challenges of rural to urban migration, such as identifying employment or housing opportunities (Xiang 2005).

Below, I provide an argument that demonstrates how informal organizations can help migrants overcome these obstacles to protest, helping them acquire the resources necessary to take action. First, I examine the types of resources most useful to migrant workers seeking to engage in protest activity, focusing particularly on the role of information. Second, I examine the ways migrant workers can acquire information that helps to facilitate protest activity through *urban ties*; the links that develop between migrants with no prior connections when operating in the cities.

MOBILIZING RESOURCES FOR PROTEST: THE UTILITY OF INFORMATION

Taking advantage of emerging protest opportunities requires that migrant workers are somehow able to mobilize the resources necessary for protest. Access to material aid for example can help workers pay for food and housing, thus expanding the window of opportunity for protests before economic necessity forces them to return home or find another job. Material support can also help pay costs associated with the legal system, including travel between government agencies, and the costs of preparing paperwork. In the west, such material support may be provided through formal organizations. Union-established reserve funds for example help members pay for daily needs during strikes, while non-profits and legal aid centers provide free legal services.

In China however, as in other authoritarian states, channels for obtaining material support are limited. The government maintains restrictions on the ability of workers to organize outside the purview of the state. While government established legal aid centers can provide legal services, these are often difficult for many workers to access. Instead, I argue that migrant workers in China often rely on informal ties, particularly family members and hometown associates, to obtain material support.

As noted above, there is a large body of literature which examines how migrant workers rely on family members for financial support, and the chapters that follow suggest these sources can provide material support to facilitate labor protest as well. Less well understood, however, is the role information can play in facilitating protest. Below, I show how access to information facilitates migrant labor protest in four key ways: helping workers learn new protest options and strategies, navigate legal institutions, connect with others sharing similar disputes, and identify additional resources.

Information helps workers gain access to others who have direct knowledge and experience with certain protest strategies, thus providing new protest options and expanding migrant workers' "repertoires of contention" (Tarrow 2011, 30). As Charles Tilly describes; "at any point in time, the repertoire of collective actions available to a population is surprisingly limited" (Tilly 1978, 151–152). While most Americans may know how to take part in mass marches or speechmaking, few individuals know how to engage in a well organized labor strike, organize a boycott, or hijack a government website, despite the publicity these actions receive in the media (Tilly 1978, 152).

Possible options for protest available to Chinese migrant workers are circumscribed in a similar manner, in that some forms of action may be known to some groups of migrants, but not others. Migrants who have never attempted to informally negotiate a labor dispute with an employer may not know how to negotiate in the "shadow of the law," or how to take advantage of their knowledge of the industry or company, to increase their chances of success. Strikes or other public demonstrations may seem straightforward, but knowing when and where to engage in such activities to maximize the likelihood of success is not common knowledge. In such situations, interactions with migrant workers who have had experience conducting these types of activities can help them learn and employ new protest strategies. A worker who has gone through labor arbitration, for example, can teach others about the types of evidence they need and how to go about obtaining it, or how to obtain leverage when negotiating with one's employer. As the following chapters illustrate, such interactions can help workers learn and employ new protest strategies.

Like many states struggling to develop legal institutions, legal channels for labor dispute resolution in China place significant information requirements on individuals seeking to use these channels. Reform of China's labor legislation began in earnest in the early 1990s, with the *1993 PRC Regulations for the Handling of Enterprise Disputes*, followed by the *1995 Labor Law*. While more recent reforms, such as the *2008 Labor Contract Law* and the 2013 revisions to that law have made great strides codifying legal protections, China's legal labor system remains a "legal system in transition," as the government continues to simplify proceedings, while seeking to strengthen the professionalism of local labor bureau officials, arbitration personnel, and judges.

In countries with long established, well-functioning legal institutions, individuals may have a reasonable expectation of obtaining valid information from government and agency representatives regarding how to navigate the legal system, thus relaxing the knowledge requirement on those seeking to take action. One need not be an expert in the labor law if the dispute process is clear, and relevant government institutions can provide useful procedural advice. In states with immature legal institutions however, "laws benefiting the poor exist on paper but not in practice unless the poor or their allies push for the law's enforcement" (Golub 2006, 161).

Where legal procedures are still in the developmental stages such as China, the process for using them is more complicated. Legally, migrant workers have access to labor arbitration procedures, but because millions of migrants continue to work without labor contracts, they must first verify their "factual labor relationship" (*shishi laodong guanxi*) before applying. Regulations have made it possible to do so by providing pay stubs, ID cards, or other types of evidence, but the process remains vague to many migrants who are unaware of their legal rights under this process (Dong and Dong 2007, 614).

Many local labor bureaus and labor arbitration offices are also under-funded and understaffed, and personnel working in those offices often receive only limited legal training, leading them to provide misleading advice. When applying for labor arbitration in Beijing for example, one construction worker was told he needed to go to Sichuan where the company was registered (Beijing Migrant Worker Legal Aid Station). Another worker I interviewed was under the impression he had to return home to apply for arbitration ("Interview Beijing 0112" 2007). A group of workers in Changzhou, Jiangsu Province, went to three different labor bureaus, and were told each time that none had jurisdiction over their dispute ("Interview Changzhou 0705" 2008). In each case, the information workers received was erroneous.

Simultaneously, the complex nature of many migrant labor cases, coupled with their often politically sensitive nature and low probability of success, means that lawyers in China are unlikely to take these cases, and will even attempt to convince workers from taking any action at all (Michelson 2006). In short, China's legal system places significant information requirements on those seeking to use it, and under such conditions it becomes necessary to become one's own "legal expert."

Knowledge of the disputes faced by other migrant workers can also help foster a sense of shared grievances, turning once individual disputes into collective actions. In their study of contentious protests among Romanian coal miners, Osa and Corduneau-Huci noted the use of "overlapping social, occupational, and residential, networks to mobilize mine workers for an extensive strike. This occurred in the *absence* of media access, so the distribution of information (and other resources) had to occur within social networks" (Ossa and Corduneanu-Huci 2003, 620) (emphasis in the original).

This type of information sharing can facilitate protest among China's migrant population as well. Factory or construction site dormitories often act as mechanisms of labor control (C. K.-C. Chan and Ngai 2009, 291) yet these living arrangements can also provide a means of facilitating grievance sharing, coordination, and cooperation. In addition, many migrant workers are aware that larger protests receive more attention, and the idea of "strength in numbers" (*renduo liliang da*) is a common refrain. As a worker in Shenzhen told me, "if you cause enough trouble (*naoda*), the authorities will have to deal with you. If you don't, they won't have to come resolve your dispute" ("Interview Shenzhen 0320" 2008).

Grievance pooling however is not automatic. Just as migrants are not guaranteed access to legal institutions simply because they have disputes, individuals do not automatically become aware of other workers' grievances simply because they work at the same factory. The insular nature of migrant worker social interactions often increases the time it takes before grievances become public knowledge, allowing workers to engage in the level of organization necessary for action.

Access to information may also help migrants connect with one of a growing number of migrant labor NGOs, or individuals possessing knowledge of the labor law but lacking formal credentials, referred to as "barefoot lawyers," "citizen surrogate lawyers," or "public interest representatives" (*gongmin dailiren*). Legal empowerment research in the west frequently highlights the importance of "nonprofessional" resources such as paralegals, law students, or experienced laypersons in providing legal advice (Golub 2006, 169–174). In China, such sources of support have increased in recent years, particularly in regions with large migrant populations. However, gaining access to many of these organizations may not be straightforward, as state constraints on organizational activities limit their ability to connect with workers, and many migrants remain suspicious of the true intentions of unknown organizations.

State provided legal services are often poorly equipped to provide migrant workers the specialized services they require. Some cities require local law firms to provide pro bono work by staffing legal aid centers, meaning it is not uncommon for government affiliated centers to be staffed with personnel not particularly motivated toward providing aid in the first place (Liebman 1999, 228). Not all government legal aid centers offer specialized aid for labor disputes, and personnel may not be knowledgeable about the labor law, or have the time necessary to allot to migrant cases, which can be time consuming and complex. Migrants may be referred to the local labor bureau, yet this creates additional problems. Discriminatory and unresponsive personnel, a lack of legal knowledge, and local government protectionism, which views migrants' issues as problems to be resolved by their home locales, all make use of the legal system by individual, unsupported migrant workers a difficult prospect (Gallagher 2007b, 202–3).

Oftentimes, more useful to migrant workers than state-run legal aid centers are one of a growing number of social organizations focusing specifically on the problems of migrant labor. Unregistered migrant labor NGOs have mushroomed in recent years, particularly in areas with large migrant populations such as Beijing, Shanghai, and cities in the Pearl River Delta such as Shenzhen, Dongguan, and Guangzhou. While they vary considerably in size, organizational structure, and legality, many share a number of similar characteristics. Many are founded by former migrants motivated by the past exploitation they experienced firsthand, and are thus more ideologically predisposed to expending the necessary effort to resolve complex, time consuming cases. Personnel in these organizations often have a better understanding of the labor law as it pertains to common cases experienced by migrant labor.

Legal channels for labor dispute resolution may have become more accessible to migrants in recent years, but the likelihood of navigating this system is greatly improved by obtaining legal aid, and even more so by obtaining specialized legal aid from an organization focused specifically on helping migrant workers. These organizations help migrants navigate the legal system, and can even provide new strategies for action. They promote legal rights consciousness, and may also promote the collectivization of labor disputes. Gaining access to these organizations may be difficult however, as many occupy a legal gray area, and rarely have the resources to promote their activities (Cheng, Ngok, and Zhuang 2010; The Politics and Law Committee of Guangdong Province 2009).

The Role of Urban Ties in Migrant Labor Protest

Access to information can be the critical difference between migrant workers who take action to protest their exploitation and those who do not. By helping migrants learn new protest options and strategies, navigate legal institutions, connect with others sharing similar disputes, and identify additional resources, information can also shape the nature of protest activity as well. Yet if information can facilitate protest activity, how then do migrants gain access to such information?

Research into the ways informal organization facilitates protest in authoritarian states has grown in recent years, and this approach is gaining attention from scholars of Chinese protest as well (Wright 2008; Zuo and Benford 1995; Deng and O'Brien 2013; Shi and Cai 2006). Moreover, there is a large body of literature in sociology, which examines the role of interpersonal ties—connections between individuals—which can shed light on the relationship between urban ties and migrant protest. This relationship between interpersonal ties and information dissemination has been articulated most clearly by the sociologist Mark Granovetter, who found substantial variation in the ways different types of social ties behave. According to Granovetter's research, "strong ties," defined as relationships between individuals involving high time commitments or strong emotional attachments, such as those between relatives, are often a good source of material support. However, Granovetter found that these relationships are not especially useful as sources of information. This is because the similarities in background, experiences, and information that strongly tied individuals share, and the frequency with which individuals connected by strong ties interact, make it highly unlikely that individuals connected by strong ties will be able to provide knowledge not already known to the group without going outside that network of strong tie relations (Granovetter 1973, 1364).

In contrast, work by Granovetter and other sociologists have found that interactions between "weak ties," such as work colleagues and acquaintances with little prior interaction, are more likely to provide new information. Where strong ties are fully enmeshed within a network, weak ties act as a bridge between networks, linking together individuals, who, absent that bridge, have little if any contact (Granovetter 1983). As a bridge connecting different groups, weak ties can be useful conduits for information. Thus, individuals with access to weak ties will have access to a greater number of channels through which new information may be provided (see figure 1.1).

Granovetter articulated this finding most clearly in "The Strength of Weak Ties: A Network Theory Revisited":

> It follows, then, that individuals with few weak ties will be deprived of information from distant parts of the social system and will be confined to the provincial news and views of their close friends.

> Furthermore, such individuals may be difficult to organize or integrate into political movements of any kind, since membership in movements or goal-oriented organizations typically results from being recruited by friends. While members of one or two cliques may be efficiently recruited, the problem is that, without weak ties, any momentum generated in this way does not spread beyond the clique. (Granovetter 1983, 202)

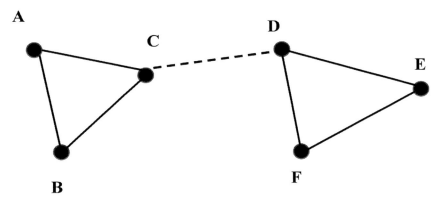

Figure 1.1.   A "Weak Tie" Between Individuals C and D Acts as a Bridge, Connecting Two Otherwise Disparate Groups of Individuals (A-B-C and D-E-F)

This insight into the roles that different types of interpersonal ties play in the dissemination of information has had a profound effect on the study of social network theory, with Granovetter's original *American Journal of Sociology* article becoming one of the most widely cited works in the field. The concept has been applied to research on the study of job searches, the spread of ideas, cultural diffusion, and many other social phenomena where information access and information searches are critical.[5]

Given the widespread application of social network theory, and its growing application to the study of popular protest and contentious protest, there is reason to believe these findings may have implications for the study of Chinese migrant labor protest as well. The migrant labor community has a reputation for remaining isolated from larger society, even after moving to the cities. Previous research has focused on the development of migrant labor neighborhoods sprouting up in major cities, with names like "Zhejiang town," or "Hebei town" (Piante and Zhu 1995; J. Zhang 2012). Even within these neighborhoods, research has shown that decades of state and social predation has provided incentives for migrants newly arrived to urban areas to rely on "trusted" individuals; family members or others with whom they have a history of interactions (L. Zhang 2001; Lu and Song 2006). To the extent migrant workers in urban China do remain isolated; "strangers in the city" relying primarily on family members or hometown associates, they may, as Granovetter found, be "deprived of information from distant parts of the social system," and "confined to the provincial news and views of their close friends" (Granovetter 1983, 202).

This is not to suggest that Chinese migrant workers do not reach out when trying to resolve a labor dispute. As I show in the chapters below, migrant workers cast a wide net when originally searching for information helping them to act. However, I also show that those who rely exclusively on rural ties will be less successful in obtaining new and useful information, which could expand their available strategies for action. Information that is useful in helping migrant workers bargain with employers or navigate China's labor arbitration system is relatively esoteric, with only a small percentage of the migrant labor population having experience in these matters. As social network theory argues, the more esoteric the information, the more useful it becomes to expand one's information search to include more individuals, helping to increase the likelihood of finding someone with access to this information.

My conversation with a group of construction workers in Beijing seems to fit this description of social interactions. I spoke with a small group of five migrant construction workers who had all come from the same village in Xin County in Henan Province, and had all been working on a building project in the *laojuntang* neighborhood in Beijing, on the east side of the city between the fourth and fifth ring roads. After working for three months without a contract, the group was finally paid, but were given only half their agreed upon salary of 1000 RMB per month. When asked how they might resolve a nonpayment issue, one worker stated he had no time to read newspapers, and television was "useless" (*meiyouyong*). When asked if there was anyone who could provide advice on how to proceed, he responded "no, we are all from the same hometown, we all work as migrants" ("Interview Beijing 0119" 2007). With no connections to individuals outside this network, workers in this group were limited in their knowledge of potential responses to what was already available within the group.

Yet as an increasingly large and important component of the labor class, migrant workers are gaining more and more opportunities to break out from these traditional social circles. It thus makes sense to examine whether new connections that are created during this process of social integration are useful in facilitating information sharing among Chinese migrant workers, much as they have been found to be useful for information sharing in other contexts.

Building on this insight, this book provides evidence that examines how such urban ties act as bridges between otherwise disconnected groups of migrant workers. It develops new arguments which show how access to *urban ties*, individuals with whom migrant workers develop connections while operating in the cities, can act as conduits for knowledge, helping them obtain information that facilitates protest. Workers with access to urban ties are thus more likely to engage in protest.

The chapters that follow also provide insight into when and under what conditions migrants engage in different types of protest activity, including informal negotiation, use of legal channels such as labor arbitration or the courts, or violence. Moreover, as described in the following chapters, violent protest often occurs when alternatives are limited, and information derived from urban ties can increase the number of available protest options, providing workers with knowledge of informal bargaining strategies, helping them navigate the legal system, or locating support to do both. In short, increasing their knowledge of alternative protest options can help workers avoid more costly, violent strategies.

CASE SELECTION, RESEARCH DESIGN, AND DATA COLLECTION

To test this argument regarding the impact of migrant workers' social ties on protest activity, it was necessary to identify a large migrant labor population with access to a variety of protest strategies. To that end, I selected three regions, spending thirteen months in Beijing, the Pearl River Delta (including Shenzhen, Guangzhou, and Dongguan), and the Yangtze River Delta region (including Nanjing and Changzhou). For roughly a year I traveled through these regions interviewing aggrieved migrant workers about their disputes and what, if anything, they did to resolve them.

All three regions have large migrant populations; together they comprise a significant portion of the total migrant population nationwide, making them important areas for any national study on migrant labor protest. Despite its small population relative to other provincial level political units, Beijing is home to approximately 3% of China's migrants. The Yangtze River Delta region of Jiangsu and Zhejiang Province (including Shanghai), and the Pearl River Delta region in Guangdong Province, contain approximately 23% and 20% of this population respectively (National Bureau of Statistics 2012b).

All three regions also have high levels of legal institutionalization, and are home to a large percentage of the total number of labor dispute cases entering the labor arbitration and court system nationwide. As shown in table 1.2, over one third of the total number of labor cases, laborers involved, and laborers involved in collective disputes occurred in these regions, as well as one fifth of the nation's total collective labor cases (National Bureau of Statistics 2013). Thus, while China's legal system is still a work in progress, migrants in these regions have access to and attempt to use legal channels that may not be available to migrant workers in other regions.

These three regions are similar in that they all possess large migrant labor populations and advanced legal development. They vary significantly however in the nature of their economic and social development. Beijing for example is well known for employing a large percentage of its migrant workforce in the construction and service industries, while Guangzhou is commonly referred to as China's manufacturing heartland. Employment of the migrant worker population in the Yangtze River Delta region is mixed, with migrants in Nanjing and Changzhou employed primarily in the manufacturing and service industries (Labor Injury Office of the Nanjing Municipal Human Resource and Social Security Bureau 2011). Moreover, many of the nation's specialized migrant labor organizations are located in Beijing and the Pearl River Delta, especially Shenzhen, Guangzhou, and Dongguan. Similar organizations in the Yangtze River Delta, while increasing, are less common.

While migrant labor protests have climbed dramatically in recent years, migrant workers engaging in protest remain a small fraction of all exploited migrant labor, and relying on random selection from a population of aggrieved migrants would likely identify few individuals who took action. To ensure I was able to talk to migrant workers who had indeed engaged in protest, while still developing a dataset that could claim to be representative, I collected data on two groups of migrant workers: those who I was sure had engaged in protest, and those who may or may not have acted. Respondents

Table 1.2. Labor Cases in Selected Field Sites as a Percentage of National Totals 2012

Region	Labor Dispute Cases	Laborers Involved	Collective Labor Cases	Laborers in Collective Disputes
Beijing	10%	7%	6%	6%
Jiangsu	9%	8%	3%	4%
Guangdong	16%	18%	11%	26%
Total	**35%**	**33%**	**20%**	**36%**

Source:(National Bureau of Statistics 2013)

in the first group were identified through cooperation with labor arbitration offices, legal aid centers, and NGOs of various sizes and registration status.[6] With their help, I distributed a fixed questionnaire used to collect data on the composition of available social ties, views of media and government institutions, and basic socioeconomic data such as age, income, and education.[7] I refer to these interviews throughout the book as *Strata I*.

This book also uses a second dataset derived from in-depth, open ended interviews with randomly selected migrant workers who experienced labor grievances. As a result of the rise in population mobility and internal migration over the past two decades, traditional methods used to survey the migrant population in China have become increasingly unreliable. While all urban residents are still expected to register with local neighborhood committees, official population lists omit large numbers of short term, unregistered migrant workers. Migrants that do register are on average more educated, affluent, and have more stable employment.

Other sampling strategies, such as identifying migrants through their worksite, would create incentives to answer questions untruthfully, or not participate in the project at all. To get around these challenges, I followed a two-step process. First, I relied on local press reports, Chinese academics, and local research assistants to create a list of potential "working class neighborhoods," within each selected city. These neighborhoods were largely located in suburban and peri-urban areas with high proportions of migrant labor. Second, I selected neighborhoods from this list and conducted initial evaluation visits, identifying locations conducive to approaching potential respondents.

While neighborhoods were randomly selected, the selection of specific field sites within those neighborhoods was purposeful. Interviewing in the middle of an open market for example would have drawn the attention of a crowd, local employers, and local authorities, making data collection impossible. Instead, I approached workers on entrances to nearby public gathering places such as markets or local food stalls, or within industrial zones, yet outside the factory gates and away from unwanted public attention. Once I identified a qualified worker who agreed to be interviewed, we arranged to conduct the interview at a more private location, such as the respondent's home. I worked primarily in the late afternoon and early evenings from 4 to 8 pm, to engage the majority of workers on a normal day shift, changing times periodically to interview workers who may be working the night shift. Each field site was visited an average of five times. In total, I collected a wealth of data on 102 individuals using this sampling process, which I refer to throughout the book as *Strata II*, and data on 180 individuals from the first process described above (*Strata I*).

Combining purposeful and random sampling is an unconventional technique, yet necessary to examine a highly mobile population in a state where accurate census data is unavailable. Moreover, as I show in chapter 5, the basic socio-economic characteristics of the workers interviewed for this book, such as age, education, or income, are similar regardless of which strata they were derived from; whether they were identified through coopera-tion with one of the migrant labor organizations (*Strata I*) or through the sampling strategy described above (*Strata II*), suggesting these two groups are indeed comparable.

BOOK SUMMARY AND OVERVIEW

The remainder of this book proceeds as follows. In chapter 2, I describe what it means to be a "migrant worker" in China, examining the growth of the Chinese migrant labor population over the past three decades. Chapter 2 also examines common grievances those migrants face today, as well as the dif-ferent types of protest strategies they employ when seeking to resolve those grievances. Specifically, I provide a spectrum upon which I place different protest strategies, defining core migrant labor protest actions in terms of informal bargaining, legal action, strikes and mass protests, and violent protest.

Chapter 3 examines the past three decades of economic, social, and politi-cal changes in China which have facilitated migrant workers' transition from social outcasts with no place in urban society, to new urban citizens. In chapter 3, I investigate these changes, which have created the space for migrant workers in urban society to engage in the larger, more varied and more frequent protests seen today.

While migrants' social standing has greatly improved over the past three decades, state and market forces, such as the denial of organizational capac-ity, a system of institutional exclusions, and limited access to information, continue to create challenges to migrant workers seeking to protest labor exploitation. These forces create challenges for migrants seeking to resolve labor disputes, particularly when seeking to do so through legal channels, administrative measures, and government monitoring and legal enforcement. Chapter 4 examines the challenges to institutionalizing migrant labor dispute resolution through these processes.

Chapters 5 and 6 demonstrate how migrant workers rely on informal ties to obtain resources necessary for protest activity, how different ties provide different resources, and how information derived from urban ties can be critical to facilitating protest activity. Chapter 5 employs statistical analysis to investigate how different social ties affect protest activity through a series of logistic regression models, demonstrating how information from urban ties facilitates protest activity in general and nonviolent protest specifically. Chapter 6 sheds light on the causal mechanisms behind these relationships through a series of cases selected from my interviews with migrant workers. Each case illustrates how urban ties help workers identify new dispute options and strategies, facilitate collective action, navigate the legal system, and identify new sources of support.

Chapter 7 examines the role of "information communication technology" (ICT) in Chinese labor protests, focusing particularly on its impact during the spring 2010 automobile strikes. Interest in the influence of new technology on popular protest has increased substantially in the past few years, particularly in the wake of the revolutions in the Middle East (the 'Arab Spring'), and the twitter revolution in Iran. Chapter 7 explores the precise nature of technology's role in Chinese migrant labor protests, examining the benefits and limitations of ICT in its ability to support labor protest in an authoritarian state.

In chapter 8 I examine the impact of Chinese migrant labor NGOs, unregistered citizen lawyers, and other labor activists on migrant labor protest activity. Relying on conversations with NGO representatives, grassroots organizations, and migrant labor rights activists, I show how these actors can help workers better navigate the legal system, bargain more effectively with employers, or even conduct unlawful protest activities in ways that are more likely to achieve success. In chapter 9, I conclude by looking at some of the implications of this book's findings; for China as well as for other authoritarian states undergoing similar economic and social transformations.

NOTES

1. This book employs a broad definition of labor protest, to include both individual and collective appeals to state-sanctioned institutions such as labor mediation, arbitration, or the courts, collective actions such as strikes and public demonstrations, informal bargaining with employers, as well the use of violence. Each of these types of protest is described in detail in chapter 2.

2. Examples of migrant workers engaging in such behavior are provided in chapter 6.

3. Growth in the number of strikes in China over this time is described in detail in chapter 2.

4. The law was adopted by the Standing Committee of the Eighth National People's Congress on July 5, 1994, becoming effective January 1, 1995.

5. See, "The Strength of Weak Ties: A Network Theory Revisited" (Granovetter 1983) for a brief summary of some of this work.

6. The status of these organizations ranged from "Officially registered as an association with the Ministry of Civil Affairs," "Official registered as a business with the Ministry of Commerce," and "Unregistered."

7. Appendix A contains an English copy of the questionnaire.

Chapter Two

The Current Condition of Migrant Labor in China: Common Disputes and Strategies for Action

In the spring of 2011, with canisters of gasoline and lighters in hand, Mr. Li and some of his fellow workers threatened to set fire to their Shenzhen factory's warehouse if their boss did not release the groups' employment contracts and physical examination records. Mr. Li and his colleagues hoped to prove that they had been poisoned while handling industrial chemicals at the factory, and these documents were needed to move forward with a labor arbitration case. While this threat of arson succeeded, even after obtaining his records, Mr. Li could not navigate the arbitration process. He spent three months, only to be dismissed by the official behind the counter at the local labor bureau:

> The [expletive] government kicked me around like a ping-pong ball. The labor bureau is a lion in the way [they act] against workers' from getting their rights. The officials never tell you all the documents you need to present. Today they say you need this. Tomorrow they say you need that.

Facing defeat, Mr. Li decided to employ the same violent strategies that had gotten him this far.

> There was a small [expletive] in the bureau responsible for filing cases. I first spoke nicely to him. He said: are you blind? Cannot you see your occupational disease verification is wrong? I waited outside until that [expletive] was off from work. I approached him. I told other colleagues to hold on and watch my back. He said: what are you doing? I said I wanted to apologize. I wanted to treat him to dinner. He said: I am busy. I said: you are busy, but I spend nearly

three months to file my case and realize my rights. Please give me a favor.
That guy said: what if I don't. I said we would kill your child. [1]

Workers often turn to violence strategies such as this after being stymied by
the courts. One worker I interviewed who was injured on a construction site
in Beijing first visited the local labor arbitration bureau, but:

> [I] couldn't find out what to do, and didn't know the company's official name,
> or how to contact the boss. There was no way. In the end we wasted three
> months, so we [this worker and a group of fellow villagers] went back to the
> site looking to fight ("Interview Beijing 0111" 2007).

Yet not all workers choose violence. As described in chapter 1, according to
the ACFTU's legal department director in Beijing, migrant workers are responsible for roughly 70% of all labor arbitration cases in that city, suggesting a significant number of migrant workers are indeed using the legal system. In Shenzhen, a city made up primarily of migrants, 50,000 workers used
labor arbitration and the courts in 2010 (J. Chan and Pun 2010). In Guangzhou, another city with a large migrant labor population, the number of labor
dispute cases have increased almost 100 times, from just over 434 cases in
1993, the year China promulgated the *PRC Regulations for the Handling of
Enterprise Labor Disputes* (HELDR), to over 40,000 cases in 2011 (Statistics
Bureau of the Municipal Government of Guangzhou various years). Still
other workers avoid using either violence or the legal system, instead employing skillful and inventive means to individually bargain with their employers directly, or engage in strikes or other non-violent collective actions.

Migrant workers often employ multiple strategies when taking action as
well; first attempting to negotiate directly with an employer, then appealing
to the court system, or engaging in strikes or mass protest, or even violence
when the first two fail. Yet not every worker seeks to use the court system,
and certainly not every worker employs violence. Many choose to take no
action at all when faced with a labor grievance. Others employ multiple
strategies, yet do so at different points in their struggle, and not simultaneously. Thus, an important question this book seeks to answer is when and
why migrant workers choose from among these different possible options,
and why they decide to switch from one strategy to the other.

This chapter begins to provide an answer to that question by introducing
the concept of migrant labor in contemporary China. The first section examines the different ways migrant workers have been classified in post-reform
China, and examines the growth of China's migrant labor population. The
second section looks at the common grievances that migrants face, including
traditional grievances, such as unpaid wages and labor injuries, as well as
emerging grievances that have appeared more recently, including access to
labor and social insurance, unlawful and illegal dismissal, and worker injury

compensation or compensation for the onset of occupational illness. This section also examines the emergence of interest-based protests among China's migrants, such as protests for higher wages or better working conditions. The third and final section of this chapter examines the different strategies that migrant workers employ, including informal bargaining, use of labor arbitration and the courts, strikes and non-violent mass protest, and violent action.

WHO ARE CHINA'S MIGRANT WORKERS?

Key to any definition of migrant labor in China is the household registration, or *hukou* system; the government system of population management and control, which classifies citizens based on their place of birth (urban or rural) (F.-L. Wang 2005; Young 2013). Precursors to the *hukou* system, such as the "mutual responsibility" (*baojia*) system, can be found throughout the dynastic period, and were used to collect taxes, control population movements, implement government policy, and distribute social benefits (Young 2013, 29).

China's current *hukou* system has its roots in the industrialization strategy of the 1950s, which was designed to extract resources from the countryside in support of rapid urban industrialization. This in turn created massive rural-urban wealth disparities, and provided incentives for peasants to migrate into the cities. Such a model for economic development however was predicated upon an immobile rural population, and in order to maintain this model, a system for restricting peasant urban migration was essential (K. W. Chan 2009, 199–201).

The core of such a system was established in 1958, when the PRC issued new regulations to provide each citizen with an urban or rural classification, and stipulated that all internal migration be subjected to approval from the government of the destination area (K. W. Chan 2009). While this did not halt rural to urban migration completely—the state continued to move peasants in and out of the cities as economic production plans required—over time, rigid implementation of the *hukou* system helped to institute a new social class structure for the benefit of the urban minority at the expense of the rural majority (Solinger 1999, 34–36). While much has changed about the *hukou* system, particularly since the start of economic reform and opening in the late 1970s, the class structure it produced continues to exert substantial influence on Chinese society, having a profound effect on migrant labor protest activity today.

Defining the Migrant Labor Population

Since their reemergence in the post-reform era, China's migrant workers have been notoriously difficult to classify. Born in the countryside yet working in urban areas in the non-agricultural sector, migrant workers have never fit neatly into China's traditional worker-peasant or urban-rural classifications. As a result, initial definitions of what constituted a migrant worker tended to be vague, with different definitions resulting in widely varying estimates of the population. These classification problems have made it difficult to conduct cross regional comparisons or comparisons of the migrant labor population over time.

Definitions of migrant labor have focused largely on two factors; the length of time a rural resident was employed in non-agricultural work, and the distance that one traveled to find employment. While these two criteria are found in most definitions of migrant labor, how they have been used in practice has varied considerably. Some definitions were so broad as to include any individual with either rural or urban residency in transit in the cities during the time of research.[2] Other studies used three days as a minimum duration in the cities, while more restrictive definitions used three months; the time after which it was necessary to apply for a temporary residence permit for rural resident holders to remain in urban areas (Solinger 1999, 17). Measures of distance varied as well. Some studies of the migrant labor population focused specifically on inter-provincial migration. Others included intra-provincial migration, or even considered all rural farmers who have "migrated" out non-agricultural work, even if they remained living within their home county.

Definitional differences can be seen across scholarly publications, Chinese government agencies, and even within the same government agency in different studies. In 1996, for example, the Ministry of Agriculture (MoA) and Ministry of Labor's[3] joint survey of rural migration began to include individuals with a rural *hukou* registration who migrate for at least one year (Cai, Park, and Zhao 2008, 191–92). The 2000 National Bureau of Statistics (NBS) Census however defined migrants as those who moved to their current residence from outside their home township or urban district, and lived in a new residence for at least six months in the prior year. Yet these statistics also included individuals who fit those criteria even if they had an urban registration (*hukou*) status (National Bureau of Statistics 2000).

These definitional differences have had a significant impact on the public discussion of the migrant labor population in China, both in the Chinese and the international media. Most estimates of the migrant labor population found in the press for example include both inter and intra provincial migrants, a population which, by 2013, had surpassed 262 million (National Bureau of Statistics 2013). When describing the actual labor migration process, however, reports tended to concentrate primarily on migrants who travel from one province to another; traditionally from the poorer central and western provinces to the affluent cities on China's coast. That inter-provincial migrant labor population however, had only reached 123 million by 2012, an extraordinary number to be sure, but only about 47% of the total (National Bureau of Statistics 2013).

As the migrant population has grown in significance, both in terms of its size and importance to the national economy, state agencies tasked with tracking internal migration, such as the Ministry of Public Security (MPS), MoHRSS, and the MoA, have grown increasingly sophisticated in their data collection and analysis. Many now conduct surveys in rural areas where migrant workers are more likely to be registered with the government, allowing them to collect more accurate and representative samples (Department of Rural Social Economy Surveys, National Bureau of Statistics 2008). Others organize their surveys to occur during Spring Festival, when many migrants return home to be with their families ("Bureau of Statistics: Chinese Migrant Workers Totaled 225.42 Million at the End of 2008" 2009, 225).

Estimating the Migrant Labor Population

Estimating the size of any itinerant population is inherently problematic, and this is true for China's migrant workers, who frequently change jobs or move without registering or notifying local authorities. Furthermore, many migrants work in the informal sector and are employed with unregistered companies, while others use fake names or the names of siblings when in the cities, making it more difficult to track population movements ("Peasant Migrants Creates Both Opportunity and Challenges for Society [Nongmingong Liudong Wei Shehui Fazhan Dailai Jiyu Yu Tiaozhan]" 2008).[4]

Despite this lack of precision in measuring the population, all estimates point to enormous growth in China's migrant population over the past three decades. While early estimates in 1989 placed the "national inter-provincial flow of migrant workers" at roughly 10 million, by 1993, this number had more than doubled to over 20.2 million, using the same measure ("Peasant Migrants Creates Both Opportunity and Challenges for Society [Nongmingong Liudong Wei Shehui Fazhan Dailai Jiyu Yu Tiaozhan]" 2008). By other accounts, the number of migrants had doubled in just a few years to approximately 60 million by the early 1990s.[5] By 2000, NBS estimated that over 113 million peasants had begun began working in the secondary and tertiary sectors of the economy, with 28 million crossing provincial borders (Ministry of Labor and Social Security and State Statistics Bureau Rural Investigation Team 2002).

By 2005, inter-provincial migration had increased to approximately 80 million, while the number of Chinese peasants employed in nonagricultural work overall had reached 200 million (see table 2.1). In 2009, the NBS reported 225 million peasants transitioning to nonagricultural employment, with over 140 million migrants employed outside their home township ("Bureau of Statistics: Chinese Migrant Workers Totaled 225.42 Million at the End of 2008" 2009). By the end of 2010, the NBS reported that the number of migrant workers nationwide had reached 242 million, including both intra and inter-provincial migration, while the number of peasants "going out and employed in the workforce" (*waichu de jiuye*) had reached 153 million (B. Xu 2011).

Table 2.1 illustrates some of the multiple definitions that have been used over the years to estimate and classify China's migrant labor population. The middle column lists, in millions, the number of "peasants going out to work" (*waichu nongmingong*), which the Bureau of Labor Statistics defines as urban residents employed in the non-agricultural sector outside their home for at least six months (National Bureau of Statistics 2010).

The right-hand column of table 2.1 compares this metric of "peasants going out to work," which has been used relatively consistently, with other measures that have been used to gauge the size of the migrant labor population over the last three decades. While none of these statistics are as consistently available as the estimate of "peasants going out to work," combined, they provide a more complete picture of the evolution of the migrant labor population over the past three decades.

WHY PROTEST? A TYPOLOGY OF MIGRANT LABOR DISPUTES

What are the main sources of unrest for China's migrant workers? As illustrated in chart 2.1, the vast majority of migrant labor disputes can be categorized into four types: unpaid wages (including overtime pay), labor injuries, illegal dismissal, and unsafe working conditions. The frequency of these different dispute types varies by industry and region. While unpaid wages are still a serious issue in the construction industry, illegal dismissal and labor contract violations remain common in the manufacturing industry. In addition, while less common, protests over a lack of social benefits, such as medical and pension insurances, appear to be growing. Table 2.2 notes the percentage of migrant workers interviewed during this research that reported experiencing each type of grievance.

Given the ubiquity of labor disputes among migrants, it is not surprising that 19% of my interview respondents reported experiencing multiple grievances. In the words of one worker who laughed when I asked if he had ever experienced a labor dispute, "I have about one every year. Which one would you like me to talk about?" ("Interview Guangzhou 0504" 2008). When this occurred, respondents were asked to discuss their most recent case, or what

Table 2.1.   Migrant Labor Population Growth: 1978–2011 (millions)

Year	Peasants going out to work*	Other Descriptive Statistics of the Migrant Population
2012	163	262 - "migrant workers"
2011	159	253 - "migrant workers"
2010	153	242 - "migrant workers nationwide"
2009	145	230 - "migrant workers"
2008	140	225 - "migrant workers"
2007	135	150 - "mobile population"
2006	132	
2005	126	200 - "Peasant employed in nonagricultural work force"
2004	118	90 - "Migrants moving to cities above the county level"
2003	110	40.3 - "Migrants engaging in intra-provincial migration for 1+ months"
2002	102	39 - "Migrants engaging in intra-provincial migration for 1+ months"
2001	89.9	36.8 - "Migrants engaging in intra-provincial migration for 1+ months"
2000	106	28.2 - "Migrants engaging in intra-provincial migration for 1+ months"
1999	102	
1998	95	
1997	86	
1996	80	
1995	75	<20 - "Peasants who migrated out of their home province"
1994	70	40 – "Temporary residents"
1993	62	22 – "National inter-provincial migration"
1992	51	
1991	42	
1990	22	
1989	30	10 – "National inter-provincial migration"
1988	26	
1987	28	
1985	25	

1983	3
1980	2.5
1979	2

(waichu gongzuo 外出工作) For a definition of this term, see (Yang and Yang 2010).

Source: (Yang and Yang 2010; National Bureau of Statistics 2013; National Bureau of Statistics 2012; Xu 2011; International Labor Organization 2007; Research Office of the State Council 2006; Cai, Park, and Zhao 2008; Ministry of Labor and Social Security and State Statistics Bureau Rural Investigation Team 2002; "Chen Xiwen: Social Development Opportunities and Challenges from the Flow of Migrant Workers [Chen Xiwen: Nongmin-gong Liudong wei Shehui Fazhang Dailai Jiyu yu Tiaozhan]" 2008)

they considered to be their most egregious grievance if occurring in the past two years.

In addition to these *rights-based* protests, in which migrant workers demand that existing legal benefits and protections be upheld, migrant workers have begun engaging in a small but important number of *interest-based* protests as well, making demands for new rights and privileges not currently codified by law or private contract (A. Chan and Siu 2012). One of the unique characteristics of the 2010 strikes in the Nanhai Honda factory for example was the fact that workers were demanding an 80% wage increase, changes to the wage scale, and the right to hold new elections for the factory's union leadership (A. Chan and Siu 2012, 90). These new demands marked a clear break from the vast majority of migrant protests, which focused on rights-based issues such as unpaid wages or other legal rights violations.

The 2010 Honda strikes were not the first instances of migrant workers' interest-based protests. Indeed, some of the workers interviewed during the course of this research took action to improve working conditions rather than retrieve unpaid wages or redress other rights-based grievances. Yet these interest-based protests remain only a small minority of the overall number of migrant labor protests. Only 13% of respondents interviewed for example complained of poor working conditions, an interest-based grievance, while only 20 individuals from that group chose to act on that dispute.

As described in detail in chapter 5, evidence suggests that interest-based grievances, such as poor working conditions are harder to act on compared to rights-based grievances, as they are often subjective and lacking in specificity compared to traditional rights-based grievances such as unpaid wages or labor injuries.

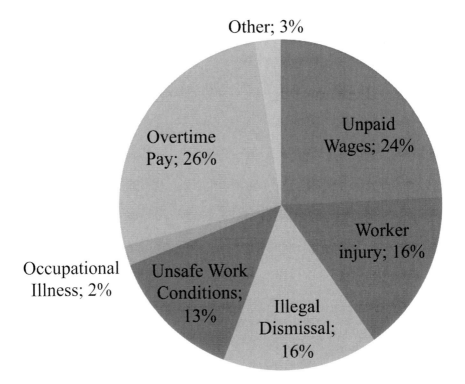

Chart 2.1. Labor Disputes as Reported by Interview Respondents. Source: Author's Interviews

Unpaid Wage Disputes

Wage issues are by far the most common form of dispute experienced by migrant workers, with employers simply refusing to pay wages, paying only a portion of workers' promised salary, or failing to pay overtime. Half the workers interviewed during my research complained of either not receiving overtime pay (26%) or receiving none or only a portion of their wages (24%).

Since 2001, when the Bureau of Statistics first began publishing national-level statistics on the types of labor cases entering arbitration and the courts, the percentage of remuneration cases has remained relatively constant, with roughly one-third of all labor arbitration and court cases caused by unpaid wage issues (see table 2.2).

Of all the grievances faced by migrant workers, unpaid wage issues have received the most government attention, and as examined in chapter 3, since the 2000s, resolving this issue has been a core component of the government's new policy orientation towards migrants. Since the Ministry of Labor began releasing national level statistics on workers receiving back wages in

Table 2.2. Labor Remuneration Cases as a Percentage of Total Labor Arbitration and Court Cases (2001–2011)

Year	Total Cases	Cases caused by remuneration issues	Percentage of total cases
2001	154,621	45,172	29%
2002	184,116	59,144	32%
2003	226,391	76,774	34%
2004	260,471	85,132	33%
2005	313,773	103,183	33%
2006	317,162	103,887	33%
2007	350,182	108,953	31%
2008	693,465	225,061	32%
2009	684,379	247,330	36%
2010	600,865	209,968	35%
2011	589,244	200,550	34%

Source: (National Bureau of Statistics 2013)

2002, the number of workers receiving back wages has declined from its height in the early to mid-2000s. Simultaneously the amount of wages being repaid has progressively increased. As illustrated in graph 1, the number of workers receiving back wages reached its apex in 2004 at almost 9 million. Between 2004 and 2010, this number steadily declined, only to increase again in the latter half of this decade, reaching roughly 6.2 million workers in 2012.

At the same time, the amount of money being repaid to workers has increased throughout the early 2000s and into the next decade, reaching 2 billion RMB in 2012, or roughly 316 million USD (see graph 2.2).[6]

Analyzing these types of government statistics is always fraught with difficulty. Like statistics on crime or corruption, it is uncertain whether the decline in the number of workers receiving back pay from 2004 onward is due to an improvement in the government's ability in combating the problem, workers simply giving up on government channels, employing other strategies, or workers giving up all together. Similarly, does the rise in the total wages retrieved imply improved government performance in this area, or a growth in the problem overall? These issues notwithstanding, the government has clearly managed to increase the amount of wages retrieved per worker; from RMB 295 per worker in 2002 (36 USD), to approximately RMB 3,225 per worker in 2012 (510 USD). This is a sizable increase, even after accounting for inflation and increased wage rates during this time.

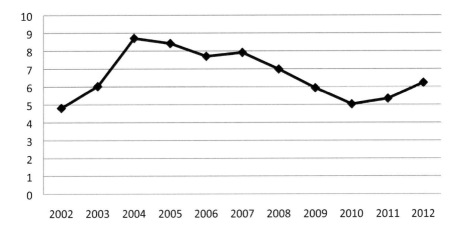

Graph 2.1. Number of Workers Receiving Back Wages 2002-2012 (Millions). Source: (National Bureau of Statistics 2013; "Labor Law Enforcement Recovers 20.08 Billion Yuan in Wages for Workers [Laodong Zhifa Wei Laodongzhe Zhuifa Gongzi Deng Daiyu 200.8 Yiyuan 劳监执法为劳动者追发工资等待遇200.8亿元" **2013)**

Although national-level statistics regarding the amount of remuneration returned to migrant workers specifically are less readily available, other indicators suggest that the central government has made unpaid wages to migrants a particular focus of its efforts. According to MoHRSS, various government organizations helped over 1.5 million migrant workers retrieve almost 3 billion RMB in back wages in 2010 ("Ministry of Human Resources and Social Security: Migrant Worker Wage Arrears Phenomenon Effectively Curbed [Renli Ziyuan Shehui Baozhangbu: Nongmingong Gongzi Tuoqian Xianxiang Dedao Youxiao Ezhi]" 2010). The government also reported helping almost one million migrant workers retrieve roughly 2.2 billion RMB in wages over the first seven months of 2011 alone ("National Trade Union System of Wage Arrears Helps Migrants Recover 2.2 Billion [Quanguo Gonghui Xitong Qian 7 Yue Wei Nongmingong Zhuihui Tuoqian Gongzi 22Yi] 全国工会系统前7月为农民工追回拖欠工资22亿" 2011).

Unpaid wage issues remain particularly egregious within the construction industry. Many construction projects for example are contracted and subcontracted multiple times, with each level of the process responsible for an independent workforce. At the lowest level of this process are individual labor contractors (*baogongtou*), who are often migrant workers themselves; individuals promising to complete one component of the overall project by using low cost labor from their hometown (Swider 2008). Thus, it is not uncommon for example to see twenty workers from a village in Sichuan

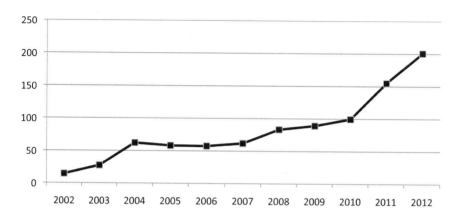

Graph 2.2. Wages Retrieved by PRC Government 2002-2012 (RMB 100 Millions). Source: (National Bureau of Statistics 2013; "Labor Law Enforcement Recovers 20.08 Billion Yuan in Wages for Workers [Laodong Zhifa Wei Laodongzhe Zhuifa Gongzi Deng Daiyu 200.8 Yiyuan 劳监执法为劳动者追发工资等待遇200.8亿元" **2013).**

charged with completing one part of a construction project, while fifteen workers from a village in Hunan complete another.

This informal and diffuse employment structure provides ample opportunities for exploitation. Labor contractors may simply abscond with workers' wages if they receive payment directly from higher levels in the contracting process. Other times labor contractors may be shorted themselves, either through project cost overages or simple corruption. Regardless, as those at the tail end of the process, it is often migrant workers who suffer.

The PRC government has taken steps to manage the unpaid wage issue, particularly within the construction industry, where it has promulgated a host of regulations over the past two decades. Articles in the 1995 *Labor Law* for example require workers to be paid each month, while numerous local regulations prohibit paying wages directly to contractors (Standing Committee of the Shenzhen Municipal People's Congress 2004). In 2004, the PRC Ministry of Construction and MoHRSS jointly issued the *Interim Measures on Wage Payments to Migrant Workers in the Construction Industry*, which suggested that migrant workers' wages should be held and distributed through bank accounts, rather than paid directly to labor contractors, and that relevant enterprises should establish a "guarantee fund" (*baozhangjin*) for use if management delays or stops payment (PRC Ministry of Labor and Social Security and Ministry of Construction 2004).

Local level governments have also begun implementing their own measures as well. In 2010, Chengdu began a "two cards" system, which requires the construction company, the contractor, and any subcontractors to open a "dedicated account for migrant workers' wages" (*nongmingong gongzi zhifu zhuanyong zhanghu*). Under this system, workers are provided with both wage and information cards. These cards are used to draw money directly from the bank on a monthly basis, and protect information relevant to the workers' employee relationship with the construction company, thus helping workers to verify their labor relationship in the event of a dispute (Chengdu Municipal Government 2010). In April 2011, the Yunnan provincial government promulgated a "three fund" system, requiring construction companies to establish a reserve and wage guarantee fund, and the local government to set up an emergency fund. Many local governments have also set up emergency funds to pay off striking workers to avoid unrest from spreading.

Despite these regulatory advancements, and the increasing government attention to the problem over the past decade, many companies and contractors continue paying wages irregularly, upon completion of specified project goals or even at the end of the entire project.[7] According to a 2007 report by the Chinese Academy of Social Sciences, only 31% of construction workers received their wages every month in accordance with the law (Z. Wang 2007). A 2009 study by the Hong Kong labor organization Students and Scholars Against Corporate Misbehavior (SACOM) interviewed 1,284 construction workers across six cities, all employed by *New World China Land* (*Xin Shijie Zhongguo Dichan*), one of China's largest construction companies. Every one of the interviewed workers reported having their wages delayed or deferred (Students and Scholars Against Corporate Misbehavior 2009).

Migrants in manufacturing experience wage issues as well, and are often forced to pay sizable deposits upon starting work, or have a portion of their wages deducted during a probationary period. Such practices were outlawed in 2000 by the promulgation of the *Regulations on Labor Market Management* (*laodong lishichang li guiding*), which prohibits forcing workers to pay deposits, or allowing employers to retain workers' personal documents or identity cards (*shenfenzheng*), another common practice (Brown 2010, 66–67). Yet both persist. In their 2007 comparative study of migrant labor in the Pearl and Yangtze River Delta regions for example, Professors Liu Linping and Wan Xiangdong of Sun Yat-sen University found that roughly 20% of all workers starting a new job in the manufacturing or service industries in these two regions were forced to first pay a deposit. In the Pearl River Delta alone, about 25% of all manufacturing workers surveyed were forced to pay a deposit before starting work. Nor is this a problem associated only with smaller or unregistered manufacturers, as 30% of workers employed at sites with more than 3,000 employees paid deposits as well (Liu and Wan 2007, 13).

Workers are also frequently denied their wages when employers simply decide to close their factory. This problem became particularly apparent during the 2008 global recession, as numerous export producing factories in the Pearl River Delta shut down. In one case, the owner of one of China's largest textile dye companies left behind 200 million in unpaid debts to both employees and suppliers, who in turn withheld wages to their employees, creating a vicious cycle of wage disputes (D. Lee 2004).

Labor and Work Related Injuries

Workers experiencing wage arrears issues usually continue to work another day. For workers injured on the job however, their experience limits opportunities for future earnings, and if serious enough, can throw whole families into poverty. Dangerous work environments, the use of heavy machinery without proper training or equipment, long hours, and the constant push for greater productivity, all contribute to labor injuries. In 2010, China's State Administration of Work Safety reported approximately 80,000 work related fatalities and over 363,000 worker injuries nationwide (H. Wang 2011). Research on migrant labor injuries in the Pearl River Delta, conducted by the NGO China Labor Watch, found a strong correlation between the prevalence of injuries and the duration of workers' shifts. This same report found that approximately 40,000 fingers are severed in industrial accidents each year in the Pearl River Delta alone ("The Long March: Surveys and Case Studies of Work Injuries in the Pearl River Delta Region" 2007, 2).

Migrants also constitute the majority of the workforce in the nation's most dangerous industries such as coal mining and chemical production (Xinhua 2006). By some estimates, more than half of China's coal mining labor force is comprised of migrant labor (Brown 2010, 106). Coal mining in China is particularly dangerous. In 2012, a State Administration of Worker Safety Circular reported that the death rate in China's coal mines was roughly .374 deaths per million tons of coal, compared to an average rate of .02 deaths per million tons in developed countries (China Labour Bulletin 2013). In 2013, the state reported 1,049 coal mine deaths, compared to 20 in the United States that same year ("China Says It Saw a Drop in Mining Deaths in 2013" 2014).

While a growing number of migrants do have injury insurance, in practice, migrants often face difficulties certifying their injuries. Employers purchase only a fraction of the insurance required for their workforce, and, like Mr. Li described above, deny employees access to the paperwork necessary to pursue a case. One native Sichuan worker I interviewed in Dongguan had her right hand caught in a machine press, which had shaded to a dark purple in color; swollen and bloated. It hung limp and useless at the end of her forearm. After the accident, her boss gave her a few hundred RMB and fired her. Having no money for medical treatment, she sought none, until the condition of her hand grew slowly worse, and she became permanently hand-icapped ("Interview Dongguan 1101" 2008).

Sixteen percent of my interview respondents had been injured at work, ranging from relatively minor injuries, which allowed for a full recovery, to more serious accidents like the one described above, where respondents lost the use of their limbs. Some lost the ability to work altogether, and had become completely reliant upon friends and family members. While danger-ous, the higher wages earned in high risk industries can be very attractive to uneducated, unskilled migrants. One worker lamented leaving his mining town in Guizhou to come to Dongguan, laboring twelve hours a day, seven days a week for less than 1,000 RMB a month in a leather goods factory. When I commented that his current work was safer, he laughed and said that as a miner he could earn twice his current salary, helping him pay for his son and daughter's schooling ("Interview Guangzhou 0502" 2008).

Illegal Dismissal

Another 16% of my interview respondents complained of being illegally dismissed from their work without compensation. The 1995 *Labor Law* spec-ifies conditions for contract termination, such as thirty days notice to em-ployees or the trade union before an employer may substantially cut its workforce ("Labor Law of the People's Republic of China" 2002). These regulations were buttressed in the 2008 *Labor Contract Law*, which stipu-lates how much compensation is owed to workers based on length of service. For many migrant workers however, the reality of the situation is far differ-ent, and such regulations are often unenforced. Many workers are dismissed after requesting the resolution of other grievances, such as overtime pay,[8] injury insurance,[9] or injury compensation.[10]

Data on the number of labor disputes caused by illegal dismissal nation-wide is limited. According to central government statistics, the number of labor arbitration and court cases caused by "reliev[ing] or end[ing] the labor contract" (*jiechu, zhongzhi laodong hetong*), has varied significantly over the past decade, ranging from a high of 23% in 2007, to a low of 5% in 2010 (see table 2.3).

Growth in the number of illegal dismissals as a dispute was suggested during interviews with multiple NGOs in the Pearl River Delta, who noted that illegal dismissal cases have become a larger percentage of their overall case load, particularly after the *2008 Labor Contract Law,* which further clarified the process for hiring and firing workers ("Interview with Migrant Labor NGO Representative, Shenzhen" 2008). Overall, the growth in com-plaints over illegal dismissals suggests that migrant workers' demands for the implementation of existing laws are expanding beyond basic wage issues. Why this is the case is examined in detail in chapter three.

Table 2.3. Labor Arbitration and Court Cases Caused by Illegal Dismissal 2001–2011

Year	Total Cases	No. Caused By Ending the Labor Contract	Percentage of Total Cases
2001	154,621	29,038	19%
2002	184,116	30,940	17%
2003	226,391	40,017	18%
2004	260,471	57,021	22%
2005	313,773	68,873	22%
2006	317,162	67,868	21%
2007	350,182	80,261	23%
2008	693,465	139,702	20%
2009	684,379	43,876	6%
2010	600,865	31,915	5%
2011	589,244	118,684	20%

Source: (National Bureau of Statistics 2013)

Poor or Unsafe Work Conditions

Like disputes over low rather than unpaid wages, complaints about poor working conditions are another example of the interest-based disputes that are beginning to appear. Moreover, many migrants also suffer from unsafe, unsanitary, and hazardous working conditions, which can lead to the immediate injuries described above, as well as long term occupational illness. Thirteen percent of the workers interviewed during this research complained of poor working conditions, with 2% suffering occupational illness derived from those conditions.

Unsafe or poor working conditions can take many forms. For migrant workers housed on their worksite, whether in construction or manufacturing, dormitory conditions are often cramped and unsanitary, causing a wide variety of health issues. In a three month joint survey of almost 4,000 migrants in Beijing, Shanghai, Shenzhen, and Guangzhou conducted by the Chinese company *39 Health Net* and the publication *Southern Weekly*, researchers found chronic fatigue, dizziness, and respiratory diseases to be common ailments (Z. Xu and Zhang 2008). In the 2009 SACOM study cited above, 80% of the construction workers housed on site suffered from varying degrees of respiratory illness (Students and Scholars Against Corporate Misbehavior 2009). In 2010, the Chinese newspaper, *Legal Daily*, estimated there are at least one million occupational illnesses cases in China, 90% of which involve pneumoconiosis, a lung disease caused by inhaling large amounts of dust and other particulate matter (China Labour Bulletin 2010).

Pneumoconiosis cases specifically are notoriously difficult to resolve through legal or administrative channels. The length of time before symptoms manifest varies greatly depending upon the quantity of dust inhaled, but it can be years before they emerge. Because China's current regulatory framework assumes that workers have an ongoing relationship with their employer, once this relationship is severed, obtaining compensation or reimbursement for medical treatment can become extremely difficult. Many relevant regulations for example call on the employer to pay for medical treatment or to provide compensation, yet if the employer has already severed this relationship, it becomes unclear how to proceed. In addition, long onset times makes it extremely difficult for workers to prove they contracted the disease from one specific employer, particularly if they have worked for multiple employers in the same industry over a number of years (China Labour Bulletin 2010).

These problems, combined with the difficulties receiving an official diagnosis and classification of an occupational illness, can push workers toward desperate action. Faced with the prospect of burdening their families with debilitating medical bills, some workers choose to take their own life. Others such as Mr. Li described in chapter 1, resort to violence. While the government has been primarily concerned with wage issues, which have often been a source of collective action among migrant labor, the desperation of many workers afflicted with occupational illnesses can make them a surprising catalyst for labor violence.

PROTESTS ACTIVITY: INFORMAL BARGAINING, LEGAL CHANNELS, STRIKES, AND VIOLENCE

Migrant grievances range from the traditional, such as unpaid wages and labor injuries, which have existed as long as Chinese farmers have been traveling to find work, to newer grievances, such as labor contract disputes and demands over injury and pension insurance, which have emerged as legal rights and protections have expanded. Migrants have also begun to protest over interest-based disputes as well. As important as the causes of unrest, however, are the strategies that migrant workers use to seek resolution. Whether workers engage in informal bargaining, use of arbitration and the courts, strikes, violence, or some combination of multiple strategies at different points in time, workers' protest have profound effects on Chinese political and economic development.

Many workers employ a combination of strategies during the lifetime of their dispute, yet they do so at different stages in the dispute process. Below,

I provide a spectrum of migrant labor protest activities based on the costs commonly associated with each strategy in terms of time, resources, and the potential for retribution (see figure 2.1). For example, workers may first attempt to informally bargain with their employer, either alone or in groups. Unlike strikes and other mass protests, such informal bargaining is not an overt, public confrontation. Instead, it is a low-level appeal for dispute resolution, often cleverly employing the strategic use of private information, such as knowledge of the inner workings of the company or of an industry. Such informal bargaining disavows public goals in favor or a private resolution, and while it is not without its risks, it is often less time consuming, is less financially costly, and poses less of a risk than taking an employer to court, engaging in strikes, or participating in violence.

Compared to informal bargaining, legal action is more costly given the time and money frequently involved, and workers often seek to use this strategy after informal negotiation fails. If these legal channels are unavailable, previous research has shown that migrants may become radicalized, moving toward strikes and other types of collective protest (C. K. Lee 2007). Finally, violence as a conscious strategy may be a final resort when action through other means is unavailable, though violent actions carry a high risk, given the potential for lost wages, physical retribution, and state punishment.

While many workers make use of multiple strategies, the question remains why workers select certain strategies over others, when and why workers switch strategies, and why some workers fail to take any action at all. The final section of this chapter introduces the broad spectrum of Chinese migrant labor protest options, including informal bargaining, use of labor arbitration and the courts, strikes and mass protests, and violence.

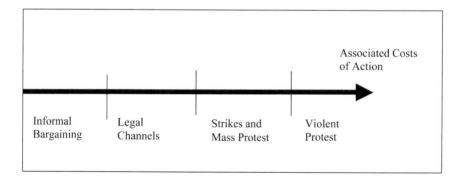

Figure 2.4.   A Spectrum of Migrant Labor Protest Escalation.

Informal Bargaining and Negotiation

When experiencing a labor grievance, many migrant workers first choose to confront their employer directly through informal bargaining and negotiation. Almost one third of all workers interviewed during the course of this research attempted some meaningful type of direct appeal or negotiation with their employer. Yet in the uneven power relationship that exists between labor and management in China, it can be very difficult for workers to obtain the leverage necessary to negotiate independently. Many migrant workers have difficulty simply finding an interlocutor within the workplace, as employers refuse to negotiate. Managers on the shop floor often argue that they have no authority to make decisions. Other times, as in the case of bankrupt factories or delayed construction projects, the responsible parties have already fled.

Yet sometimes workers are able to succeed through direct negotiation, and this is especially true when they have some form of leverage, as well as the courage and opportunity to use it. One group of temporary workers (*linshigong*) employed on a renovation project for an apartment building in Beijing for example had not been paid as promised upon the project's completion. One of the workers however was aware that the contractor had been "fooling the landlord by using inferior products and cutting corners."[11]

Rather than resorting to violence or taking their information to the authorities, these workers simply confronted the labor contractor with this knowledge and asked that the contractor paid their wages. Upon hearing this implied threat, the contractor immediately agreed to pay as promised.

Confronting one's employer directly may be faster than government appeals or the courts, yet it does hold some danger. When challenging their employers, workers have little protection from retaliation by angry bosses, and examples of workers being attacked after making demands are not uncommon. In one highly publicized example in Nanjing in early January 2008, a group of construction workers was severely attacked after demanding the payment of back wages, with one having his hand cut off ("Requesting Salary Rebuffed: A Nanjing Migrant Worker Has Hand Cut Off [Taoxin Bucheng: Nanjing Yi Nongmingongshou Bei Kanduan]" 2008).

Legal Channels for Dispute Resolution

Since the early 1990s, when the PRC first acknowledged the potential for conflict between labor and management in a modern capitalist economy, government policies towards labor disputes have oscillated between neutral third party enforcement of the law and direct intervention. While the former position seeks to establish a system of transparency and predictability within China's labor relations system, this has at times led to an increase in labor dispute cases, and escalation of disputes towards higher levels of the system through the appeals process. As a consequence, the government has not wholly given up on state-managed mediation, despite the fact that this may at times undermine the arbitration and court systems.

As described in detail in the chapters that follow, the government first began to establish a legal framework for labor dispute resolution in the late 1980s, although migrant workers would not began to gain access to this system until the mid-1990s with the promulgation of the 1995 *Labor Law*. Since then however, an increasing number of workers have sought to use this system. Graph 2.3 charts the number of labor dispute cases entering the courts between 1993 and 2011, which have increased dramatically in the past two decades. The formal legal labor dispute system received a significant boost in 2008, with the passing of the 2008 *Employment Promotion Law*, *Labor Contract Law* and perhaps most importantly, the *Law on the Mediation and Arbitration of Labor Disputes*. These laws removed some of the more onerous obstacles workers faced when seeking to use the legal system, allowing for an explosion in the number of labor arbitration and court cases.

Within the formal dispute resolution framework, labor arbitration is often considered the first step, with Labor Arbitration Committees responsible for reviewing and rendering verdicts on arbitration requests (National People's Congress Standing Committee 1995, Article 79). Theoretically comprised of

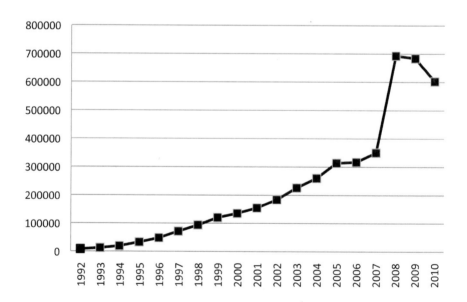

Graph 2.3. Labor Dispute Cases in Arbitration and the Courts 1993–2011. Source: (National Bureau of Statistics, China Labor Statistics Yearbook, various years)

three members, in reality the sheer number of applications for labor arbitration has swamped the system, and the arbitration process is often conducted by only one arbitrator, who may work in that capacity full or part time. This is especially true after the promulgation of the *Labor Contract Law* and the *Labor Dispute Mediation and Arbitration Law* in 2008, which lowered costs associated with arbitration by abolishing application fees, leading to a large jump in the number of arbitration and court cases.

The labor arbitration process itself is also increasingly taking on characteristics found in litigation, with workers hiring lawyers and obtaining professional legal advice during proceedings to match the legal representation retained by most employers (Taylor, Chang, and Li 2003, 167; "Interview with Labor Arbitration Official, Hefei" 2011). Thus, while the *2008 Mediation and Arbitration Law* abolished application fees, the growing litigiousness in the arbitration process has had the opposite effect, increasing the costs associated with the formal system ("Interview with Labor Arbitration Official, Hefei" 2011).

If either party disagrees with the arbitration decision, they may initiate a lawsuit under Chinese Civil Procedure Law. Like arbitration, China's court cases have risen exponentially in recent years, with labor arbitration and court cases increasing in areas with large migrant populations even faster. In 2008, the year the *Labor Contract Law* came into effect, 13 judges in the Tangxia town court in Dongguan alone handled 7,540 cases, or approximately 600 cases per judge, compared to the national average of 42 cases per judge annually at that time (He 2008). In 2010, the Anhui Provincial Arbitration Commission heard over 400 cases with a staff of five full time and five part time arbitrators ("Interview with Labor Arbitration Official, Hefei" 2011). This sharp rise in demand has in part encouraged the government to push disputes towards administrative channels, including informal dispute mediation, while cautioning courts against being too stringent with the implementation of new laws (Xie 2009).

For many migrant workers, legal appeals may be an attractive strategy, yet for migrants facing complicated cases that lack evidence, or limited resources to hire a lawyer, legal options are often unattainable. Meanwhile, as labor arbitration and court cases have skyrocketed, the central government is increasingly concerned with the impact of so many cases reaching into higher levels of the appeals process (Minzner 2011).

As a result, many migrants opt for direct government intervention, including appeals for the intersession or mediation of labor bureau officials, petition offices, or other government agencies such as the local police. In total, 21% of the respondents interviewed during the course of this research first made a direct appeal for intervention at the nearest labor bureau after their dispute took place. An additional 8% of all interview respondents made appeals to other agencies, such as local petition offices or the local police.

How successful were these direct appeals? By themselves, direct government intervention had limited results. While many of my own respondents sought out government intervention, only 7% were successful convincing any government agent to intervene directly. One woman I interviewed was the exception in this regard. A twenty year old from the outskirts of Yangchun in southern Guangdong Province, she had been working in a small electronics factory in the Baoan district of Shenzhen since December 2006. The factory was small, employing fewer than 100 workers. Before beginning work, her employer made her commit to a period of two years, deducting a portion of her pay each month, and promising these funds would be paid in full at the end of the two year contract. After two years however, her employer refused to return the wages as promised.

Deducting a portion of one's salary (*kouqian*) is a common practice. However, unlike many migrants who lacked physical evidence of their labor exploitation, this worker did at least have pay slips documenting both her pay and the amount deducted. After some initial difficulties in searching out the local labor bureau (she became hopelessly lost looking for their office on more than one occasion), she was finally able to contact them and describe her situation, after which authorities invited her employer to the bureau offices to discuss the manner. When the employer refused, the bureau uncharacteristically dispatched a team to the factory to follow up, threatening to fine the factory if the back wages issue was not resolved. This began a process of negotiation between the bureau and the employer, after which the employer agreed to return most of the deducted wages ("Interview Shenzhen 0322" 2007).

To be sure, this is a rare case in which a local labor bureau intervened directly on behalf of a single migrant worker without that worker bringing any pressure to bear. However, in this instance, the worker did have a number of factors in her favor. Unlike many, she had physical documentation of her dispute. She was also a young woman who spoke Cantonese, and was from Guangdong Province, and so while not a local (*bendiren*) from Baoan, she may have evoked sympathy from the local labor bureau. However, even when such informal mediation efforts are successful, such extralegal administrative appeals circumvent normal legal procedures, eroding the legal system which the PRC has worked so hard to create.

More common are examples of migrant workers who experience government intervention as a perfunctory process, with police or labor bureau officials arriving on the worksite after receiving numerous complaints, only to leave without resolving the problem. In contrast to the example above, a 23 year old woman from Guangxi Province had been working 16 hour days, 29 days a month in a small electronics factory in the outskirts of Shenzhen. Starting in August of 2007, her employer began to withhold wages for her and about 20 other workers, all young women about the same age. [12]

After not receiving their wages for three months, she and some other workers called the police. The police arrived, talked briefly to the employer, and left without allowing the workers to tell their side of the story. According to the respondent, this was because the police were "bought off" with gifts of cash.[13] The police also presumably provided the employer with information on which workers complained. After they left, the entire group was summarily fired without their unpaid wages being returned ("Interview 0302" 2007).

Strikes and Mass Protest

Nonviolent strikes and protests represent another form of bargaining, which may be aimed at either the employer or local government officials, and often occur after informal bargaining or legal appeals have failed (C. K. Lee 2007). Though present in the 1978 state constitution, the right to strike in China (*bagong*) was replaced in the 1982 constitution by references to "work slowdowns" (*daigong*) or "shutdowns" (*tinggong*) ("China's Constitutional Framework" 2014). But despite this legal ambiguity, strikes have increased in frequency, intensity, and even organizational sophistication throughout the past decade.

While still leery of strikes as an exercise in social organization, and cognizant of the role of labor in the political transitions of other authoritarian states, there is some evidence to suggest that strikes are no longer seen by the government as inherently destabilizing, and are increasingly viewed as a normal part of a market economy by many Chinese policy makers. In the March 2011 National People's Congress for example, NPC delegate Zeng Qinghong, who is also the general manager of the Guangzhou Automobile Group and President of the Guangdong Provincial Automobile Industrial Association, submitted a proposal to legalize "the economic right to strike within the framework of the law" ("Chinese Legislator Calls for Restoration of the Right to Strike" 2011; Zeng 2011).

Estimating the number of strikes in China is exceedingly difficult. There are no publicly available government statistics on the number of strikes nationwide, and while different government agencies may provide statistics on "mass incidents," or "public order disturbances," the different methods used to compile these statistics from year to year makes comparison over time difficult ("2005 National Social Order and Public Stability Criminal Records Fall for First Time After Rising [2005 Quanguo Shehuizhian Wending Xingshi Lian Shouci Huiluo] 2005 全国社会治安稳定 刑事立案首次回落" 2006; Minzner 2007).

Since the 1990s however, a number of different sources suggest that China has witnessed a marked increase in the number of strikes and "spontaneous incidents" involving migrant workers (C. K. Lee 2007, 6–7). In Shenzhen for example, "large and important" labor disputes as categorized by the municipal labor bureau increased from only 11 recorded protests in 1989 involving 317 workers, to 511 such protests in 1999 (C. K. Lee 2007, 163). In 2008, sociologist Yu Jianrong estimated the number of strikes nationwide to be roughly 30,000, although this should only be viewed as a rough estimate, given its reliance on government statistics that conflate strike activities with other incidents of mass protest (Yu 2008).

Other local data can provide a more consistent frame of reference. For example, since 1993, the Guangzhou Municipal Labor Bureau has, relatively consistently, provided data on the number of "strikes" (*bagong*) or "sudden mass incidents" (*tufa qunti shijian*) dealt with by municipal labor inspection organs. In 1996, the city's labor inspection organs reported dealing with 256 strikes involving over 21,000 workers. By 1998, the number of workers involved in strikes had risen to 38,000. In 2000, the labor inspection organs stopped referring to strikes in their official statistics, instead referring to "sudden incidents" involving thirty or more workers. By the end of the decade in 2010, labor inspection organs had dealt with 388 such incidents. Graph 2.4 below provides the number of strikes and sudden mass incidents officially reported in Guangzhou from 1993 to 2011.

Perhaps the most well known recent example of migrant labor strike activity was the 2010 automobile strike wave, which began in the spring of 2010 at the Nanhai Honda factory in Foshan. Lasting 18 days from May 17 to June 4, at its peak the strikes at Nanhai included some 1,900 workers. The initial Nanhia Honda strike was soon followed by strikes in other Honda suppliers; in Fengfu Honda in Foshan (June 7–9), Honda Lock in Zhongshan, Guangdong (June 9–18), and Nihon Plast in Zhongshan, Guangdong (June

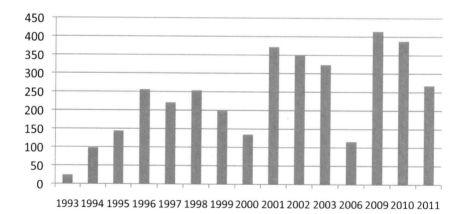

Graph 2.4. "Strikes" and "Sudden Mass Incidents" Reported by Guangzhou Labor Inspection Organs, 1993–2011. Source: (Statistics Bureau of Guangzhou City various years)

17–19). Strikes then spread to suppliers for other car manufacturers, including Ford, Nissan, and Toyota. In the three months between May and July, the Hong Kong Liaison Office of the International Trade Union Federation estimates that at least 13 separate strikes took place in different auto parts manufacturers across the country ("Implications of the Strike in Honda Auto Parts Manufacturing Co Ltd (CHAM)" 2010).

Within the Pearl River Delta, strikes among China's manufacturing workers appear to be an almost daily occurrence, and many of the workers interviewed during the course of this research admitted to participating in strike activities. One worker in Dongguan for example described how an entire workforce of approximately 4,500 workers decided to strike in front of the factory gates in the Qingxi district, an industrial region known for producing electronics, after becoming increasingly angry with the high costs of arbitrary fines and penalties placed on workers by the factory. According to the respondent, the workers occupied the area in front of the factory for two days until the police arrived.

While the strike allowed workers to retrieve a portion of their wages, the respondent indicated he was unhappy with the outcome ("Interview Dongguan 1103" 2008). Yet these types of collective actions sometimes have unintended consequences. In this case, the process of striking provided an opportunity for 40–50 more militant workers within the factory to identify and connect with each other, allowing a useful social network to develop.

More recently, researchers and labor activists have been making use of social media to estimate the number of labor strikes and protests. Since 2008, the website China Strikes has used crowd sourcing techniques to estimate the number of labor strikes nationwide. The website allows individuals to submit information regarding known protests directly from their cell phones or by filling out a form online (Elfstrom 2014). Between 2008 and January 2013, China Strikes has recorded 563 protests. Since 2011, the labor rights NGO *China Labor Bulletin* has been collecting and coding instances of labor protest activity as well. Between January 2011 and February 2013 alone, the organization recorded 678 different strikes and protests ("CLB Collective Labour Incidents Map" 2014).

While increasingly useful as a broader gauge of strike activity, particularly in the absence of official data, use of social media to estimate the number of strikes and protests can be problematic. Use of social media as a reporting tool suggests that statistics will likely be skewed towards areas with greater internet accessibility. In addition, it is unclear how well known these documentation attempts are among China's workers, especially China's migrant labor population. Absent the availability of government statistics however, resources such as these provide useful frames of reference. Moreover, as internet access and use of social media in China continues to spread, such crowd sourcing research techniques will likely improve.

Violent Protests

The final category of migrant labor protests activity involves the use of more violent and unorthodox forms of collective action. Statistics regarding the number of violent protests are unavailable, and protest activity within this broadly defined group may indeed vary significantly. Whatever their form however, violent protests all possess the ability to disrupt social order in ways informal bargaining, use of legal channels, or routine strikes do not. Whether it is migrant workers attacking police and burning police vehicles during the Xintang riots in the summer of 2011, the Foxconn riots in Taiyuan the fall of 2012, a handful of workers disrupting traffic by climbing scaffolding, buildings, or bridges and threatening to jump, or a worker setting himself on fire in the middle of a public square, these acts of protest constitute a significant threat to the party's social contract, which promises to maintain the social stability necessary for economic growth in exchange for political acquiescence.

Much like strike statistics, estimates regarding the number of violent protests, and migrant workers engaging in violence, are hard to come by. The available evidence however does suggest a general pattern of growth in migrant labor violence over the past decade. According to research from Sun Yat-sen University, from 2001 to 2005, the number of migrant workers in the Pearl River Delta region participating in "mass incidents" increased from roughly 160,000 in 2001 to over a quarter of a million in 2005 (Ping 2008).

In November 2008 after the full impact of the international economic crisis, the number of mass incidents over unpaid wages in Beijing involving migrant workers rose roughly 146% from the previous year, with the number of participants in these incidents rising 132% (Dong 2009). That same year at the Hong-Kong owned Kaida toy factory in Dongguan, several hundred recently laid-off workers rioted after failing to come to an agreement with the factory owner. When police arrived, the violence only escalated. In the end, a reported 500 workers destroyed factory equipment and facilities, as well as a number of police vehicles (Xinhua 2008).

Other workers engage in single acts of violence which are no less disruptive. In 2009 alone, one migrant worker committed suicide by slitting his wrists at a crowded Guangzhou railway station, another engaged in a suicide bombing of a hotel in Foshan, and a third murdered two managers at the jewelry factory where he worked before taking his own life (Foster 2009; Eli Friedman 2012). More recently, a 2011 survey by the Foshan municipal ACFTU found that approximately 45% of all surveyed migrant workers had attempted to protect their rights through "mass incidents" (*quntixing shijian*), while 16% of survey participants agreed that "causing big trouble can resolve things" (*shiqing naodale jiu hui jiejue*) ("45% of Migrant Workers Protect their Rights Through Mass Incidents" 2011).

Riots can often result from unresolved grievances that eventually bubble over. In a Foxconn factory employing roughly 79,000 workers in Taiyuan, Shanxi Province for example, workers often complained of poor working conditions, overcrowded dormitories, unsanitary conditions, and militant security guards. In September 2012, these grievances led to a riot involving around 2,000 workers. Rioters broke windows, destroyed factory equipment, and forced the factory to go off line. Forty people were reportedly injured during the event, and five thousand police were called in to reestablish order (Agence France Presse 2012; Jim 2012; Barboza and Bradsher 2012).

Only a minority of the migrant workers I interviewed during the course of this research turned to violence in response to labor disputes. This minority however employed a wide array of violence, including attacks on security guards employed at the workplace, manhunts designed to track down labor contractors who abscond with wages, destruction of property, worksite occupation, and attacks against employers. Workers often utilize these strategies in the hopes of resolving disputes more quickly than formal channels would allow, either through capitulation by management, government invention, or a combination of the two.

Violent protest has long been part of the "repertoire of contention" of Chinese peasants and workers, with specific tactics being handed down from generation to generation via native place ties and local community associations (Perry 1994). Almost a century later, today's migrant workers operate in a similar manner, relaying on these ties to facilitate and organize violent activities.

Labor violence directed at employers is not an uncommon outcome either. Small scale workplace violence is often characterized in the mainland press as spontaneous or criminally motivated, but not all examples can be so clearly categorized. Many are calculated responses designed to enact revenge. In 2008, the wife of a small clothing factory owner in Zengcheng city in southern Guangdong was stabbed to death by a former employee over a dispute involving a mere 50.8 RMB (US$ 7.47). Workers in this factory were paid piece meal on a monthly basis, providing a record of their work to the factory on the 5th of each month, to be paid for the preceding month. If workers failed to turn their records in by the 28th, they forfeited their pay. When one worker turned her ticket in late, she was rudely told she had forfeited her wages. Vowing to return to "get revenge" (*zhaoren lai shoushi ni*), she later came back to the factory with four family members, murdering the wife outside the factory door ("Wife of a Small Factory Owned Stabbed to Death Outside Factory Gates [Xiao Gongchan Laobanniang Changmenkou Bei Tongsi]" 2008).

There are no statistics available to analyze the percentage of labor disputes that turn violent in this manner, yet attacks of this intensity illustrate the potential for violence which percolates just below the surface. Migrant workers who spend much of their time at a basic subsistence level have little in the way of a social safety net to catch them should something go wrong. Under such pressure, it is not surprising that disputes often turn violent.

Finally, it is not unheard of for desperate migrant workers to engage in public acts of self immolation or take revenge against their employers, particularly when they lack the capacity for larger collective action, yet are unable to simply give up. In these cases, workers can resort to self immolation or lash out in violence. In the winter of 2007 for example, a 23 year old migrant worker from Yunnan Province and his wife agreed to work in a handbag factory in the Longgan district of Shenzhen. The couple lacked a contract, relying only on an oral agreement, and agreed to be paid twice a year at the rate of 67 RMB per day (US$ 9.80).

Paying workers in one large lump sum rather than on a monthly basis has the added benefit for employers of decreasing workers' mobility, thus providing the factory with a more stable workforce. Yet sometimes this strategy can backfire. After working for just a short time, the couple received a call from the husband's grandfather, saying that the couple's one year old son had fallen ill. Desperately needing to return home, but lacking a labor contract or any type of social or medical insurance, the couple had no option other than to approach their employer, explain their situation, and ask for their wages. The employer refused, even after the couple agreed to take 50% of what was owed them. After being rebuffed, the husband responded by setting himself on fire in the middle of his employer's office (Zhou 2007).

Migrant workers in contemporary China employ a number of protest strategies, including informal bargaining, legal appeals, routine strikes, and violence. Yet opportunities for protest were not always so expansive. In the first few decades of economic reform, Chinese migrant workers were highly constrained in their behavior. With little rights and protections in the cities, migrant workers in the early years of economic reform faced a tenuous existence, fraught with threats of violence, extortion, extralegal imprisonment, and deportation back to their hometown. The process by which migrants' urban environment has changed over the past three decades, allowing for greater protest opportunities, is the focus of the next chapter.

NOTES

1. Interviews with workers arranged by labor rights NGO in Shenzhen, 13 June, 2011.
2. Definitions of the migrant labor population used by Guangzhou in 1989 for example included any individual in the city on business, on vacation, or visiting relatives or friends. See Statistics Bureau of Guangzhou City, *1990 Guangzhou Statistics Yearbook*, (Guangzhou: China Statistics Press, 1990).
3. As part of a greater bureaucratic restructuring effort, the PRC Government, during the March 2008 meeting of the National People's Congress, announced plans to merge the Ministry of Personnel and the Ministry of Labor to form the Ministry of Human Resources and

Social Security (MoHRSS) (*Renli Ziyuan he Shehui Baozhangbu*). See, "New ministry resolves 'split' in labor market," *China Daily*, 14 March, 2008, http://www.china.org.cn/government/ NPC_PCC_sessions2008/2008-03/14/content_12567148.htm.

4. It was not until after working and living together for a few months for example that I learned that my research assistant, Mr. Tang, had actually been using the name and registration card of a relative.

5. One source lists the national population of "migrants" [English] at 60 million as early as 1992, while another lists the "floating population" [English] at 60 million by 1994. For the former, see Zhou Yan and Bai Xu, "3 Decades On, China's Migrants Still 'Outside Looking In,'" *Xinhua News* [English], 12 August, 2008, available at http://news.xinhuanet.com/english/ 2008-12/08/content_10472326.htm. For the latter see Huang Ping and Zhan Shaohua, "Internal Migration in China: Linking it to Development," Paper presented at Regional Conference on Migration and Development, Lanzhou, China, 14-16 March, 2005, pp. 3.

6. Using an average 2012 exchange rate of 1 RMB = .158 US Dollar.

7. A 2005 survey of 82 construction workers in Shenzhen alone found that approximately half were paid only upon completion of the entire project, while the rest were paid either at the end of the year, upon completion of certain tasks, or intermittently. See "Research on the Labour Situation of Migrant Workers in the Construction Sector of Shenzhen," *Worker Empowerment Newsletter*, 24 April, 2007.

8. Interview SZ 0441, 0450, 0460, 0461, March, 2008.

9. Interview NJ 1042, 1052, September, 2007.

10. Interview BJ 0235, March, 2008, Interview GZ 0619, January, 2008.

11. "*laoban youdian hunong fangdong, jiushi cailiao youdian ci huozhe shi tongguojianliao,* " Interview BJ 0114, 15 September, 2007.

12. Labor intensive manufacturing companies often recruit young women, rather than men, as they are more obedient to authority, less likely to protest poor treatment, and less likely to take action over exploitative conditions. This sentiment is widely held among migrant workers themselves, and was expressed to me during this interview. See for example Tan Shen, "At the Pearl River Delta: the Relations of Women Migrants to Foreign Invested Enterprises and Local Government," Paper Presented at the Annual Meeting of the American Sociological Association, San Francisco, California, 1998, available at http://www.sociology.cass.cn/english/papers/ P020050202556602962322.pdf.

13. The respondent used the phrase (*hongbao*), literally "red envelope," which describes gifts given during the Spring Festival.

Chapter Three

From Wandering Beggars to New Urban Citizens: The Changing Landscape for Migrant Labor

Migrant labor protests in China today are a common occurrence, whether they emerge as informal bargaining between workers and employers, labor arbitration or court cases, strikes, or workplace violence. Yet migrants in China did not always have the same opportunities for protest they enjoy today. As a group, they were subject to severe movement restrictions and limitations on their ability to live and work in urban areas. How has this change come about? How have migrants made this transition from "wandering beggars" to "new urban citizens"; acknowledged as accepted, if still second class, members of urban society? This chapter examines the changing structure of protest opportunities available to migrant workers through an examination of the key political and economic events which have made this transformation possible.

The emergence of migrant labor as a segment of the labor force capable of engaging in significant protest activity speaks to a broader question in comparative politics; how do new protest opportunities emerge in authoritarian states? Opportunities for protest are structurally dependent, and actors' "political opportunity structure" expands or contracts depending in part on the various political, social or economic changes taking place in their environment (Meyer 2004, 126). In democracies, meaningful elections may provide such opportunities. The election of pro labor administrations for example may embolden workers to push for greater protections (Tarrow 2011, 73). In authoritarian states, openings may emerge from the creation of new institutions, regime liberalization, declining state power, or massive demographic and economic upheavals (Tarrow 2011, 77–78). Differences in opportunities for protest also vary by social class. When windows of opportunity arise for some, obstacles to action may emerge for others (O'Brien 2008, 14). In China for example, students and intellectuals are traditionally seen as the moral voice and conscience of the state, and are provided with space to protest government policy. Workers and peasants in contrast are often treated much more harshly when speaking out against the state (Wasserstrom 1991).

For Chinese migrant workers, changes which have expanded protest opportunities over the past three decades have occurred in three stages; the creation of migrant labor as a separate class in the 1980s, the emergence of a labor protection regime in the mid-1990s, and the integration of migrant labor into that regime, coupled with the creation of migrant specific protections, beginning in 2003–2004. As economic reforms in the early 1980s provided opportunities for farmers to leave the countryside, they formed the beginnings of a new labor class, which did not fit neatly into the traditional worker-peasant dichotomy. Flocking to the cities in search of work, millions of migrants joined the urban labor force throughout the late 1980s and early 1990s, providing the labor force necessary to build the country's modern metropolises, and the low wage workforce upon which the nation's manufacturing industry was built.

However, the retreat of the state from that workplace, replaced by an unregulated labor market, provided conditions ripe for exploitation. As China continued with economic reforms, the Jiang Zemin regime in the late 1990s began creating the framework for China's current labor protection regime, both as a means to manage the state's increasingly complex labor market, and to legitimate central government policy.

As migrant workers were not considered members of the working class, they were largely excluded from this regime. Yet the demographic shift which brought millions of migrants to work in China's major metropolitan centers in the south and east coast, most notably in the country's vital export production sector, began to alter political decision makers' assumptions regarding the potential costs of excluding migrants from urban society altogether. Thus, as part of an effort to reaffirm party legitimacy, the Hu Jintao regime in 2003–2004 began tackling some of the more egregious forms of social injustice and inequality. For migrant workers, this shift in policy meant relaxing restrictions on internal migration, recognizing their social status as workers rather than "wandering peasants," highlighting their contributions to economic development, and integrating them into the existing labor protection regime. These policy shifts provided migrants with more legal protections in the city, while expanding their opportunities for protests. Moreover, as new legal protections were bestowed on migrants, the government's need to advertise these protections helped promote a growing sense of legal rights consciousness (*falu quanli zhishi*) among the migrant labor population. The Hu Jintao regime's positive and sympathetic rhetorical shift also helped create a greater sense of efficacy among migrants, leading in part to changing demands and expectations in the workplace. Cognitive changes such as these are an important step in the transformation of migrant labor from passive workers to active protest participants. Previous research has shown that when political authorities acknowledge and respond to the demands of excluded social groups, otherwise fatalistic individuals begin to assert their rights, responding to these new cues (Piven and Cloward 1979, 3). In China, while the government first began granting protections to migrants as a response to their growing economic importance, publicizing those protections further promoted their use. By codifying these commitments into laws and regulations, the central government created the legal framework which made possible the larger, more frequent migrant protests to come.

THE CREATION OF CHINA'S MIGRANT LABOR

China's post-reform labor migration has its roots in the dismantling of the rural commune system, which freed up vast amounts of surplus rural labor (Solinger 1999, 45–46). Economic and market reforms, first begun at the Third Plenum of the 11th Central Committee in December 1978, both dismantled the socialist rural economy, freeing peasants from forced work on the communes, while downgrading many of the rudimentary social services afforded to peasants in the countryside. These disincentives to stay on the farm were matched by a number of incentives to migrate to urban areas in search of employment.

First, agricultural reforms began allowing Chinese peasants to sell their surplus product in the cities, providing the additional food supply needed to sustain a new urban workforce which lacked the grain rations provided to urban residents. Economic policies favoring east coast development shaped the direction of migration as well, as foreign investment began to appear in the Pearl and Yangtze River Delta regions, areas which would become the destination for the majority of the nation's inter-provincial migrant workers.

Government policies allowing companies to keep a portion of their earnings, and increased flexibility in urban hiring practices, paved the way for a construction boom in the early 1980s, largely supported by cheap rural labor. Between 1978 and 1988, nonagricultural employment in the cities increased 6.3% per year, compared to only 1.3% in the rural economy (Bannister 1993, 242).

Regulation and Control

Peasants seeking to move into towns and cities at this time benefited from the fact that neither the central nor local governments were unified in their approach towards this new wave of rural to urban migration. Students of Chinese politics have long studied the obstacles to implementing central-level policies at the local level, and attempts to regulate and control the migrant labor population at this time are no exception (Lieberthal and Oksenberg 1988). Depending upon their bureaucratic purview, agencies at both the central and local levels of government disagreed whether to support or restrict migration. At the central level, although national guidelines relaxed movement restrictions in order to support the emerging manufacturing and construction sectors, senior party officials, including Politburo member Yao Yilin, Standing Committee member Qiao Shi, and Premiere Li Peng, expressed their concerns that rapid growth in the urban population would affect infrastructure and stability in the cities (Solinger 1999, 52–55).

Government actors at the local level faced mixed incentives. Local labor bureaus, who were responsible for maintaining full employment among urban citizens, expressed concerns regarding the impact of additional labor on the employment situation. Public health and housing agencies expressed concern over the stress to the urban infrastructure and the urban welfare system. Meanwhile, agencies tasked with generating income, such as local industrial and commercial bureaus, supported labor migration as a means to generating increased revenue. Some agencies faced mixed incentives. Public security bureaus, which were primarily tasked with maintaining social order, were naturally cautious, yet saw new fines and fees as opportunities for revenue generation (Solinger 1999, 66–70).

Such a mixed set of incentives made it difficult for the government at either the central or local level to fully regulate the population flow once incentives to migration had been created. For example, the 1981 *State Council Notice on Strict Control Over Rural Labor Entering Cities to Work and Agricultural Population Becoming Nonagricultural Population* reported that approximately 6 million peasant workers were moving from the countryside to towns and cities each year, often unofficially "through the back door" (*zuohoumen*) (State Council of the People's Republic of China 1981). Moreover, the notice warned that this was an issue of serious concern which, left unattended, would adversely affect economic reforms and urban employment.

In response, the State Council notice called for stricter control over peasants' urban migration, while also denying them access to urban citizenship, illustrating both the difficulty and importance of controlling migration flows in the eyes of the central government (Emerson 2009). The *1983 State Council's Regulations Concerning Cooperative Endeavors of City and Town Laborers* relaxed these policies slightly, allowing farmers to move to local market towns. Yet so concerned was the central government with maintaining stable urban food prices, migrants were only allowed to do so if they could supply their own food in the cities (Solinger 1999, 49).

Despite agencies' incentives either to support or oppose labor migration, few had any incentives to spend resources on the protection and welfare of migrants once they reached their destinations. Not only were migrants without proper papers subject to forced detainment and repatriation by the state, their ambiguous status as something between peasants and workers meant they fell outside traditional protections reserved for the working class. The millions of migrants who found employment within the reemerging labor contracting system for example, were subject to the whims of contractors' goodwill. A 1986 interview with a labor contractor sums up the prevailing sentiment of the time. When asked about the migrant labor on his work crew, this contractor stated that not only did he not keep records of any of the migrants who worked for him, he and he alone received the wages, distributing them to his crew as he saw fit. How he rewarded "his" workers was none of the state's concern (Korzec 1988, 125–126).

Left unprotected by the state, migrants were also blamed for any growth in urban crime. Ironically however, clustered in their own neighborhoods in the cities, and lacking adequate security and protection, migrants were more likely to be victims rather than perpetrators of crime. Away from home and disconnected from their traditional social circles, migrant workers made easy prey for criminal elements. In addition to fines, fees, and other extractions imposed by local public security organs, emerging criminal gangs began focusing primarily on extorting migrant labor, kidnapping migrant women in transit, and selling them into prostitution. "Vampire gangs" preyed on unsuspecting migrants, luring them by the promise of good jobs, and then forcing them to sell their blood for money (Solinger 1999, 136).

Yet the dangers of exploitation were not enough to stem the tide of rural to urban migration, as peasant farmers reacted primarily to the opportunities for higher wages. While urban-rural income disparities declined throughout the early 1980s, largely as a result of the dismantling of the rural collective production system, by 1984 it had begun to increase, leading to the largest rush of peasant migration since the initial reforms.

In response, the State Council, in October 1984, issued the *Notification on the Question of Peasants Entering Towns and Settling*, allowing peasants to obtain a new, nonagricultural registration, provided they could raise their own funds, supply their own food, and obtain housing. Even then however, the document still formally prohibited migrants from moving into larger regional centers such as county seats, despite the widespread and ongoing practice occurring informally (Solinger 1999, 50). It was not until the end of the decade in 1989, with the State council's *Regulations on the Management of Temporary Labor*, that companies were finally allowed to officially sign individual labor agreements with migrant workers, thus legitimating an employment relationship that had existed for much of the decade.

1990-2000: The Decline of the State Sector and the Rise of Migrant Labor

Economic reforms in the 1990s took a serious toll on workers in China. Within the state sector, State Owned Enterprise (SOE) reform led to the layoff of millions of SOE workers. While the official unemployment rate in urban areas remained between 3% and 4% for most of the 1990s and into the early part of the next decade, unofficial estimates range anywhere from 18.8% in 1995, 15.3% in 1997, and 11% as late as 2002 (Lee 2007, 51).

This transition to a more freewheeling, market orientated economy created vast amounts of new wealth, yet it also led to a massive rise in income disparity and social upheaval, as income equality across almost all possible measures grew throughout the 1990s. By the middle of the decade, China had not only experienced one of the most dramatic increases in economic growth in modern times, but it had also created one of the most unequal distributions of wealth in all of East Asia (Riskin, Zhao, and Li 2001, 3).

While the state sector was in decline, migrant workers were finding jobs in the burgeoning construction and manufacturing sectors along China's southern and eastern coast. By 2004, migrants comprised over 90% of the workforce in the construction industry (S. Liu 2004). Factories in these areas were fast becoming reliant on cheap migrant labor as well, as migrant labor grew to account for a growing proportion of the overall population of China's most developed cities.

Perhaps no city typified the rural to urban migration process during this time more than Shenzhen. Unlike historically rich Beijing, Shanghai, or Guangzhou, the history of Shenzhen is largely a history of China's economic reforms. With a population of roughly 30,000 in 1979, the decision to make Shenzhen the nation's first Special Economic Zone through the promulgation of the "Regulation on Special Economic Zones" in 1980, helped transform it into one of China's largest and most dynamic cities. Graph 3.1 charts Shenzhen's enormous population growth during this time. In 1983 before the first major migration wave, temporary residents, individuals without Shenzhen permanent resident status, made up about one third of the Shenzhen population. By 2002 however, nonpermanent residents constituted over 80% of the total municipal population (Statistics Bureau of the Municipal Government of Shenzhen 2008).

As China experienced high rates of growth throughout the 1990s, cadres' career progression were significantly tied to their ability to continue delivering this growth, often at the expense of workers' rights (S. P. S. Ho 1994). Quantifiable targets such as GDP growth, tax revenues, and other economic indicators were favored over "soft targets" involving environmental or labor protections (O'Brien and Li 1999). Moreover, cadre evaluation systems also incorporated the opinions of leaders at lower levels, which, for cadres at the

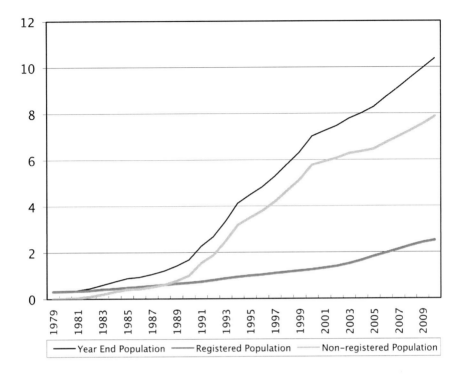

Graph 3.1. Shenzhen Migrant Population Growth 1979–2010 (millions). Source: (Statistics Bureau of the Municipal Government of Shenzhen, various years)

township level, could include the opinions of enterprise managers and village leaders at that locale (Edin 1998). This promotion structure created ample incentives for local level cadres to favor economic growth at the expense of workers' rights, while creating opportunities to collude with the private sector at the expense of migrant labor.

By the early 1990s, strict militaristic factory regimes had become common, giving rise to "localistic despotism," whereby collusion between foreign investors, local business interests, and local officials ensured that the enforcement of labor regulations often stayed outside the factory gates (Lee 1998). In addition to common forms of labor exploitation such as unpaid wages and unpaid overtime, scholars have catalogued more extreme issues; frequent use of corporal punishments, confinement to factory grounds, forced labor, and enslavement (Chan 2001). Instances of workers literally being "worked to death" (*guolaosi*) were not unknown.

In the manufacturing and construction industries, labor injuries, labor related illnesses, and labor related deaths, increased at an alarming rate. In a November 1993 fire in the Shenzhen-based Zhili Toy Factory, 87 mostly female workers were killed while 47 others were injured (Chan 2001). According to government statistics, within the first 10 months of 1993 alone, over 28,200 industrial fires killed approximately 1,400 workers and injured 50,000; estimates which no doubt exclude the growing informal sector, and the hundreds of thousands of unregistered migrants employed in that sector (Poole 1996). By the end of the 1990s, approximately 31 workers were injured every day in Shenzhen, while one worker died every four days (K. Liu 2004, 18–19).

Policy Response in the Jiang Zemin Regime

As the social consequences of economic reform and restructuring continued to emerge, the state was forced to take action, lest social unrest undermine stability and the state's capacity for further economic reform. In response, the Jiang Zemin regime followed a two pronged approach. First, the state sought to expand social services, particularly services to laid-off workers and unemployed urban residents. By the mid-1990s, the national unemployment insurance system, which had previously covered only state sector workers, had been expanded to cover those in the private sector as well. Under the 1999 *Regulations on Unemployment Insurance*, an insurance scheme was created whereby employers would contribute 2% of their total expenditures, while employees would contribute 1% of their salaries. Covered workers were eligible to receive unemployment subsidies for a period based on their prior length of employment (Lee 2007, 52).

Migrant workers however were excluded from this new social safety net. Though the state had expanded the unemployment insurance program in the mid-1990s to include the non-state sector, the many unregulated, private enterprises most likely to employ migrant labor were also least likely to participate. In addition, having never worked in the state sector, migrant workers did not qualify to receive aid from the state's newly established reemployment centers. As rural residents, they also failed to qualify for the basic living allowances provided to their urban counterparts. Thus, while the mid-1990s saw the creation of multiple components of a social safety net for labor in China, migrant labor, the country's fastest growing segment of the workforce, remained largely excluded from those protections.

The second pillar in the government's labor policy lay in the creation of a legal system for resolving labor disputes. Promoting a "rule of law" system more generally had been a key task for the party since the beginnings of economic reform, and was seen as a way to guard against a return to the political and social chaos enacted under the personal dictatorship during the Mao era.[1] A functioning legal system would also provide the predictability and stability necessary to attract foreign investment (Gallagher 2007).

Early aspects of the labor law regime can be traced to the late 1980s. On 31 July 1987, the state council's *Interim Provisions for the Handling of Labor Disputes in State Enterprises* established the three tiered dispute resolution process of mediation, arbitration, and litigation. Yet this process applied only to those working within the state sector (V. H. Ho 2003, 38) and was thus irrelevant to the 10 million plus interprovincial migrant workers at the time ("Peasant Migrants Creates Both Opportunity and Challenges for Society [Nongmingong Liudong Wei Shehui Fazhan Dailai Jiyu Yu Tiaozhan]" 2008). Regulations outlined in the 1987 *Interim Provisions* were expanded in August 1993, with the promulgation of the *PRC Regulations for the Handling of Enterprise Labor Disputes* (HELDR). The HELDR replaced the *Interim Provisions,* making this three tiered system relevant to the private sector as well, while the central government issued new regulations dictating wage, benefit, health, and other labor conditions (V. H. Ho 2003, 38–39).

On 5 July 1994, after years of deliberation and debate, the National People's Congress promulgated the *Labor Law of the People's Republic of China,* which removed distinctions between workers employed in SOEs, private firms, or foreign owned enterprises, while solidifying the concept of divergent interests between workers and management. The *Labor Law* also enshrined the concept that the responsibility of mitigating conflicts between these two interests fell upon the state and the legal system, a reversal from Mao-era notions highlighting informal dispute resolution and a politicized role for mediators and disputants, who were urged to view issues from the interest of the state.[2]

Like the social welfare programs described above however, urban workers, not migrants, were the primary targets of early legal reforms. By forming a national labor market, the 1995 *Labor Law* protects some basic rights of all China's workers. Yet the new law was highly ambiguous regarding the definition of workers, and makes no mention of migrant workers specifically (Ngok 2008, 56). As a result of this ambiguity, migrant workers continued to be left out of the general definition of what constituted urban residents or urban workers.

MIGRANT LABOR POLICY REFORMS UNDER HU JINTAO

Labor migration was a key component in the PRC's economic reforms, providing the cheap labor necessary to attract foreign direct investment and spur economic growth. Throughout the 1980s and 1990s however, the state concerned itself with either exploiting the economic benefits, or mitigating the potential costs, of this demographic shift. This is illustrated in the majority of central government policy documents referenced above, which focus overwhelmingly on control and regulation, rather that providing protections and benefits.

Central government policies to migrants began to change under the Hu Jintao regime, which embarked upon a series of significant reforms that expanded the space available for migrant workers to live and work in the cities, increasing their ability to protest labor exploitation. Through inclusion into the ACFTU, changes in party rhetoric, and the promulgation of new government regulations removing both social stigmas and economic and social restrictions, the early years of the Hu Jintao regime began a process whereby migrants came to be recognized as members of the working class.

Sources of Policy Change

Although the policy making process in China remains opaque, multiple factors appeared to contribute to this policy change. Unlike the previous regime under Jiang Zemin, the Hu-Wen regime appeared more focused on tackling the issue of social inequality. At the November 2002 Sixteenth Party Congress for example, which affirmed Hu's status as the next CCP General Secretary, the party released a political report entitled "Building a well-off society in a well-rounded way," reaffirming the goals of "long reign and perennial stability," and noting this would be accomplished only by increasing social justice and raising the standard of living for the general population, including China's rural citizens (Lam 2006, 316). Thus, expansions in protections for migrants should be viewed as part of a larger policy goal of improving the lives of the China's "disadvantaged groups" (*ruoshi qunti*), and the growing concern on the part of China's leaders that growing social inequality may lead to social unrest (Tanner 2004).

The growth in the migrant labor population likely played a role in the new regime's reevaluation of its policy as well. From the time Jiang Zemin came to power in 1989, to the 16th Party Congress in 2002, the number of "peasants going out to work" (*wailai wugong*) had increased over three-fold, from 30 million to over 100 million (Yang and Yang 2010). By the early 2000s, migrants made up the majority of workers in the manufacturing and construction sectors, and as described above, made up the overwhelming majority population in some of China's largest cities.

Large-scale demographic changes of the kind which took place in China in the early 2000s have often been a catalyst for broader policy reform, as the forces of urbanization and industrialization compel policy makers to reevaluate the state's relationships with emerging social groups (McAdam 1999, 41). As Chinese manufacturing and construction grew more reliant upon migrants for continued growth, ignoring the most grievous aspects of migrant labor exploitation became increasingly problematic.

This reliance on the migrant labor population became clear in 2004, when areas relying overwhelmingly on migrant labor began to experience significant labor shortages. Long hours, stagnant pay, and the constant threat of labor exploitation compelled a growing number of migrant workers to engage in what some have referred to as a "silent protest" against their treatment (Kwok 2004). Growing job opportunities in rural areas, rising wages in the agricultural sector, and reform of the agricultural tax made it increasingly hard to attract workers into traditional manufacturing regions. By 2004, a MoHRSS survey conducted in the Pearl River Delta estimated that the region faced a shortage of 2 million workers, forcing some manufactures to scale back production (Shi 2004). As migrant workers became reluctant to take jobs in the more grueling and notorious sectors of the economy, it became commonplace to read of the growing migrant labor shortage (*laodongli duanqie*), making it impossible for many factories to operate at full capacity (Zhao 2004).

To counter this shortage, some companies raised wages, while important manufacturing cities such as Dongguan began to raise the local minimum wage (Harney 2004). Yet long hours of unpaid overtime often ate into any wage increase, while a myriad number of fines and fees absorbed the rest. Indeed, this continued to be a problem voiced by workers during interviews I conducted in Dongguan after Spring Festival in the late 2000s. While many factories hung banners over the front gates promising higher monthly wages, workers remained suspicious, believing any wage hike was sure to be followed by fines, fees, or longer work hours. In the words of one worker; "yes, they promise higher wages now, but then they'll just punish us whenever they like" ("Interview Dongguan 1103" 2008).

China's continued demographic shift was joined by a generational shift in the migrant labor population as well. Unlike their predecessors, who began migrating to the cities in the 1980s and 1990s, had spent time in rural areas doing agricultural work, and had experienced the hardship of China under Mao firsthand, many of China's "new generation" of migrants (*xinshengdai*) born after 1980 lack agricultural experience, had already spent a significant amount of time in the cities, and had been raised under conditions of relative prosperity. This new generation of migrant workers was younger, more educated, assertive, and well positioned to take advantage of new opportunities for protest as they emerged throughout the 2000s (All-China Federation of Trade Unions Editorial Department 2010).

A growing number of migrant labor organizations devoted to the legal rights and protections of migrants began to appear at this time as well, thus creating another source of government concern. While organizations designed to provide social services to migrant workers began to appear in the early 1990s, the new decade witnessed a significant increase in their numbers. In 2002, 1,500 migrant workers joined the Tangxia Migrant Workers

Association in Zhejiang Province, an organization established with the help of village officials, in the hopes of combating the rise in native place associations and local labor violence (Pan 2002). That same year, organizations in Beijing such as *Migrant Women's Home* and *Little Bird*, as well as Pearl River Delta organizations such as the *Panyu Migrant Document Service Center*, the *Institute For Contemporary Observation*, and the *Nanshan Women Worker Service Center*, had begun providing a range of social and legal services to their local migrant communities.

Thus, both emerging policy priorities, and fundamental structural changes to the migrant labor population and labor market, likely influenced the Hu Jintao regime's policy changes. These reforms, according to State Council Development Research Center Director Han Jun, amounted to a change in government's policy on migrants from "forbidding the flow to accepting the flow, and finally encouraging the flow" [of migrant workers] (Xinhua 2004).

This process of reform would greatly expand the space available for migrants to live and work in the cities, and by doing so, expand the space migrants had to engage in labor protest activity. Migrants also gained legal access to government and government related institutions, and, at least on paper, were freed from many arbitrary fines, fees, and detention policies.

This period also witnessed a symbolic and rhetorical shift in the government's language toward migrant labor, moving away from the view of migrants as "transient laborers," or "blind wanderers," outside the scope of proper society, and towards greater recognition of their contributions to the nation's economic development and modernization. The rhetorical shift in the government's attitude toward migrant labor, evident in highly symbolic events such as Premiere Wen Jiabao personally meeting with migrant workers to resolve wage issues, provided a strong signal to migrants regarding their importance, modifying the ways in which many would frame their disputes ("'Premier Wen Helps Recover My Payment!'" 2003). Scholars of popular protest have long held that signals such as these are important for encouraging activists to pursue further action. As sociologist Doug McAdam noted in his analysis of the U.S. civil rights movement, "the belief that conditions are subject to change are largely a function of the response of other groups to the aggrieved population" (McAdam 1999, 106). The government's changing position vis-à-vis migrant labor sent strong "cognitive cues," modifying and increasing migrant labors' own expectations regarding how they should be treated at the workplace.

Legislative and Policy Reform 2003–2006

Evidence of a subtle shift in the government's position towards migrant workers can be seen as early as 2001, with the promulgation of a joint circular, published by both the National Development and Reform Commission and the Ministry of Finance, which called for the removal of the myriad fees on migrant labor moving into urban areas, as well as the abolition of temporary residency fees (National Development and Reform Commission and Ministry of Finance 2001). Two years later, the period between 2003 and 2004 witnessed a dramatic growth in the number of policy statements and legislation focusing on migrant labor rights, shifting the central government's overall focus to one that, while still concerned with the effects of migrant labor on urban areas, gave voice to issues of rights and protection. As these pronouncements were reported by the domestic press, they increased public awareness of migrant labor issues more generally.

One of the most important documents in this early period was the January 2003 *Circular on the Protection of the Legal Rights of Migrant Workers* (Circular no. 1) (State Council of the People's Republic of China 2003b). This document explicitly acknowledged the problems migrants faced in the cities, stating that "currently in a few regions, migrants entering the cities in search of work still encounter a few irrational restrictions, migrant legal rights are not effectively safeguarded, and the phenomenon of wage arrears, wage deductions, and chaotic fees etc. are critical" (State Council of the People's Republic of China 2003c). The circular discussed a wide range of migrant labor rights and protections, calling on local governments to abolish prohibitions on migrants working in certain industries, implement temporary residence permit programs, clean up wage arrears (particularly in the construction industry), and increase inspections of migrant labor worksites. The *2003 Circular* also called on local governments to limit the detainment and repatriation of migrants who lacked official documentation, a program which had long been a source of abuse, as well as an informal funding source for local governments. Finally, the circular called for the general removal of social stigmas associated with migrant workers, recognizing their contributions to economic development (State Council of the People's Republic of China 2003c).

The *2003 Circular* is one of the earliest government documents acknowledging such a wide range of problems. However, like many high-level policy pronouncements, it was vague in its language and unspecific in regards to its implementation. Moreover, its sympathetic language towards migrant workers was balanced by language which recognized the issues urban governments face when managing migrants, noting that "migrant workers entering the cities in search of work create new problems of social public order and urban management," hinting at the limits of the central government's support for migrant labor rights at this time.

The Sun Zhigang Incident

One key aspect of the *2003 Circular*, the issue of forced repatriation back to their hometown for migrants who lacked proper documentation, came to the forefront shortly after the circular's promulgation. On 17 March 2003, Sun Zhigang, a 27 year old graduate student from Wuhan University, who had recently moved to Guangzhou to work for a garment manufacturing company, was detained by the local police for not having his residence card. Three days later, he died while in state custody at a local detention center. Although the official cause of death was heart attack, an autopsy conducted by doctors at Sun Yatsen University showed he was beaten to death. The story went unreported in the Chinese press for almost a full month, until a former classmate of Sun's who worked at the Supreme People's Court intervened and contacted the *Southern Metropolitan Daily*, which finally published an article about the case on 25 April 2003 (Zheng 2003).

Throughout the 1980s and 1990s, migrant workers had generally garnered little public sympathy from the urban populace, as city residents often viewed them as the source of urban society's ills rather than its victims. Previous work on popular protest however has demonstrated how the identification of a sympathetic subject can do much to influence the public's framing of an issue, even in a state with limited media freedoms such as China (Tarrow 2011, 106–22). Regulations allowing the arrest and detention of any migrant worker without proper papers had been in effect for over two decades. At the time of the Sun Zhigang case, the government had at least 850 such detention centers throughout the county, where migrants were commonly subject to violence, extortion and blackmail (Lam 2006, 120). However, the fact that the victim in this case was a successful college student; a respected position within Chinese society, elicited much more sympathy from the general public, compared to the hundreds of similar cases of abuse targeting less educated migrant workers. Ironically, the ramifications of this public outcry over the death of a well educated graduate student would have major implications for China's migrant labor population overall.

Reform of the repatriation system for unregistered migrants was likely already on the government's agenda at the time of the Sun Zhigang case. However, the public response was overwhelmingly sympathetic, creating a large public outcry regarding the treatment of migrant labor in general. Memorial websites soon appeared online, attracting tens of thousands of viewers, while a similar number of readers published comments denouncing the government's treatment of migrants (Tai 2006, 264–66). Lawyers and academics drafted open letters denouncing the inhumane nature of the government's internal deportation system, while online petitions directed to the Supreme People's Court and Supreme People's Procuratorate protesting the treatment of migrants began to appear (Tai 2006, 266). In less than three months on 22 June 2003, the government introduced new regulations, replacing the 1982 Regulation on "Custody and Repatriation of Homeless Beggars," which had provided the legal basis to detain migrants without temporary residence cards or work permits (Human Rights in China 2003).

With the changes to the 1982 Regulations, migrants were no longer subject to repatriation as an everyday aspect of normal urban existence. To be sure, harassment by government authorities and expulsion from urban areas still occurs. Extralegal detainment for political activists, particularly petitioners, still exists, while government authorities may remove or temporarily relocate migrant labor during extraordinary circumstances. In the run-up to the 2008 Olympics, the Beijing government removed hundreds of thousands of migrants and other socially undesirables from the city (Bu 2008), while the Shenzhen municipal government expelled over 80,000 individuals in 2011 as part of the city's anti-crime efforts before the national University Games.

Such events however are no longer an aspect of everyday life for migrant labor. While still second class citizens, migrants have become an accepted facet of urban society, and reforming the Custody and Repatriation System was an important step to expanding freedom of movement and urban legitimacy for China's migrant labor population. This increased freedom of action in urban areas, without the constant fear of forced expulsion from the cities, has in turn helped to expand migrants' opportunities for protest activity.

Addressing Migrant Grievances: The Wage Arrears Campaign

Nowhere was the government's migrant labor policy shift more evident than in the decision to begin addressing the issue of unpaid wages. As described in chapter 2, unpaid wages (*tuoqian gongzi*) have long been the primary source of migrant labor disputes. As a national issue, migrant wage arrears had been mentioned prominently in policy documents such as the January *2003 Circular*. However, not before 2003 had the government enacted a sustained campaign designed to resolve migrant wage arrears issues. The use of campaigns (*yundong*) as a policy tool has a long tradition in Chinese politics, involving the expenditure of significant government resources and increased public attention on a specific subject over short bursts of time. Campaign topics often reflect the importance that the central government attributes to a specific policy priority, and in this case, the government campaign against unpaid wages was a reflection of the increasing importance attached to this issue.[3]

The public beginnings of the government's wage arrears campaign can be traced to Premier Wen Jiabao's fall 2003 inspection tour in Yunyang County in Sichuan. In a meeting with local peasants, the premier heard from Xiong Deming, a local woman who complained that her husband was owed over 2,000 RMB in back wages from his job as a construction worker. Within a few hours after the personal intervention of the premiere, Xiong's husband, along with over a dozen other village migrant workers, had received their pay. Xiong Deming quickly became a national news celebrity, receiving thousands of requests for aid from other migrants. The encounter was nominated as one of the top domestic news stories of the year by Xinhua News Agency, greatly increasing national attention devoted to the wage arrears issue (Lam 2006, 60).

This well publicized meeting signaled the start of a national wage arrears campaign, and a flurry of policy documents and legislation soon followed. First, the central government began publishing policy pronouncements calling on local governments and businesses to take seriously the issue of wage arrears, while developing mechanisms that, if properly implemented, could combat future occurrences. In September 2003, MoHRSS and the Ministry of Construction jointly issued the *Circular on Resolving Migrant Worker Wage Arrears Issues in the Construction Industry,* which called on local labor bureaus to establish an information system within local enterprises to verify the disbursement of wages (*qiye gongzi zhifu xinyong zhidu*), and to double its efforts in inspecting the conditions of migrant labor in their areas (Ministry of Labor and Social Security and Ministry of Construction 2003). This was followed later in the year with the State Council's *Circular of the General Office of the State Council on Settlement of Delinquent Construction Project Costs in the Construction Business* (*circular no. 93*), which further exhorted local governments to "fully recognize the necessity and urgency of resolving the issue of migrant labor wage arrears in the construction industry." The notice went on to argue that these issues seriously influence both the development of the construction industry, and social stability more generally (State Council of the People's Republic of China 2003a).

By early 2004, the government's wage arrears campaign had come more clearly into focus. In February 2004, the Ministry of Construction issued *An Urgent Circular on Stepping up the Resolution of the Issue of Migrant Labor Wages*. The circular reiterated the government's position that resolving the wage issue was important for maintaining social stability, while lauding the government's success in obtaining back wages for migrants from government invested projects. The circular noted that it had returned almost 24 Billion RMB, or 75.66% of all outstanding wages, while resolving 95.22% (15.92 Billion RMB) of all wages owed from 2003. The notice also called upon government agencies at all levels to resolve all back pay issues in the construction industry occurring in 2003 by June of that year, while resolving all wage issues occurring prior to 2003 by June of 2005 (Ministry of Construction 2004).

A month later, Premier Wen's 5 March 2004 work report at the 2nd Plenum of the 10th National People's Congress again made clear the importance the central government had attached to the wage arrears issue. In describing the principal tasks for the new year, the premier reiterated the State Council's decision to "basically solve the problems of default on construction costs and wage arrears for migrant rural workers in the construction industry within three years," while stating that enterprises and managers who refused to pay back wages to migrants must be held accountable in accordance with the law (Wen 2004).

This high level policy statement was followed by a September 2004 joint circular from the Ministry of Construction and the MoLSS entitled *Joint Circular on Provisional Methods for Managing Wage Payment to Peasant Workers in the Construction Sector* (Ministry of Labor and Social Security and Ministry of Construction 2004). Like previous pronouncements, the circular called for enterprises to sign labor contracts and pay legal minimum wages. The notice also stated that enterprises needed to pay wages directly to employees, rather than to labor contractors.

In 2006 on the heels of the wage arrears campaign, the state council issued its most comprehensive migrant labor policy document to date, entitled, *Some Opinions of the State Council on Resolving the Problems Faced by Migrant Workers* (State Council of the People's Republic of China 2006). This forty point document outlined the importance of migrant labor to the manufacturing and construction industry, and identified the government's policy goals of gradually establishing a unified urban and rural labor market, protecting migrant labor rights, and increasing public services available to migrant workers. The document called for stricter implementation of local minimum wage laws and the labor contract system, while the pro-migrant labor rhetoric of the document helped set a more positive tone.

The state council document also recommended abolishing discriminatory hiring practices and reforming the occupational injury insurance, retirement, and pensions systems to include migrant labor, a goal that was further advanced with the promulgation of the 2011 *Social Insurance Law* (State Council of the People's Republic of China 2006).

Later in 2006, Vice Minister of Labor and Social Security, Hu Xiaoyi, called for the continuation of the work of all government organizations to resolve unpaid wage issues, suggesting the issue had not been completely resolved by the 2005 timeline outlined in previous government pronouncements. Specifically, the vice minister called for the introduction of four measures to guarantee workers' wages; a system of inspection and control for migrant worker wages, a cash deposit system (*baozhengjin*) which would compel construction companies to establish accounts for the payment of migrant wages, universal salary standards for part time workers, and a system to guarantee the distribution of migrant wages (Wang 2007).

Throughout this three-year period between 2003 and 2006, these policy documents were matched by a flurry of articles and editorials stressing the necessity of resolving the wage arrears issue for the good of economic development and social stability.[4] Yet to what extent was the government's campaign successful in resolving this issue? Like most campaigns, the energy needed to prosecute the wage arrears issue at such a high level of intensity was simply unsustainable. And despite highlighting the billions of dollars in back pay retrieved, government admonishments to resolve the unpaid wage issue continue to remain a staple of the Chinese media in the run-up to the New Year holiday; a spring festival tradition as predictable as firecrackers and dumplings ("End Begging for Wage, Editorials" 2011).

Yet the government's wage arrears campaign also helped change public perceptions of the wage arrears issue, and provided the legal and rhetorical cover for migrants to protest against this form of exploitation. While unpaid wages remain a serious issue, changing government policy and rhetoric recognizing the unjust nature of withholding migrants' wages legitimized protests against this activity. Employing national policy as a way to justify protest at the local level is a time tested strategy, both in China and elsewhere (O'Brien 2011). Central level policy pronouncements provided migrants with this justification, allowing them to more freely oppose unfair practices such as wage arrears and unpaid wages by providing a level of policy cover and moral legitimacy unavailable in earlier decades.

The Union's Changing Stance Toward Migrant Workers

Taking its cue from the state's changing migrant labor rhetoric, China's union began taking important steps to change its migrant labor policy throughout the 2000s as well. Union membership had been on a steady decline throughout the economic reform era, as state enterprises privatized and emerging private sector firms were weary of allowing the union to establish new branches. In his 2000 speech to the ACFTU Executive Committee for example, ACFTU Chairman and Politburo member Wei Jianxing reported that only 5% of workers employed in private enterprises were union members, while this number declined to 3.4% for workers employed in township and village enterprises (Howell 2009). Even where union branches did survive, new state policies, which provided more power to enterprise management to allocate union funds, placed financial control of enterprise unions in the hands of management. Enterprise level union cadres were often treated like any other employee, and could be fired for acting on behalf of workers.

Union response to this decline in membership base and shop floor influence largely followed a three pronged approach; influencing labor legislation at the central level, establishing a presence in the emerging private sector through the creation of new union branches, and reevaluating its position on migrant labor by recognizing migrants as members of the working class, while engaging in a widespread campaign to recruit migrants workers into the union.

The union's policy change towards migrant labor was solidified in the August 2003 *Notice on Better Protection for the Legal Rights of Migrant Workers*. In accord with the government's broader campaign to protect migrant labor rights more generally, this document marked a dramatic shift in the union's recognition of migrant labor as workers rather than peasants, arguing that "laborers entering the cities are burgeoning workers who rely on wages as a source of income, and already constitute an important segment of our country's work and staff members" (All-China Federation of Trade Unions Editorial Department 2003). Referring to the growing number of labor disputes among migrant workers at the time, the document rails against worker injuries and unpaid wages, argues that the trade union is "duty bound" (*yibu rongci*) to protect the rights of migrant workers, and called for the adoption of measures to help bring migrant workers into the union (All-China Federation of Trade Unions Editorial Department 2003). Later that year, the Party Central Committee and the State Council jointly issued the *Opinions on Several Policies Promoting an Increase in Farmers' Incomes*, which reaffirmed the idea that "farmers were already an integral part of the industrial workforce," a nod to non-traditional, rural workers operating in non-agricultural sectors of the economy (H. Liu 2004).

Following the publication of the ACFTU's *2003 Notice*, the union embarked upon a recruitment campaign targeting migrant labor, stating that over 34 million migrants had "flocked to join the trade union" within a month ("Migrant Workers Flock to Join China's Trade Unions" 2003). In addition, the union set a goal to recruit at least six million new migrant workers each year for the next four years. By 2007, the ACFTU boasted that it had organized over 40 million migrants (Xinhua 2007). By 2008, this number had increased to 66 million ("Trade Unions Extend Aid for Migrant Workers in Financial Crisis" 2009).

Given the ACFTU's publicly announced goal of recruiting six million migrants annually, it is not surprising that year end statistics matched these estimates. Many migrants however appeared to join the union in name only. Because the ACFTU often relies on a top-down strategy of establishing new branches through collaboration with management, rather than engaging in grass roots organizing, many members do not sign membership forms, pay union dues, or participate in union activities aside from the occasional recreational activity ("Migrant Workers Flock to Join China's Trade Unions" 2003). Thus, for many migrant workers, as well as for many workers overall, the union was, in the words of one worker I interviewed "only ornamentation" ("Interview Shenzhen 0404" 2008). Regardless, by 2004 it was clear that the union had followed the party's new line towards migrant workers as an important segment of the working class in need of protection, a sharp change from just a few years ago when migrants were considered outside the union's purview.

To be sure, barriers that prevent migrants from obtaining union protections persist, and are discussed in detail in chapter 4. However, the union's policy shift towards migrant labor, from interlopers operating outside proper urban society to members of the working class, was a critical step in shaping migrant workers' opportunities for future protest. As union members, migrants were now part of a social group lauded by official party and government rhetoric. This helped underwrite the emerging narrative that migrant workers should both feel proud of their contributions to the development of a modern China, and were deserving of the same rights and protections as other workers in society. Practically, the union, in conjunction with other government agencies such as the Ministry of Labor and Ministry of Construction, began to address some of the more egregious labor issues during this time period, such as the issue of wage arrears in state owned construction sites.

CONCLUSION: LAYING THE FOUNDATIONS FOR FUTURE PROTEST

Research on popular protest and social movements has demonstrated how broad social processes, including industrialization, changes within the structure of the labor market, and demographic shifts, have the potential to shift authorities' calculations regarding how to managing its relations with emerging social groups (McAdam 1999, 40–41). In China, the economic changes which took place in the late 1990s and the early 2000s in part affected the central government's calculus regarding migrant workers and their place in society. Mass urban migration, the creation of a unified labor market, and the state's retreat from the market and subsequent rise in labor exploitation, all contributed to the creation of migrant workers as a distinct social group. This group faced both traditional grievances common to all workers in China, and unique grievances specific to their place in Chinese society, and the stage of Chinese economic development.

As migrant workers' became increasingly important as an engine for economic growth, the level of extreme exploitation that they faced, in part a reflection of the growing level of social inequality and civil unrest in China more broadly, appeared to influence decision makers' calculations. Such levels of labor exploitation seemed increasingly untenable, and changes were needed to safeguard future growth and social stability. While high-level decision making in China remains opaque, this appeared to be the general logic behind official statements, such portions of Jiang Zemin's 16th party work report, which referenced the growing problem of low wages and public disorder, as well as the general rhetorical policy line espoused in the early years of the Hu Jintao regime (Jiang 2002).

The central government's change in policy can be seen in the growth of edicts, regulations, and legislation in the early 2000s, which provided migrants new legal protections, as well as social legitimacy, by recognizing their contributions to economic development. Changes in the policies of detaining and repatriating unregistered migrants provided increased freedom of movement, while growing access to the labor arbitration and court system expanded the number of options available for migrant protest. To be sure, obstacles to using China's labor arbitration and court system remain, and are discussed in detail in chapter 4. Yet institutional reforms, such as the removal of arbitration fees, and the increased availability of legal support, have led to a growth in the use of the legal system among migrant labor.

Symbolically, the government's new policy position towards migrant workers—that as members of the working class migrant labor had the right to protections like other workers—helped spur a sense of legal rights consciousness. This provided a fundamental criterion necessary for increased protest activity; a change in migrant labor's subjective interpretation of their situation from helplessness to optimism and expectancy. These policy changes had long lasting pragmatic and symbolic impacts, expanding the space available for migrants to protest their exploitation, and the number of dispute options available, and changing migrants subjective understanding of their rights as members of the working class.

By themselves, such changes however were insufficient to guarantee the growth in migrant labor protest activity that we see today. Although they provided the prerequisite space to act, migrant labor continues to face a host of obstacles to protest, ranging from the inability to engage in formal, independent organizing, to the challenges inherent in obtaining the financial and informational resources necessary for action in an authoritarian state. Understanding these obstacles, and the strategies migrant workers use to overcome them, is the focus of the second half of this book.

NOTES

1. China's legal system is also often referred to as one of "rule by law" rather than "rule of law," acknowledging the party's position as unconstrained or only loosely constrained by the nation's legal framework. This book uses the more common "rule by law" terminology. See Neil J. Diamant, Stanley Lubman, and Kevin J. O'Brien, eds., *Engaging the Law in China: State, Society and Possibilities for Justice* (Stanford: Stanford University Press, 2005); Stanley Lubman, *Bird in a Cage: Legal Reform in China After Mao*, (Stanford: Stanford University Press, 1999); Ronald C. Keith and Lin Zhiqiu, *Law and Justice in China's New Marketplace*, (New York: Palgrave, 2001); Randall Peerenboom, *China's Long March Toward Rule of Law*, (Cambridge: Cambridge University Press, 2002).

2. Mary Gallagher and Junlu Jiang, "Guest Editor's Introduction," *Chinese Law and Government*, vol. 35, no. 6, (2002), pp. 3-15; Ho, *Labor Dispute Resolution in China*, pp. 37.

This is not to suggest that the legal system in China has been thoroughly depoliticized. The appointment of officials from the Ministry of Public Security to positions on the Supreme People's Court, or the reassignment of notable legal scholars such as He Weifang from Beijing to the western provinces, suggests an oscillation in the politicization of rule of law in China. See Carl Minzer, "Back and Forth From Beijing," *New York Times*, 29 May, 2009.

3. On the campaign process in China, see for example Andrew Wedeman, "Anticorruption Campaigns and the Intensification of Corruption in China," *Journal of Contemporary China*, vol. 14, no. 42, 2005.

4. Such examples abounded in the Chinese press during this time. For a small sample, see "Government to Tackle Farmer Workers' Wage Arrears Issue," *Xinhua*, 10 March 2004, http://www.china.org.cn/english/10th/89799.htm; "Migrant Workers' Wage Arrears No Longer Owed" [weile nongmingong gongzi buzai beituoqian] *Guangming Daily*, 26 June 2005, http://www.gmw.cn/01gmrb/2005-06/23/content_255982.htm. See also the *People's Daily* news portal devoted to migrant labor rights issues, "Concern for Migrant Workers, Protect Migrant Worker Rights and Interests [guanzhu nongmingong baohu nongmingong quanyi], *People's Daily*, http://www.people.com.cn/GB/shizheng/8198/30572/.

Chapter Four

The State, the Market, and Challenges to Institutionalizing Migrant Labor Protests

Since 2003, as part of the government's broader policy of promoting social stability through the creation of a "harmonious society" (*hexie shehui*), the Chinese government's strategy for addressing rising social and economic inequality has included the integration of migrants into the national labor protection regime. The importance of migrant labor to the national economy, combined with increasing demographic pressure and the growing presence of migrant labor in China's major cities, meant older policies focusing exclusively on social control have grown untenable. As a result, new policies beginning in the early 2000s have helped to legitimize migrants as members of the working class, while also providing them with greater freedom of movement and protections in the cities.

Despite these changes however, opportunities for protest remain constrained. This is particularly true for migrant workers seeking to use the formal legal system or government channels to resolve their disputes. Prohibitions against formal organization, lax labor monitoring and enforcement mechanisms, and unresponsive legal institutions, all pose challenges to the *institutionalization* of migrant protest through use of labor arbitration, the courts, or collective bargaining. These factors also inhibit the prevention and mitigation of migrant labor disputes through labor monitoring or policy enforcement by government agents.

Weak state enforcement of legal protections, and state controls on civil society, are problems for all Chinese citizens. However, migrant workers face obstacles to institutionalizing disputes in ways other social groups do not. The informal employment of many migrant workers for example makes collecting the evidence necessary to take action via labor arbitration or the courts a difficult proposition. The growing use of complex labor relationships, such as those involving labor contractors and labor dispatch services, has created new obstacles for government monitoring and enforcement institutions, making it difficult for the state to enforce the law. Additionally, despite their newfound legitimacy, the hostile urban environment faced by many migrant workers, characterized by institutional exclusion, social biases, and an exploitative environment, combined with the lack of an urban social safety net, encourages migrants to discount sources of information that cannot be readily verified by trusted sources. This limitation on migrant workers' informational access in turn limits the number of protest options and strategies available. This chapter examines each of these obstacles in turn.

THE ROLE OF THE STATE

Nothing influences Chinese migrant workers as much as the party-state itself. As an authoritarian regime which retains a monopoly on political power, the Chinese government consciously influences the manner in which all groups in society operate, organize, and interact. For migrant labor, this influence takes the form of organizational and associational restrictions, institutional exclusion via the household registration (*hukou*) system, and limited governance capacity of the state's labor institutions tasked with monitoring, investigating, and resolving labor disputes.

Restrictions on Organizing

The capacity to organize is fundamental to the development of labor rights, allowing labor to bargain with employers on an even footing (Offe and Keane 1985, 184–91). The arrangement of interests groups in Chinese society however, which are vertically organized to facilitate state control, roughly resembles what comparative political scientists have described as a "state corporatist" model (Schmitter 1974).

China's civil society model of state corporatism however does not preclude repression, and labor's right to organize outside the party continues to be forcefully prohibited (Deyo 1989, 106–11). While legally recognized grass roots organizations have emerged in areas such as environmental protection, AIDS prevention, women's rights, and even migrant legal rights and cultural activities, the CCP still prohibits workers from organizing for the purpose of collective bargaining. It was no coincidence that the only arrests before the 4 June 1989 Tiananmen demonstrations reached their apex were made on workers, and one of the greatest concerns for the party leadership was the full participation of labor in the demonstrations (Wright 2008; Zhang

2002). Given this situation, it is unsurprising that the All-China Federation of Trade Unions (ACFTU), China's umbrella organization and the sole legal labor organization in China, is controlled both organizationally and financially by the party, deriving its authority from its institutional position vis-à-vis the CCP, as opposed to its ability to organize and mobilize workers (F. Chen 2004).

This is not to suggest that the ACFTU is unable to ever provide support for China's workers, but workers are much more likely to receive union help if their dispute is individual in nature as opposed to collective, limited in scope, apolitical, and employs only state sanctioned protest strategies, such as appeals to labor arbitration or the petition system (F. Chen 2004).

Straightforward, apolitical labor disputes in which the union is most likely to intervene however make up only a small portion of migrant labor disputes, whose cases are often more complex as a result of the complicated and informal nature of their employment. Migrant workers are less likely to receive union support for other reasons as well. The ACFTU's top down strategy for establishing new branches, which it implements by engaging ownership and managers as opposed to organizing workers, creates a union presence with little shop floor impact. The grassroots organization of 17 Wal-Mart unions in the summer of 2007 for example provides an exception which proves the rule. While the majority of Wal-Mart enterprise unions were established through a traditional top-down method of Chinese union organizing, the few unions which did organize workers at the grassroots level were more active in supporting worker rights ("China Labor News Translations" 2008). This grassroots organization strategy however is extremely rare. One interview respondent in Shenzhen summed up migrants' view of the union succinctly, saying "union representatives are appointed by the employer, and are helpless to safeguard the rights and interests of workers" ("Interview Shenzhen 0444" 2008).

Other research has also described migrant workers' pessimistic assessments of the union's ability to represent them on the shop floor. In the spring of 2006, the Unirule Institute of Economics in Beijing conducted a survey of 1,117 workers in nine provinces, 63% of which were migrants. When asked which channels were the most effective in resolving disputes, less than 1% selected the union (J. Zhao, Zhou, and Song 2007). Of 372 migrants surveyed by researchers at Sun Yat-sen University in Guangzhou, only 7 stated they would rely on the trade union to voice their dispute, while only 8 of the 59 migrant workers who were injured at the workplace brought their dispute to the union (L. Liu and Wan 2007, 19–22).

ACFTU actions after the 2008 economic crisis only highlight the challenges that the union faces when seeking to represent China's workers. One key state policy in the wake of the global crisis, enacted without union opposition, was to simply suspend the enforcement of the labor law. Thus, in early 2009, Guangdong officials publically stated that employers suspected of "normal crimes" should not be prosecuted, and that enforcement agencies should not take any action that may negatively impact the company, even if legal violations were found. One official in Foshan, Guangdong Province went so far to say that the newly promulgated *Labor Contract Law* should not be enforced (Eli Friedman 2012).

Throughout this period, the only action taken by ACFTU as an organization in support of workers was to announce a "mutually agreed upon action" between workers and employers, whereby employers would take vaguely worded steps to avoid laying off workers, while workers in turn promised to avoid taking collective actions to protect their rights. Such weakly worded requests for cooperation did nothing to tamp down the explosion of protests that took place during this time.

The inability of the union to represent workers extends to union cadres at the enterprise level, the level of organization where union personnel have the most interaction with workers, but ironically are most tightly constrained in their actions. This problem is often acknowledged by enterprise-level union cadres themselves. During a 2010 union training seminar in Sichuan, one union cadre gave voice to his frustrations, arguing: "The [enterprise] union's expenses should be independent from the enterprise, [they should] have more consultations with employers, organize workers' representatives, strengthen communication and coordination, and should be given the authority of a trade union branch" (Trade union official #1 2010). Another training participant was more succinct, stating "The [enterprise] union officials should not be assigned by the enterprise. The union needs to be independent from the enterprise" (Trade union official #2 2010).

Interviews conducted with migrant workers support this pessimistic outlook regarding the utility of the union. When asked about their relationship with the union, only 28 of 266 respondents stated that their workplace had a union representative, while seven were unsure. Only 16 of the 265 respondents were union members, while a mere 16 others participated in union activities (see table 4.1). In the words of one respondent, "the union is currently only ornamentation" (*gonghui xianzai jiu shi baishe*) ("Interview Shenzhen 0404" 2008).

The party-state limits migrants' organizational capacity in other ways as well, most importantly through restrictions on the right to strike. The right to strike in China remains a controversial subject. China's 1982 state constitution removed any reference to workers' right to strike, yet the right to strike is also not expressly prohibited under the law.

This lack of clarity at the national level has led to local level experimentation. In November 2008 for example, the Shenzhen Municipal People's Congress published the *Shenzhen Special Economic Zone Regulations on the Promotion of Harmonious Employment Relations* (*Shenzhenshi Shenzhen*

Table 4.1.   Migrant Worker Union Participation

	Union Presence at the Workplace?	Union Membership?	Participate in Union Activities?
Yes	28 (11%)	16 (6%)	16 (6%)
No	238 (89%)	249 (94%)	251 (94%)
Total	266	265	267

Source: Author's Interviews

Jingji Techu Hexie Laodong Guanxi Cujin Tiaoli), which changed the local labor relations dynamic by no longer insisting that the trade union's main concern during labor strife was to assist management in resuming production. This development caused some international labor organizations to argue that the new legislation put Shenzhen workers in China "one step away from the right to strike" ("Trade Union Official Says China Is Just One Step Away from the Right to Strike" 2008). However, the document also included provisions allowing government officials to order a 30 day "cooling off" period, during which time strike activities were suspended. Because the litigation provides no limitations on this provision, others caution it could be used to suppress labor activity (Congressional Executive Commission on China 2008).

Other experiments regarding migrant workers' role in the union have received attention in recent years as well. Following the Honda strikes in 2010, much was made in the US press regarding the decision to experiment with direct elections of worker representatives in Guangzhou. Yet unions in Guangdong, Zhejiang, and Shandong have been conducting similar experiments throughout the past decade, though the experiments have faced significant resistance from both foreign businesses and the union leadership itself, which fears a loss of leadership power (Howell 2009, 803).

Collective bargaining, another important institutional mechanism for protecting workers' rights, exists in China as well, albeit with serious limitations. The push to create a collective contracts system, more formally known as the "equal consultation and collective contract system," began in the mid-1990s. By 2009, over 836,000 collective contracts had been signed, covering over 1.4 million enterprises and 115 million workers (All-China Federation of Trade Unions Editorial Department 2012). However, because the ACFTU has a monopoly over collective bargaining, the power of collective bargaining agreements to protect workers' rights is constrained. Enterprise level union cadres are appointed by management, and often lack training in contract negotiation and the collective bargaining process. As a result, many contracts are simply templates provided by local or provincial unions, containing little if any context specific information or clauses relevant to that specific workplace or its workers ("Breaking the Impasse: Promoting Worker Involvement in the Collective Bargaining and Contracts Process" 2007, 8).

Like the Shenzhen regulations described above, local legislation in the mid-2000s provided optimism that workers would be given greater freedoms to engage in collective bargaining. Article 20 of the 2004 *MoHRSS Regulations on Collective Contracts* for example stated that if no union was present, a majority of workers could nominate and approve their representatives ("Breaking the Impasse: Promoting Worker Involvement in the Collective Bargaining and Contracts Process" 2007, 4). Provisions in the 2008 *Labor Contract Law* however removed any possibility of such negotiations, stating that in the event of no union presence, worker representatives will be selected under the guidance and direction of the next highest level union organization, effectively cutting off the legal opening for workers to elect their own leadership (National People's Congress Standing Committee 2007 Article 51).

Institutional Exclusion

State limitations on workers' ability to organize affects both urban workers and migrants alike, but China's *hukou* system, which categorizes citizens based on their place of birth, redistributing resources to the urban at the expense of the rural population, plays a key role shaping migrant labor dispute behavior (F.-L. Wang 2005, 2–13). While *hukou* controls have relaxed considerably in the past decade, many Chinese academics and members of the political elite remain supportive of some form of the *hukou* system as a key component of the rural social safety net. For example, under the current *hukou* system, migrants who keep their rural status retain the right to farm a piece of land back at their registered place of residence (Wing Chan and Buckingham 2008, 596) and many argue that retaining this link between migrant workers and the land protects the nation from developing a permanent urban underclass of landless laborers, a phenomenon common in other developing countries (H. Wang 2006; Huang and Zhan 2005). During the height of the 2008 global economic recession, when many factories in the Pearl River Delta went out of business, access to this rural based support system, combined with a lack of an institutionalized social safety net in the cities, created disincentives for migrants to stay in urban areas, thus acting as a deterrent to urban protest activity.

In addition, many Chinese sociologists have noted how the continuation of a system that is explicitly discriminatory against rural citizens, denying them the same status as urban citizens, combined with the traditional "second class citizen" status (*erdeng gongmin*) of peasants in Chinese society, creates among migrants a sense of "inferiority" (*zibei*) compared to their urban counterparts (Y. Liu 2000, 33). This sense of inferiority can in turn create added barriers to action, as many migrant workers express helplessness, or a sense of being constrained (*yayi*), after experiencing unfair treatment at the workplace (Y. Liu 2000, 84–85). Recognizing this problem, a number of organizations have emerged in larger cities such as Beijing and Chengdu with the goal of "empowering" migrant workers, helping them to understand the value of their identity as productive members of society, and helping them to be more assertive.[1]

Restrictions on migrant labor in the cities have relaxed considerably in recent years, particularly in smaller cities which have allowed greater numbers of migrants to maintain a more legitimate status. The registration process for temporary resident status however can still be arduous, time consuming, and rife with opportunities for local governments to engage in extortion and predatory behavior. Current *hukou* regulations vary considerably from place to place, and many formal restrictions have been abolished. Officially, rural laborers with plans to enter the workforce in most urban areas need only obtain a valid copy of their resident identification card (*shenfenzheng*), while women of child bearing age need a special migrant labor family planning certificate (*liudong renkou hunyu zhengming*). Once in the city, migrants staying longer than three months must often obtain a temporary residence permit (*zanzhuzheng*), which, formally, is required to conduct a wide range of everyday activities, such as renting a room or opening a bank account (F.-L. Wang 2005, 74).

The central government has reduced or abolished many of the administrative fees associated with applying for such permits, yet many continue to be illegally collected. While the Beijing municipal government was one of the first to adopt new regulations limiting the costs of temporary residence permits in 2002 for example, reports of migrants being charged multiple fees of hundreds of RMB continued into 2007 ("A Journalist's Investigation in Beijing: The Procedures for the Application of a Temporary Residency Permit Is Chaotic; Types of Application Fee Are Confusing" 2002). Decentralization of the system of population management has also created a lucrative source of extra-budgetary income for local governments, and reports of abuse leading to unrest are not uncommon. In 2008, hundreds of migrant workers rioted in Zhejiang Province, burning police vehicles as they protested the physical abuse one migrant received when he was beaten by security guards while trying to obtain a temporary residence permit ("Migrant Workers Riot in East China: Rights Group" 2008).

Local governments place restrictions on housing purchases as well. For example, many cities required residents without local *hukous* to prove they have paid taxes for a consecutive number of years before being allowed to purchase an apartment, while local residents are provided home loans at cheaper rates. While home prices in places such as Beijing and Shanghai are far beyond what most migrant workers can afford, such policies simply reinforce the differences between local residences and migrant workers, solidify-ing migrants' second class status.

Relaxing restrictions on rural to urban migration in the past decade has provided new employment opportunities, particularly as the government has relaxed many of the *hukou* restrictions on finding employment in specific sectors of the economy previously open only to local residents. However, the complexity of the current registration system, and its vulnerability to abuse, continues to alienate migrants from the state, decreasing their confidence in the ability of state institutions to provide effective governance. Costs in terms of both time and money associated with registration deters many migrants from doing so, increasing their likelihood of finding employment in the informal economy, which is less regulated and more open to abuse ("Inter-view 48, Beijing NGO Director" 2008).[2] Many unregistered migrants for example take jobs in informal and unregistered, "opened and closed facto-ries" (*kaiguanchang*), named for the frequency in which they are open, shut down by local authorities, and reopen. In these types of situations, labor relationships are often only oral agreements, while government monitoring is lax, and workers' likelihood of experiencing exploitation increases.

Labor Monitoring and Enforcement

The state's capacity to carry out its monitoring and enforcement duties great-ly influences migrant dispute behavior as well. Effective and efficient government mechanisms for monitoring legal compliance can facilitate the labor dispute resolution process, making procedures transparent and straight-forward. Institutional reform in China however has largely failed to keep up with the rapid changes in the labor market and the economy more generally. Although significant reform involving labor supervision and investigation agencies have occurred in the past two decades, many of these institutions still face limited capacity, and in some cases limited commitments to moni-toring and enforcement, either for fear of adversely affecting local economic growth or as a byproduct of government nepotism. In other cases, loopholes in new legislation are sought out by employers, with the government con-stantly a step behind.

MoHRSS labor investigation bureaus have historically been understaffed, and despite the government's changing policy and rhetoric in favor of mi-grants, this did not appear to translate into significantly larger budgets for labor inspection bureaus. In 2005, for example, Shenzhen, home to one of the largest migrant labor populations in the country, had only one full-time labor inspector for every 20,000 workers (Hu 2006, 168). Jiangsu province, a common destination for inter-provincial migrants, had one for every 36,000 workers (Quan 2007). Nationally, the number of enterprise inspections has climbed steadily, rising from under one million enterprises inspected, covering 71 million workers in 2002, to just over 1.81 million enterprises covering 90 million workers by 2008, the year China's much anticipated *Labor Contract Law* was passed during a high tide in the government's focus on labor rights issues. Since 2008 however, the number of inspected enterprises has grown only slightly, reaching about 1.85 million in 2011 (National Bureau of Statistics 2013).

Other government and legal institutions have been slow to reform as well. Like other workers, migrants may utilize the three tiered dispute resolution system consisting of mediation, arbitration, and the courts, often referred to as "one mediation, one arbitration, and two trials"; describing the general path of most disputes, and the right of both sides to appeal the first court ruling. Effective use of this system for migrant labor however is limited, and suffers from difficulties the state has faced integrating aspects of the system with China's rapidly changing economy, the rise of new employment relationships, and high information requirements on migrant workers seeking to use this system. At the same time, China continues to oscillate between favoring pre-reform channels of dispute resolution such as mediation, and formal legal channels such as arbitration and the court system, creating a somewhat schizophrenic character to legal reform.

Labor Mediation

Labor mediation previously played a pivotal role in Chinese dispute resolution. Yet by the mid-1990s, the number of disputes resolved by company based Enterprise Mediation Committees (EMCs), tripartite committees comprised of a representative each for workers, the union, and management, began to decline significantly (Ho 2003, 58–59). ACFTU statistics report that EMCs nationwide declined to 153,113 in 2003, down 7% from 2002, and 56% from 1997 (Ministry of Labor and Social Security 2006). Moreover, management's ability to select union representatives means many workers do not consider EMCs to be neutral arbiters. As one worker described the mediation process in his factory, "it's an internal matter [inside the factory]. Anything that is internal is controlled by the company" ("Interview Dongguan 1103" 2008).

Since the mid-2000s however, labor mediation appears to have made a comeback, as party authorities have begun to shift back towards alternative forms of dispute resolution, including mediation (Minzner 2011). Numerous Chinese regulations call for labor arbitrators to first attempt mediation before handing down an arbitration decision, while the number of cases resolved either through arbitrators mediating rather than providing a ruling, or mediating outside the labor arbitration process altogether, has increased throughout the 2000s. From 2002 to 2011 for example, the number of grassroots labor dispute committees nationwide (*laodong zhengyi tiaojie weiyuanhui de ji-*

ceng danwei) has increased roughly four times, from roughly 165,000 committees in 2002, to over 660,000 in 2011. Guangdong has seen an even faster
rate of growth, with the number of grassroots union mediation committees in
that province expanding over fivefold; from roughly 13,000 in 2002 to over
65,000 in 2011.[3]

In 2011, in what appears to be an effort at reviving and expanding the old
EMC process, MoHRSS issued the *Regulations on Consultation and Mediation for Labor Disputes in Enterprises.* These regulations mandate the creation of new labor dispute mediation committees (*qiye laodong zhengyi tiaojie
weiyuanhui*) within large scale enterprises. In the event of a labor dispute,
these new EMCs will be responsible for seeking a settlement agreeable to
both parties. The regulations go far beyond simply reestablishing old EMCs
however, as they give the new dispute mediation committees responsibility
for supervising the implementation of negotiated agreements, monitoring
enterprise compliance of labor contracts and other relevant labor laws, and
participating in discussions on enterprise decisions that could significantly
impact workers, such as mergers or relocations. In addition, the 2011 regulations call upon local MoHRSS departments to work with local union organizations to establish an early warning system for the prevention of strikes and
protests ("China Issues New Regulations on Labour Dispute Resolution—
Seeks to Create Early Warning System" 2011).

New Employment Relationships

In addition to enhanced mediation efforts, government monitoring and enforcement agencies can limit labor disputes by ensuring that relevant laws
and regulations are properly implemented. However, new employment structures arising as a result of economic reforms have created more complex
labor management relationships that are difficult for the government to monitor effectively.

Labor dispatch (*laodong paiqian*) for example, a trilateral system separat-
ing the employment relationship from the enterprise receiving the labor, is
widely used and easily exploited by companies seeking to avoid compensat-
ing workers. Especially common in industries requiring large amounts of
short term or temporary workers (*linshigong*), the legal responsibilities of
these dispatch services and the workers' place of employment have been
hotly contested, as previous laws governing the regulation of labor dispatch
companies have been unclear. This confusion provided opportunities for
companies to claim no labor relationship with workers, or to transfer the
responsibility of even long term employees to labor dispatch companies.

One Shenzhen construction company for example, which employed large
numbers of migrant labor, would consistently dock 10% of workers' wages,
explaining it was used to pay premiums on insurance which the company

never actually purchased. When over 200 workers demanded either the reimbursement of their deducted wages, or the money owed through social insurance, the company refused to acknowledge it had any labor relationship with these workers, arguing their relationship was solely with the labor dispatch company. This dispute lasted years, and in the end, the workers received little compensation, as the complexity of the relationship between the workers, the labor dispatch company, and the construction company made the dispute difficult to resolve, with labor arbitration and the courts diverging widely in their interpretation of the law (K. Liu 2005).

Nor is this problem confined to the construction industry. After working in a warehouse for 10 years, one worker was threatened with dismissal if he did not sign a contract with a labor dispatch company, which would in the future be responsible for his wages and benefits. After signing the contract, the company dismissed the worker anyway, while also claiming they were not liable for compensation from the previous ten years (Dong and Dong 2007, 579–94).

Provisions in the 2008 *Labor Contract Law* attempted to clarify the responsibilities of labor dispatch services. Section two of the law for example sets minimum capital requirements for those seeking to register as labor dispatch companies, stipulates the need for a labor contract between workers and labor dispatch companies, and describes in detail the responsibilities of both the labor dispatch company and the enterprise receiving the work (the "accepting entity") (National People's Congress Standing Committee 2007 Article 57-67). In December 2012, the *Labor Contract Law* was further amended to increase the level of oversight on labor dispatch companies. These revisions increased the minimum capital requirements from 500,000 to 2 million RMB, required companies to use the same calculations for paying both regular and dispatched workers, narrowed the conditions under which workers from labor dispatch may be employed, and increased the fines for unlicensed labor dispatch companies (Standing Committee of the National People's Congress 2012).

Yet for government and legal institutions originally designed to manage employer employee relationships centered on a single employer, such as a state-owned enterprise, growing market complexity creates obstacles to timely and effective dispute resolution. Moreover, these problems are especially prevalent for migrant workers, who often have complex or informal relationships, and are most likely to be employed through these emerging employment models.

Similarly, the return of labor contractors (*baogongtou*), individuals who recruit workers to work as part of a larger construction project or to work within a manufacturing plant, pose a problem for the enforcement of migrant labor rights as well. The practice of labor contracting has a long history in China. As Elizabeth Perry notes, the practice was ubiquitous in cities such as

Shanghai during the Republican period, as artisans from Guangdong, manual labor from North China, and workers from Jiangsu and Anhui would return home to recruit others, forming the foundation of native place guilds and associations that shaped early Shanghai labor politics (Perry 1994, 32–64). While restrictions placed on freedom of movement in the Mao era essentially ended this practice, labor contracting is again widespread, and many migrants work informally for labor contractors from their home regions to avoid the associated registration and permit costs of formal employment. Moreover, like working for labor dispatch companies, many migrants working for labor contractors have no formal relationship with the company where they actually work. A large construction project for example may employ multiple groups of workers recruited by multiple contractors, and many workers interviewed during the course of this project did not even know the name of the parent company employing them.

Like the use of labor dispatch, the imposition of labor contractors between workers and the entity receiving the labor increases opportunities for exploitation. As described in chapter 2, if the contractor fails to receive payment from the parent company, or simply absconds with the wages, it can be difficult for workers to prove a labor relationship with the parent company without a formal contract ("Owed Wages: Unresolved After Five Years, The Difficulties of a Migrant Worker Chasing Back Wages [Yi Tao Xin She Wunian Nan Juekan Kan Nongmingong Taoxin Suqiao Zhe Nan] 道讨薪题五年难解开 看农民工讨薪诉求之难" 2006; Halegua 2008).

Labor Arbitration and the Courts

Individuals in China attempting to use labor arbitration and the courts are often required to possess a high level of personal legal knowledge to successfully navigate the system. Use of labor arbitration or the courts can be extremely complex, requiring an understanding of how the system operates both formally and informally. Many migrants for example are at a loss regarding whether to contact labor bureaus at the municipal, county, or township level, and spend time and money searching for an institution willing to accept their case. In addition, the state's institutional resources have simply failed to keep pace with demand, and as the number of dispute cases has grown, local labor arbitration and court systems have been overwhelmed.

Given this situation, it is not uncommon for officials to be less than concerned with the outcome of individual cases, and may even try to convince workers that their case is hopeless or someone else's responsibility. After being fined 3,000 RMB by their employer for asking for time off during the Chinese new year, one couple in Changzhou appealed to three different labor bureaus at different levels within the government, with each bureau refusing to take responsibility. Finally, they were told by officials at the third bureau that "this sort of thing is common, and there's really nothing we can do" ("Interview Changzhou 0705" 2008).[4]

Many government personnel working in labor dispute agencies also receive limited training on the labor law, while others simply discourage migrants from taking action. It is not uncommon therefore for workers to receive erroneous information, and if the worker in question lacks basic legal knowledge, the process of taking action through legal channels is likely to end. When applying for labor arbitration to obtain back wages in Beijing, one construction worker was erroneously told that because his employer was registered in Sichuan, he needed to return home to apply for labor arbitration, a trip costing at least a few days and hundreds of RMB (Beijing Migrant Worker Legal Aid Station). Another worker dismissed labor arbitration as an option, as he was under the impression he would have to return home to apply ("Interview Beijing 0112" 2007). In both cases, the information the workers received was erroneous, as each would have been able to take legal action in Beijing.

Use of labor arbitration and the courts may also take months, or sometimes years, to complete. Under the current system, initial labor arbitration is mandatory, but if any party objects to the arbitrator's decision, or if the losing party fails to comply, either may bring the case to court (National People's Congress Standing Committee 1995 Article 79). If either party disagrees with the initial court decision, it may be appealed. For migrant workers with few resources, or whose place of residence may be tied to their employment, the length of this process can be prohibitively costly. In fact, many employers count on long court delays, hoping to wait out the limited resources of the plaintiff ("Interview Migrant Labor NGO Representative, Shenzhen" 2012).

The 2008 *Law on the Mediation and Arbitration of Employment Disputes* sought to streamline this process, allowing for the possibility of expedited enforcement in certain situations, while also abolishing application fees for arbitration, thus significantly reducing costs (Standing Committee of the 10th National People's Congress 2007 Article 44, 47, 53). However, many workers still have difficulty navigating the arbitration process, and a growing number rely on legal representation for help. While workers who obtain the aid of a qualified lawyer at a government or union run legal aid center may be able to more successfully navigate the system without incurring additional costs, finding qualified and motivated legal aid personnel is not always easy, and many migrants lack the financial resources to hire their own legal counsel.

THE ROLE OF THE MARKET

Previous research on comparative labor politics has demonstrated how the nature of the labor market influences worker protests in many countries, shaping the timing and nature of the development of class consciousness, conditioning the degree of labor militancy, and facilitating or limiting the capacity of the working class to improve its position (Bellin 2002, 124; Kerr et al. 1960, 150–52). China is no different, and the Chinese labor market clearly conditions migrant workers' ability to engage in dispute activity. Four factors in particular, the size of the workforce, migrants' skill sets, the nature of employment, and the mobility and seasonal nature of migrant employment, influence migrants' ability to institutionalize labor protest activity.

The Impact of Surplus Labor

The mid to late 1990s in China witnessed a significant rise in the level of labor strikes and protests, as China's SOE reforms sent millions of state workers into the ranks of the unemployed (Lee 2007). Absent such types of dramatic shocks to the labor market however, a large body of labor economics research has found that the bargaining power and militancy of workers tends to decline in periods of relative slow economic growth and high unemployment, and rise in times of prosperity (Card 1990, 410–15; Nelson 1991; Nelson 1994, 1:363; Kennan 1986; Lange 1984). While labor remains cheap and plentiful, workers may endure unlawful treatment for fear of losing their jobs, constrained by what Marx referred to as "the dull compulsion of economic relations," or what James Scott simply called "the day to day imperative of making a living" (Scott 1985, 246). When labor is in tight supply, workers may be more likely to protest unlawful treatment.

This finding regarding the relationship between labor militancy and the labor market appears to reflect the situation of China's migrants. While layoffs in the state owned sector of the economy in the late 1990s led to large-scale strikes among state owned workers, the increase in the urban unemployed dampened labor protest among migrants at this time. The labor market struggled to absorb surplus labor from both former state-owned workers and the migrating rural population, and coupled with the Asia financial crisis, urban unemployment became a serious issue in many municipalities (Solinger 2001). So concerned were local governments with rising unemployment rates in the late 1990s and early 2000s that many cities began to issue discriminatory employment regulations restricting migrants' ability to work in certain sectors (Cai, Yang, and Wang 2001). From 1991 to 2003, MoHRSS reports that wages for migrant workers in the Pearl River Delta rose only 68 Yuan (US$8.2) in real terms (A. Chan 2005 fn. 5,6).

Since 2003 however, there has been a heated debate regarding the speed at which China's surplus rural labor is diminishing (K. W. Chan 2010). Government programs channeling investment into the central and western provinces have created opportunities for surplus rural labor to move to cities in China's hinterland, further diminishing the labor supply available to China's traditional migratory destinations on the east coast. Additionally, the rising age of the labor force as a result of the one child policy has significantly reduced estimates of the surplus labor force.

In light of these factors, some observers have argued that China has already reached a "Lewisian turning point," the period when the surplus labor in a developing country declines and wages rise (Cai 2007, 95–105). Relying on data from the 2005 National survey for example, researchers at the Chinese Academy of Social Sciences' Institute of Population and Labor Economics estimated that by 2009, rural China had only about 16 million remaining workers in the surplus rural labor population below the age of 30 who were likely to join the urban labor market in the near future (Cai, Du, and Wang 2009, 38). Others however argue that China retains an abundance of rural surplus labor, and will for the next few decades(K. W. Chan 2010).

While the size of China's overall rural labor supply may be open to debate, areas traditionally relying on migrant labor inflows have clearly experienced a labor shortage over the past decade. Since 2004, many companies in Shenzhen, Guangzhou, Dongguan, and elsewhere in the Pearl River Delta have complained of China's "migrant labor flood" (*mingongchao*) transforming into a "migrant labor shortage" (*mingonghuang*) (China Labour Bulletin 2007, 25) (*mingonghuang*) (Xinhua 2004). Moreover, this is also roughly the same time that labor rights organizations in the Pearl River Delta region began reporting a marked increase in protest activities among migrant workers. Others have attributed the rise in migrant labor protest activities to the labor shortage in the region as well (Wong 2010).

Limited Technical Training

A large portion of China's reported labor shortage in the past decade may not necessarily be due to the shortage of migrant workers overall, but to the scarcity of migrant labor with the skill sets required by employers. In a set of 2006 MoHRSS employer surveys, over 42% of employers stated that the number of available qualified candidates were scarce, while over 30% of employers stated that "migrant workers are not scarce, but there are not many workers appropriate for the job" (D. Chen 2007, 11). Other reports suggest the same conclusion. In 2009 for example, the Guangdong government reported roughly 750,000 outstanding job vacancies, mostly in skilled technical sectors such as computer engineering, for which most migrant workers remained unqualified (K. W. Chan 2010, 522).

When workers are highly skilled, replacing them is more expensive, allowing workers the opportunity to demand better treatment (Bellin 2002, 125). Workers with more education and technical expertise also have more responsibility, and thus more influence over decisions within the workplace, providing them with more leverage when bargaining for better conditions (Perry 1994; Walder 1986, 39–56).

Wage growth among migrant workers during this time is a complex puzzle as well. Declines in surplus labor suggest that conditions for migrants should improve, as employers are forced to raise wages to attract workers, and indeed the National Bureau of Statistics reports a rise in wages in the labor market more generally during this time ("Annual Data 1996–2013" 2014). Data regarding migrant workers specifically however suggests that while their wages have risen during this time, the rate of increase remained far lower than that of urban workers, in part because of this structural mismatch in skills desired by employers, and those possessed by the majority of the migrant population.

For example, relying on data from the *China Urban Labor Surveys* conducted in 2001 and 2005 in five cities (Shanghai, Fuzhou, Wuhan, Shenyang, and Xi'an), researchers Du Yang and Pan Weiguang found the average monthly minimum wage within these cities for all workers, including both migrants and local residents, rose 8.4% annually when adjusted for inflation. Migrant worker wages rose only 1.4% per year during this time (Knight, Deng, and Li 2011, 11–12). From 2001 to 2005, wages for migrant workers in these five cities actually fell relative to urban workers, who saw their inflation adjusted wages rise 3.2% per year, while the proportion of migrant workers paid *less* than the minimum wage increased, rising from 11% in 2001 to 16% in 2005 (Knight, Deng, and Li 2011, 18).

Other research paints only a slightly more positive picture. Using annual rural household surveys from 2003 to 2006, research from the Ministry of Agriculture found that migrants' average annual real wages grew 3.9% nationwide (Knight, Deng, and Li 2011, 13). In 2006, a nation-wide survey conducted by MoHRSS found that wages for migrants with no technical (*jishu*) training for this same three year period rose only 8.4%, not adjusted for inflation, again suggesting that migrant wages were rising far slower than average wages overall (C. Zhao and Wu 2007, 23).

Informal Employment

Scholars of labor protest in other contexts have also found that workers employed in larger, more formal settings are more likely to protest mistreatment, as common disputes such as nonpayment of wages or labor injuries are replicated in large numbers (Bellin 2002, 124; Kerr et al. 1960, 150–52). As Eva Bellin notes "the concentration of workers in ever larger factories nurtures solidarity and militancy, so much so that Marx predicted on it the rise of a revolutionary working class movement" (Bellin 2002, 124). Labor disputes within smaller or unregulated workplaces by contrast are more individual in nature, with a small number of laborers more easily replaced than a large workforce.

In China, much of the migrant workforce continues to find employment in smaller, largely unregulated and informal workplaces, which, as described above, can make it difficult to take action through institutional channels such as labor arbitration and the courts. Workers employed in these smaller settings are less likely to have labor contracts, formalized payments processes, and other criteria which help prove a labor relationship, and thus have more difficulty resolving grievances through institutionalized channels.

For example, in their survey of approximately 1,400 migrants in the Pearl and Yangtze River Deltas, Liu and Wan found that 43.6% of the worksites in their sample had less than 100 employees, with another 32.3% having anywhere between 100 and 499 employees. Approximately 70% of those in the smallest category of worksites had not signed a contract (L. Liu and Wan 2007, 10–11).

Moreover, not only are smaller, informal workplaces less likely to provide workers with the documentation necessary to use labor arbitration and the courts, other research suggests informal employment settings are precisely the types of places where workers are more likely to encounter labor disputes. For example, in a survey of 260 labor injury cases conducted by China Labor Watch, 56% were injured on a worksite of 200 or fewer workers, with approximately 37% operating in a workplace of less than 100 workers ("The Long March: Surveys and Case Studies of Work Injuries in the Pearl River Delta Region" 2007).[5]

Commitment to the Labor Force

Finally, migrant workers' time spent in the urban workforce, their mobility, and their seasonal employment, all impacts the decision of when and how to protest. Traditionally, Chinese migrant labor has been short term and seasonal, lacking the commitment to the workforce necessary to demand pensions, insurance benefits, pay raises or other benefits often provided to a stable, institutionalized workforce. The early years of Chinese migrant labor, in which migrant workers were not wholly dedicated members of the urban labor force, mirrored the story of labor in other countries. The Taiwanese industrial proletariat in the late 1970s for example was comprised largely of young, short term labor; individuals working long hours for little benefits and "selling their youth to the company" before settling down. Like their mainland counterparts, the short term nature of their employment made them hesitant to demand better treatment (Gates 1979, 396).

Analogous to Albert Hirschmann's study of organizational decline, migrant workers faced with labor exploitation in this situation may often choose "exit" over "voice," given the costs associated with engaging in protest (Hirschman 2004). Indeed, the high levels of labor exploitation and poor quality of life in China's Pearl River Delta factories is often cited as a reason for the "labor shortage" in that area, as workers choose to "use their feet to represent their interests" (*yongtui daibiao liyi*), and find other employment, rather than struggle to improve their current conditions ("Interview with Chinese Academic, Beijing, Chinese Academy of Social Sciences" 2007).

OBTAINING CREDIBLE INFORMATION UNDER AUTHORITARIANISM

Independently, state and market obstacles create impediments to migrant labor dispute activity. Combined, these factors have a multiplicative effect, compounding the challenges migrants face when attempting to take action. Treated as second class citizens and facing a predatory and often unresponsive state, Chinese migrants are forced to operate in an extremely hostile environment which impedes their ability to obtain credible information, and provides incentive to discount unverified information in favor of trusted, though less knowledgeable sources.

Unresponsive state monitoring and enforcement agencies create a permissive environment for migrant labor exploitation, and the mix of both sincere and fraudulent actors that prey on migrants in urban Chinese society makes it difficult for them to differentiate between the two. Lawyers may offer legal services to workers, yet instead charge high fees for no work (Michelson 2006). In addition, the state itself is often predatory towards migrant workers. Street level local police are difficult to appeal to, as workers who do so may be just as likely to incur more trouble. Low level government bureaucrats or employers may mislead migrant workers regarding the labor dispute resolution process. Grassroots migrant labor organizations may provide free classes on workers' legal rights, but so do for-profit training classes, the difference being that the latter often demand payment from workers after a few sessions. Even newspapers are subject to suspicion, as many migrant workers believe they "report only the good news and not the bad" (*baoxi bu baoyou*).

The idea that dangerous or difficult environments constrain the free flow of information and force individuals to rely on trusted sources is not limited to migrant workers in China. In Taiwan, student movements operating in an authoritarian environment under the Kuomintang (KMT) faced restrictions on their ability to organize, and were forced to rely on preexisting bonds of friendship to avoid repression (Wright 2008, 27–28). This same phenomenon appears to be at work in migrant labor communities in China, as workers attempt to avoid exploitation by relying on similar relationships. Unsurprisingly, large segments of the migrant labor population, including those interviewed during this research, have extremely unfavorable views of the police in urban areas where they work, who at best ignore their problems, and at worst extort them (Lu and Song 2006, 35). In the words of the wife of one interview respondent in Beijing, "I don't believe the police; the police don't care…now all I believe in is strength in numbers" ("Interview Beijing 0114" 2007). Other workers stated they did not go to the police because the police "only listen to money" ("Interview Beijing 0119" 2007).

Attitudes towards state institutional performance and credibility often shape the choice of escalation strategy, and a similar logic is at work in the case of labor disputes (Landry and Tong 2005). For migrant labor, a hostile social environment and suspicion and distrust of state and social actors decreases the credibility of state institutions, including institutions tied to the state, such as the media or state sanctioned labor markets. To avoid the exploitive situations and pitfalls that befall newly arrived migrants, information that cannot be directly verified by a trusted source, such as family, friends, individuals from the same hometown, or fellow workers, is often discounted. While this strategy provides protection against potentially exploitive situations, the cost of this strategy is that potentially useful information may be discounted or unavailable.

This type of risk-averse behavior is present in job search activities as well, as many migrant workers rely on friends or family members to provide information on possible employment. Most workers forgo state sanctioned employment centers or labor markets, and rely instead on family members or friends to provide employment information, yet those who do *not* forgo alternative information sources, earn more on average (Bian 1997). Reliance on social networks to obtain employment in other cultures is common as well, but it is important to note that China's migrant workers use this method not because they may provide higher pay—on the contrary, jobs found though these trusted sources are often lower paying—but in order to avoid exploitation.

The Andingmen labor market in Nanjing provides an illustrative example. Established in July 2002, it is one of the largest of its kind in Eastern China, designed to provide a legally regulated means for connecting short term and unskilled labor with potential employers (Jiang 2006). However, in a survey of 300 migrants interviewed at the market, 62% were unwilling to use the institution for fear of being cheated by labor market personnel, who were believed to have contacts with companies registered there (Sun 2004, 32). Many workers had heard stories of other workers who found jobs through the center, but were fired after only a few days, receiving no pay (Sun 2004, 37).

While conducting interviews with migrant workers in Dongguan just after the spring festival in 2008, it was often reported in the mainland press that factories were increasing salaries to attract workers in the face of a substantial labor shortage. Over the main gate of almost every factory hung ubiquitous red banners with white characters publicizing the rise in wages, while company representatives sat behind folding tables, waiting to help interested applicants. For each applicant however, there were many more individuals who hung back, sure that management would find ways to claw back the higher wages through the more fines and fees.

Just as migrants discount job information at the cost of potentially lucrative employment, so too do they discount unverifiable information that may help them engage in labor protest, including information found in traditional media. Media access and information flows are important factors influencing workers' opportunities for protest in authoritarian states (Tarrow 2011; Ossa and Corduneanu-Huci 2003, 612; Schock 2005, 19) and China is no exception (Zuo and Benford 1995). Positive media portrayals of workers using the legal system can encourage other workers to engage that system (Stockmann and Gallagher 2011).

For workers with little media exposure, or those who have experienced labor grievances firsthand however, the impact of these news stories may be muted. Two questions were asked as part of this research project to gauge migrant workers' views of the media; "I see examples of labor disputes in the media (television, newspapers or radio) that are very similar to my own experiences" (Q.1), and "Seeing examples of labor disputes in the traditional media (television, newspapers or radio) can help me resolve my own labor dispute"[6] (Q.2). Answers to both questions were scored on a 1–4 point scale, ranging from "strongly agree" "agree," "disagree," and "strongly disagree."

Table 4.2 compares workers who agreed (or completely agreed) with both questions, workers who disagreed (or completely disagreed) with both questions, and workers whose answers were mixed.[7] The results suggest that while most see examples of similar labor disputes in the traditional media, and believe they can be helpful, a significant number of workers were either unable to locate such examples, did not consider them to be helpful, or both.

When asked if he saw examples of labor disputes in the traditional media similar to his own, one individual working in construction in Beijing responded with an affirmative no. "Because the examples they publish [in the newspapers] are certainly those where you get your back pay. If you don't end up getting your back pay, they won't publish [your story]" ("Interview Beijing 0114" 2007). Another Beijing worker thought the examples published in the newspapers dealt only with "official" jobs, not the problems of migrant workers working unofficially for labor contractors, and thus had little relevancy to his dispute. "Here it's just fellow villagers working for fellow villagers" ("Interview Beijing 0125" 2007). Two workers, one from Shenzhen and the other from Guangzhou, each expressed absolutely no trust

Table 4.2. Migrant Workers' Use of Traditional Information Sources

N=245	**Question 1.** I see examples of labor disputes in the media (television, newspapers or radio) that are very similar to my own experiences. **Question 2.** Seeing examples of labor disputes in the traditional media (television, newspapers or radio) can help me resolve my own labor dispute
Agreed with both questions	60%
Question 1. Agree Question 2. Disagree	23%
Question 1. Disagree Question 2. Agree	5%
Disagreed with both questions	12%

Source: Author's Interviews

in the media, believing all of it to be "fake" (*jiade*) ("Interview Shenzhen 0310" 2007; "Interview Guangzhou 0505" 2008).

Limited exposure to media as a result of longer work hours and lower average incomes may help to explain its mitigated impact on migrants compared to the general working population. When asked about whether she could obtain information on dispute resolution strategies from television or newspapers, one respondent from Guangzhou, who had been injured on the job, complained she was "uncultured" (*wenhua chengdu taidi*), and never had the chance to read newspapers or watch TV ("Interview Changzhou 0723" 2008). As another worker from Beijing stated "when we don't work, we sleep, either way we don't have money for such things" ("Interview Beijing 0105" 2007).

Others saw the media more as a potential advocate, rather than a source of information, believing a media story would attract the attention of government officials and compel them to intervene. One individual sent by a labor dispatch company to work as a security guard (*baoan*) in a construction site in Beijing had been waiting for his pay for two months. While this worker was uninterested in talking to a lawyer or obtaining legal aid, he was extremely interested in talking to a reporter, believing a reporter could get the company to "admit they made a mistake" ("Interview Beijing 0102" 2007). When asked about the media's importance, one Changzhou woman spoke glowingly, stating that being interviewed by the media would be helpful. However, when it was clarified that the question being asked was about whether what she read in the paper could be helpful, her opinion changed.

She did not trust anything that she saw in the papers ("Interview Changzhou 0711" 2008).

As China's state controlled media continues to perfect its message regarding the legal system, it is not surprising that workers increasingly hold a positive opinion of labor arbitration and the courts as an option for dispute resolution. However, owing to their limited media exposure, personal dispute experience, and views of the media as advocates rather than information sources, a significant portion of the migrant labor workforce appear to face challenges in applying information available in China's media directly to their own situation.

CONCLUSION: OBSTACLES TO INSTITUTIONALIZING MIGRANT PROTEST ACTIVITY

This chapter has sought to outline the state and market obstacles migrant workers face while attempting to institutionalize labor protest through labor arbitration, the courts, collective bargaining, or other state-sanctioned channels of dispute resolution. Limited formal organization, ineffective state monitoring and enforcement organizations, and unresponsive mechanisms for legal recourse, all limit the utility of state sanctioned options. Additional obstacles arising from the nature of the labor market, such as a large, relatively unskilled, seasonal, and diffuse workforce, have hampered the development of a genuine working class movement in China.

In addition, government policies of exclusion and discrimination create additional problems for Chinese migrant labor. Different forms of treatment between rural and urban citizens through the household registration (*hukou*) system help provide opportunities for exploitation. Frequent exploitation from both state and social actors causes many workers to discount unverifiable information, and place greater emphasis on information derived from personal ties and networks. Thus the presence or absence of these networks greatly impacts the likelihood of workers engaging in dispute activity, as well as the forms these protests take.

The challenges described above suggest that for migrant labor, engaging in protest activity is extremely difficult. Yet in the past two decades, protests have been on the rise, both through legal mechanisms as well as extra-legal activities. In the next chapter, I seek to explain this puzzle by demonstrating how different social ties provide different resources, allowing migrant labor to obtain the information necessary to engaging in labor protest activity despite operating in an environment in which the institutionalization of labor protests remains difficult.

NOTES

1. See for example the work of the Beijing based social organization, *Hua Dan*, who seeks to empower migrants through small-group participatory exercises, where workers are given the opportunity to act out their grievances and develop plans of action to address them. http://www.hua-dan.org/.

2. This sentiment was also expressed by a large number of interview respondents, who connect the hassle of registration with their inability to obtain employment in the formal sector directly.

3. *China Labor Statistical Yearbook*, 2003–2012.

4. Paraphrased from interviews with two workers describing their encounter with that official.

5. My thanks to Li Qiang at China Labor Watch for providing me with the data from this study.

6. Interview questions are provided in appendix A.

7. The complete results for this graph, including all 16 possible outcomes, are provided in appendix C.

Chapter Five

Mobilizing Resources for Protest: Quantitative Analysis

The first section of this book introduced migrant labor protests as a growing concern for the party-state, and examined the evolution in the government's policy toward migrant workers over the past three decades. Relaxation of restrictions on population movement, the grudging acceptance of migrant workers as members of the working class, and changes in rhetoric and symbolism towards migrants, all provided a more stable existence in the cities. At the same time, government policies providing migrant workers with legal protections expanded their legal rights, while increased access to labor arbitration and the courts created opportunities to demand that those legal rights be upheld.

Despite these structural, legal, rhetorical, and symbolic changes however, migrant workers continue to face many obstacles when engaging in labor dispute activity, particularly when using institutionalized channels of protest, such as labor arbitration, the courts, or collective bargaining. Restrictions on formal organization, lax government enforcement and monitoring, and the increasing complexity of the labor market and use of complex labor relationships, all create obstacles for migrant workers seeking to use formal government channels.

Yet in spite of these obstacles, China has witnessed a dramatic rise in the number of migrant labor protests over the past decade, raising the key question that motivates this research—what explains the growth in migrant labor protest activity in the face of authoritarian constraints, particularly on workers' ability to obtain information and organize independently from the state?

Changes to migrant workers' urban political environment in the early 2000s, in which migrants obtained greater freedom of movement and increased legal protections, only provided opportunities for action. To take advantage of these new opportunities, migrants must somehow identify and mobilize the resources necessary for action.

The demographic changes that brought millions of migrants to the cities did more than change the political calculations of the party; they also created new opportunities for migrant workers to expand their social ties and networks. Chapters 5 and 6 analyze the ways in which migrant workers rely on these social ties to provide the resources necessary to engage in protest. This chapter begins by marshalling quantitative evidence to demonstrate how traditional *rural ties*, defined as connections between family members or hometown associates that existed before migrants moved into the cities, provide material resources, while *urban ties,* defined as connections that develop between workers with different backgrounds and experiences while operating in the cities provide information.

After restating in detail the argument regarding the importance of migrants' social ties and the resources they provide, I analyze some key characteristics of the workers interviewed during this research, including their age, income, education, and the impact of these factors on protest activity. Such characteristics have long been considered crucial to predicting protest activity, yet the data below suggests these factors alone do not fully explain workers' behavior.

I then test my arguments regarding rural ties, urban ties, and their impacts on protest activity through a series of regression analyses. First, I provide evidence to show that rural ties are more useful as a source of material support, while urban ties are more useful as a source of new information. Next, I demonstrate how access to information derived from urban ties is more likely to facilitate protest activity, and how individuals with access to information derived from urban ties are more likely to engage in dispute activity, particularly non-violent activity such as use of the legal system.

THE ARGUMENT IN DETAIL

Social links between friends, family members, coworkers, or individuals from the same hometown all have the potential to provide a wealth of resources to migrant workers, including material support or information. These resources can help migrant workers access protest strategies that would otherwise be unavailable. There is a significant body of literature in both Chinese and English for example, which describes how traditional rural ties between family members or hometown associates with whom migrants have longstanding relationships provide material resources. Theoretically, these rural ties have the capacity to provide information as well.

However, as described in detail in chapter 1, there is another body of literature in sociology and social network theory, which demonstrates how the insular nature of these traditional rural ties are less likely to provide new information to individuals within that network. Instead, work in this field has found that interactions between work colleagues, and between acquaintances that have only limited prior connection, similar to the urban ties developed by migrant workers while operating in the cities, are more likely to provide new information. This is because these relationships can act as a bridge between networks, connecting different groups of individuals who would otherwise have little if any contact. Thus, migrant workers who expand their information searches to include urban ties will have access to a greater number of channels through which they may obtain new information, compared to individuals relying primarily or exclusively on rural ties for information.

Given these posited relationships between social ties, resources, and protest activity, we should expect to see the following relationships between rural ties, urban ties, and the availability of different types of resources, namely information and material support. Table 5.1 lists these predicted observations.

As table 5.1 describes, migrant workers' rural ties are likely to be useful sources of material support. Family members, or those from the same hometown with whom one has prior connections, (i.e., hometown associates), are individuals with whom migrants are likely to have developed strong emotional bonds, have a shared history, or have similar experiences. Because of these connections, I posit that migrant workers are more likely to draw upon these types of relationships for material support, compared to relationships with other workers with whom they have met more recently in the cities, with whom they lack these emotional connections, and with whom they have less in common. However, the same factors that help create these emotional connections; the similar backgrounds and time commitments shared by these individuals, limits their ability to provide new information regarding potential dispute options or strategies.

Table 5.1.   Rural and Urban Place Ties: Predicted Observations

Social Tie (Rural or Urban)	Likelihood of Providing Information	Likelihood of Providing Material Support
Family (Rural)	Low	High
Hometown Associate (Rural)	Low/Medium	High/Medium
Friend (Urban)	Medium/ High	Medium
Fellow Worker (Urban)	High	Medium/ Low

In contrast, new urban connections which migrant workers develop while living and working in the cities may act as a bridge, connecting them with other, more diverse networks of individuals with a wider range of different experiences. Although these connections lack the same emotional sentiments commonly found among family members or hometown associates, these new ties help connect migrants with new networks of individuals that are more likely to have different work and life experiences. Thus, given their ability to link migrants to new groups of individuals with more diverse and varied backgrounds and experiences, urban tie relationships can be useful resources for obtaining new information regarding how to prosecute a labor dispute.

INTERVIEW RESPONDENTS: BASIC CHARACTERISTICS

Factors such as income, education, and dispute size have long been considered important variables in the study of labor politics and labor protest. Contrary to Marxist predictions for example, which focused on the potential for revolution within the most downtrodden and dispossessed segments of the proletariat, educated and affluent workers have often been at the forefront of labor movements (Geary 1984; Perry 1994, 242–43). Other factors, as straightforward as the size of the grievance for example, have been shown to be an impetus for protest activity (Gurr 2011). While this book argues for the importance of social ties in facilitating labor protest activity, these other factors cannot be ignored, and table 5.2 provides basic information from my interview respondents on these key characteristics, including their age, education, income and the monetary value (in RMB) of the dispute in question.

Personal Income

Traditional Marxist views of labor have held a special place for the poorest members of the working class. However, skilled and affluent members of the labor force are often highly active participants in labor protest, owing to their greater financial resources. This appears to be the case in China as well, as better skilled and higher compensated workers have been at the forefront of many labor actions. During the early years of the PRC for example, factory workers in Shanghai protested strongly against state policies that negatively affected their wage and compensation levels, standing in stark contrast to the orthodox views of labor's unquestioning support for the new regime at this time (Chen 2013). Despite being privileged members of Chinese society, Shanghai's workers took action in defense of their interests again during the Cultural Revolution (Perry 1997).

Unlike SOE workers before economic reforms, no one could reasonably consider migrant workers to be privileged members of Chinese society. The average income for the migrant workers interviewed during this research for

Table 5.2. Interview Respondents—Basic Characteristics

	Strata I (Test Sample)	Strata II (Control Sample)	Total
N	167	104	271
Average Age	32	28	30
Average Education	Some High School Experience (4.88/7)	Middle School Graduate (4.43/7)	Some High School Experience (4.71/7)
Average Income	1,382	1,311	1,354
Average Dispute Value (RMB)	22,648	6,180	16,002

Source: Author's Interviews

example was significantly lower than the average incomes for urban Chinese workers within the same industry and geographic regions (see Table 5.3). Incomes from the test and control samples however were almost identical, with respondents in the test sample having an average monthly income of 1,382 RMB, compared to 1,311 RMB in the control sample.

As table 5.4 illustrates, the data suggest that protest activity tends to increase with income, with higher income individuals engaging in more frequent protest activity. For example, respondents making over 2,500 RMB per month engaged in the highest average number of protest activities. Meanwhile, workers with a monthly income of less than 1,000 RMB engaged in similar levels of protest as those making 1,000 to 2,000 RMB per month. While high income respondents did engage in the highest average levels of protest activity, lower income respondents were not particularly submissive, engaging in protest at levels similar to those at medium income ranges.

Worker Education Levels

Education was relatively constant across the entire sample of migrant workers as well, whether they were selected randomly as part of the control sample (strata II), or as part of the test sample of migrants that had taken their grievance to a migrant labor NGO (strata I). Education was coded on a 7 point scale, from "no schooling" to "education beyond a high school level" including university or technical training. As shown in table 5.5, the average education score for interview respondents was 4.7/7, meaning that the average education level of respondents in the sample included some high school experience.

In general, individuals within the test sample (strata I) have a slightly higher education level (4.9) compared to those in the control sample (strata

Table 5.3. Average Wage Comparisons: Region and Industry (RMB)

Region	All Industries	Manufacturing	Construction	Services
Beijing Registered Workers	3,343	2,468	2,215	1,808
Guangzhou Registered Workers	3,444	2,450	2,906	
Shenzhen Registered Workers	3,233			
Changzhou Registered Workers	2,534			
Nanjing Registered Workers	2,659	1986	2121	1664
Project Sample	1,322 (n=236)	1315 (n=128)	1445 (n=42)	1,175 (n=41)

Source: Author's Interviews; (Beijing Municipal Statistics Bureau 2007; Guangzhou Municipal Statistics Bureau 2008; Statistics Bureau of the Municipal Government of Shenzhen 2008; Statistical Bureau of the Municipal Government of Nanjing 2008; Changzhou Bureau of Statistics 2014)

II), who had an average education of 4.4. The fact that workers in the test sample—those who were selected in cooperation with migrant labor NGOs precisely for the greater likelihood that they had engaged in dispute activity—had very similar education levels compared to those in the study overall suggests that education was not a critical predictive factor in migrant labor dispute behavior. This finding is also supported in the regression analysis provided below.

Dispute Size

Research into the importance of relative deprivation dominated early work in the study of protests and social movements (Gurr 1970). While recent work has focused on other factors, such as actors' political and social environments, and their or their ability to organize or mobilize resources, clearly some level of grievance is necessary for protest to occur. Respondents selected from migrant labor NGOs (strata I) engaged in both a higher number of labor dispute actions, and had a higher average dispute size (22,648) compared to those within the control sample (6,148). This is not unexpected,

Table 5.4.   Protest Activity by Income Level (RMB)

	0-999	1,000-1,499	1,500-1,999	2,000-2,499	2,500-2,999	3,000+	Total
Number Engaging in Protest Activity	58	86	38	24	8	7	221
Average Protests per Income Level	1.60	1.47	1.58	2.42	2.5	2.29	1.69

Source: Author's Interviews; n = 221

as workers with larger monetary disputes are often more motivated to seek aid. Yet in-depth interviews conducted with workers identified through random selection (strata II) uncovered many examples of individuals who chose to act on relatively "small" disputes,[1] while others took no action at all, despite having disputes of size comparable to those found among strata I.

The story of one interview respondent in Changzhou is illustrative of workers who took no action despite suffering significant financial exploitation. An individual from rural Zhongjiang County in Sichuan Province, a region with an average annual per capita income of 3,334 RMB (approximately US$ 490), this migrant worker first came to Changzhou in 1995, and worked in the local coal power plant in the Qishuyan area of Changzhou. The work was dangerous, and the dust particles he was constantly breathing gave him severe respiratory problems. He had no health insurance, and though he had worked at this location for years, he was still considered a part time worker, compensated in lump sum payments twice a year.

While this respondent readily showed me detailed records he kept regarding the amount of overtime he believed he was owed, which by his estimate totaled tens of thousands of RMB, and certainly qualified as a substantial dispute, when asked why he did not appeal to the local labor bureau, he said labor bureau officials would just "talk law" and "say things he doesn't understand" ("Interview Changzhou 0716" 2008). In addition, determining the monetary size of complex migrant labor disputes such as labor injury cases, long term illness cases, or cases involving unlawful dismissal, can also be extremely difficult, particularly when the worker never acted upon those cases. In short, dispute size addresses motivation, but fails to address issues of resource mobilization or resource availability, which ultimately allows migrant workers to act on that motivation. This same migrant worker for example, who complained of not knowing what to do, also complained of not knowing where to go or who to talk to in order to find that information. After being in Changzhou for years he still cited immediate family members as his best source of information, stating that he knew almost no one outside a few

Table 5.5. Total Protest Activity by Educational Level

	Test Sample (Strata I)		Control Sample (Strata II)	
	Percentage	Protests/Person	Percentage	Protests/Person
None	.7%	1	0%	0
Elementary	7.8%	1	12.8%	.69
Middle School Experience	10%	1.33	11.8%	.92
Middle School Graduate	31.2%	2.04	33.3%	.88
High School Experience	12.3%	1.8	12.8%	.85
High School Graduate	27.1%	2.54	20.6%	1.24
Some University/ Technical school experience	10.8%	1.9	8.8%	.78
Average	4.9/7		4.5/7	
N	100%	167	100%	102

Source: Author's Interviews

fellow villagers from Zhongjiang County who also worked at the power plant, illustrating a key obstacle to action for many migrant workers.

Types of Protest Activity

Chart 5.1 lists the percentage of interview respondents who engaged in each type of protest activity; informal bargaining, use of the legal system, non-violent strikes, and violence. Information on respondent's protest activity was collected through both a fixed questionnaire, and through open ended interviews.[2]

Migrant workers often take the least costly action when seeking to resolve a labor dispute, changing strategies when the path of least resistance is re-stricted, unavailable, or ineffective. This general logic is reflected in the distribution of protest activity among the respondents, with more workers engaging in less costly activities, and progressively fewer workers engaging in activities as the costs associated with those activities increase.

For example, 52% of interview respondents sought to engage in informal bargaining with their employers, while 40% of workers interviewed took action through labor arbitration or the courts. As described in chapter 2, neither strategy is completely costless; workers who take their bosses to

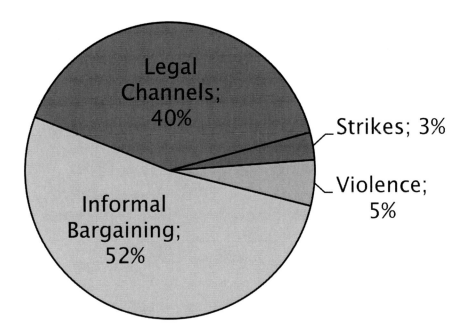

Chart 5.1. Labor Protest Activity by Type (Percentage). Source: Author's Interviews.

labor arbitration or the courts may face retribution. At the very least they may be forced to find another job, though cases where workers face physical retaliation from their employers after taking such actions is not uncommon.

Migrants who take any type of action to protest their treatment remain only a subset of the total number of migrants facing exploitation, and those who engage in high cost and high risk behavior, such as participating in strike activity, or engaging in violence, remain an even smaller subset. This is reflected in the decrease in the percentage of interview respondents who sought to engage in this high cost activity. Only 3% of interview respondents for example admitted to engaging in strike activity, while 5% of workers stated they had engaged in violence.

Strikes remain illegal under Chinese law, and although officials in some locales may be sympathetic to labor's plight, workers who engage in strikes and mass protests not only face possible retribution form employers, they may face retaliation from the state. This is particularly true if workers take a leadership role, or if the strike activity expands to include multiple locations. Finally, while strikes operate within a legal grey area, worker violence is clearly a violation of the law and subject to criminal prosecution by the state. Moreover, mass migrant labor violence of the kind that took place in Xintang in 2011, or Foxconn's Taiyuan plant in 2012, are precisely the type of behavior that threatens local investment and state control, and local investment is not likely to be looked upon kindly by local officials.

Factors traditionally considered to play a key role in the formation of dispute activity, including income, education, and dispute size, are clearly influential in shaping migrant workers' dispute behavior. The evidence above for example suggests that workers with larger incomes or higher levels of education have more personal resources at their disposal, and their resources helped them to take action. In addition, workers experiencing larger, more costly disputes may have added motivation to act, though they may still lack the capacity to do so. Absent such personal resources however, workers must turn to other means to engage in protest activity, and the next section provides additional analysis to demonstrate how migrant workers may overcome resource limitations by relying on both rural and urban ties.

RURAL TIES, URBAN TIES, AND PROTEST ACTIVITY

Below I examine the impact of rural and urban ties on protest activity. First, I investigate the impact of rural and urban ties on the likelihood of engaging in protest activity more broadly. Rural ties, and the material and financial support they provide, have long been considered critical to migrants newly arrived in the cities seeking to acclimate themselves. While not understating the importance of such material support, this research however finds that information, particularly information derived from urban ties, is highly correlated with protest activity.

Second, I investigate the impact of rural and urban ties on specific types of protest activity, including informal bargaining, use of the legal system, nonviolent strikes and demonstrations, and violence. While workers often employ multiple types of protest strategies over the lifetime of their dispute, the fact that migrants commonly employ these different strategies at distinct periods of time during the dispute process allows us to examine when workers change strategies and why they do so. The data below supports an argument that information derived from urban ties is positively correlated with nonviolent protest, such as the use of labor arbitration and the courts, or informal negotiations and bargaining.

Social Ties and the Likelihood of Protest

To test this argument regarding social ties, the resources they provide, and their impact on migrant labor dispute behavior, I first examine the data through the following logistic regression model of the form:

logit(π) = α + β INFO_U + β INFO_R + βMATAID_U + βMATAID_R + βMATAID_B + z + ε.

The dependent variable in this model is protest activity, and logit(π) is the logit function of the probability of engaging in such activity, including use of the legal system, informal bargaining, nonviolent strikes and protests, and violence. INFO_U is a dichotomous coding of the worker's source of best information as indicated by the respondent, coded one if the migrant worker's best source of information was an urban tie and zero if that worker's best information was derived from other sources, such as newspapers, television, or radio. Similarly, INFO_R is coded as one if the worker's best information was obtained from a traditional rural tie, and zero if obtained elsewhere.

Workers' material support was measured using three variables, MATAID_U, MATAID_R, and MATAID_B. MATAID_U was coded one if the worker obtained material support from an urban tie, and zero if the worker obtained material support from any other source. MATAID_R is coded one if the worker obtained material support from a rural tie and zero if derived elsewhere. Finally, MATAID_B was coded one only if that worker had to access to material support from both urban and rural ties. MATAID_B was coded as zero if the worker was unable to rely on both tie types for material support.

In the formula above, z refers to the other variables in the model described below. AGE is a measure of the respondents' age at the time of the dispute, measured in years. SEX indicates whether the respondent is male or female. EDUCATION is a measure of the respondent's formal education, coded one through seven.[3] INCOME is a measure of the worker's monthly salary in logarithmic scale. Manufacturing and construction are used to identify the respondents that work in those industries, and are coded 1 if employed in that industry and zero if employed elsewhere, respectively. TYPE is a variable used to control for the two types of interviews included in this research, and is coded zero if the worker was randomly selected (strata II), and one if accessed through one of the migrant labor organizations (strata I).

To control for regional variation, I also include dummy variables YRD and BEIJING, depending on whether the respondent was interviewed in the Yangtze River Delta or Beijing, compared to respondents interviewed in the Pearl River Delta. Finally, dummy variables were added to indicate whether the respondent's dispute was an unpaid wage issue (including unpaid overtime), a labor injury, illegal dismissal, grievance regarding unsafe working conditions, or a long term occupational illness issue. Table 5.6 reports the correlation coefficients and standard errors for each variable, as well as the Log Likelihood, Percent Classified Correctly, and Chi² for the model.

The results above provide support for the argument that workers with access to information derived from urban ties are more likely to engage in

Table 5.6.   A Logit Model of Labor Dispute Activity

Variable Name	Correlation Coefficients (Standard Error)
INFO_U	1.43*** (.48)
INFO_R	.00 (.56)
MATAID_U	-.06 (.59)
MATAID_R	.82 (.56)
MATAID_B	1.44** (.67)
AGE	.00 (.03)
SEX	.40 (.54)
EDUCATION	.15 (.15)
INCOME	.00 (.00)
MANUFACTURING	.68 (.55)
CONSTRUCTION	.71 (.61)
TYPE	2.37*** (.49)
UNPAID WAGES	1.21** (.50)
INJURY	1.35** (.68)
ILLEGAL DISMISSAL	1.18 (.76)
WORKING CONDITIONS	-.24 (.60)
OCCUPATIONAL ILLNESS	-1.27 (1.11)
BEIJING	-.47 (.67)
YRD	-.43 (.47)

N	242
Log Likelihood	-90.87
Percent Correctly Classified	83%
Prob > chi2	.0000

Source: Author's Interviews. * p<.10; ** p<.01; *** p<.001.

protest activity. In table 5.6, INFO_U was statistically significant and positively correlated with protest activity, suggesting that information derived from urban networks increases the probability of worker protest. Taking the exponential of the correlation coefficient, migrant workers were 4.18 times more likely to engage in protest activity when their best information came from an urban tie. In contrast, whether or not migrant workers were able to rely on rural ties for information had little impact on their protest behavior. Moreover, a difference of coefficients test (f-test) finds a statistically significant difference between information from these two sources (Prob. > chi2 = 0.01).

The findings provided in table 5.6 also suggest that workers' access to material support plays a role in promoting protest activity as well. However, contrary to much of the literature on migrant workers' social networks, which focuses solely on the importance of rural ties in providing such support, the results above suggest that workers who are able to rely on *both* urban and rural ties for material support are more likely to engage in protest activity. In table 5.6, workers with access to material support from both urban and rural ties were 4.22 times more likely to engage in protest. Unlike information regarding how to engage in informal bargaining, or how to navigate the legal system, which is relatively esoteric and not universally available, money is fungible. While rural ties with whom migrant workers share a strong emotional bond may be more likely to provide material support, such material support does not necessarily have to come from rural ties. It does not matter where this support comes from, so long as one has it.

Industry type is often considered a key predictor of labor protest, as high concentrations of labor in sectors such as manufacturing are thought to foster solidarity and working class consciousness. As illustrated in table 5.6 however, industry type had no appreciable effect on the likelihood of protest, with neither MANUFACTURING nor CONSTRUCTION, the two broad based sectors employing most migrant workers, predictive of labor dispute behavior.

This is not to suggest the structure of economic organization has no impact on protest activity. While better educated, technically skilled workers are often better positioned to engage in protest activity, large economic sectors such as manufacturing or construction do not appear to be powerful predictors of protest once workplace relationships are taken into account.

Workers in highly concentrated sectors, for example, may have greater opportunities to develop the urban ties necessary for protest, yet a structure of workplace relationships that creates division and sows distrust can diminish this advantage.

A brief description of the differences in workplace relationships between workers in the Honda and Foxconn companies as described in Chinese NGO reports, as well as Chinese and English media reports, illustrates this difference. Despite both companies having a large, technically skilled workforce, Foxconn actively discourages social interaction among its workers in its Shenzhen facility. Roommates for example are often assigned from different business groups, rather than from the same assembly line or department, limiting opportunities for small groups of workers to discuss topics of mutual interest. Workers sharing the same dorm room can go for days and see each other only once or twice, if at all. Some dorms combine day and night shift workers, further limiting opportunities for interaction. One Foxconn worker who lived in the same dorm room with seven others, five of whom worked the night shift, interacted with them so rarely, he was not even sure of all their names (China Labor Watch 2010). Only floor supervisors are allowed to talk on the factory floor.

Like Foxconn, workers at the Foshan Honda factory were also relatively well educated compared to the general migrant labor population. Unlike Foxconn however, the Foshan Honda workers were often recruited from the same technical schools, meaning that many had spent long periods of time with each other even before arriving at Honda. Moreover, migrant workers at Honda worked in a more relaxed atmosphere, absent the militaristic regiment which controlled the lives of the Foxconn labor force (Crothall 2010).

Finally the results in table 5.6 suggest that workers who suffer from rights-based grievances such as unpaid wages or labor injuries, are more likely to engage in protest activity, compared to workers who suffer from more complex grievances such as illegal dismissal or occupational illness, or interest-based grievances such as poor working conditions. Workers who suffered from unpaid wage issues were 3.35 times more likely to engage in protest activity compared to workers facing other types of grievances, while workers who suffered labor injuries were 3.86 times more likely to engage in protest. In contrast, workers experiencing illegal dismissal, poor working conditions, or occupational illness were no more likely to engage in protest activity than workers suffering from any other type of grievances.

Unpaid wage disputes and labor injuries are two of the most common grievances facing migrants. They are also some of the most obvious and direct forms of labor exploitation, particularly when compared to workers who experience poor working conditions, which may be viewed in a relative context, or occupational illnesses, which have a long onset time and are notoriously difficult to connect to a specific job or employer (China Labour Bulletin 2013; China Labour Bulletin 2010; China Labour Bulletin 2005).

As described in chapter 2, there has been a rise in interest-based claims among migrant workers' protesting against low wages and poor working conditions, and a subsequent debate within the literature regarding the extent to which the emergence of such claims constitutes a fundamental change in the nature of labor relations in China (Chan and Siu 2012). While migrants are certainly engaging in interest-based protests, and these appear to be occurring at a greater rate than a few years past—witness the automobile strike wave over low wages which took place in 2010—examples of interest-based protests appear far less often than right-based protests. The statistical significance of rights-based grievances such as unpaid wages and labor injuries, compared to the lack of statistical significance for interest-based grievances such as working conditions, speaks to the continued and ongoing difficulty of workers acting on interest-based grievances.

Social Ties, Information, and Nonviolent Protest

As described in chapter 3, workplace violence, attacks against employers, or destruction of property are not uncommon forms of protest among Chinese migrant labor. Such protests however incur a heavy cost to the migrants who take such actions, as they may be hurt, killed, face retaliation from employers, or punishment from the state. This of course begs the question: when do workers pursue violent or unlawful protest, knowing that they face the very real likelihood of retaliation and punishment?

One possible answer is that workers use violence because they have lost faith in non-violent forms of protest. Previous research has shown that Chinese citizens' perceptions of the legal system may be informed by the experiences of their peers. Those who hear about the negative experiences of their friends or colleagues for example may develop a sense of "informed disenchantment" towards the law (Woo 2011). Such an informed disenchantment may lead to the use of alternative strategies, including violence. Yet this explanation has difficulty accounting for the growth in the use of labor arbitration and the courts among migrant labor more generally. Moreover, if individuals may develop a negative impression of the legal system by talking with others who have firsthand experience, they may presumably also learn from the same individuals how to avoid making the same mistakes, and navigate the legal system more smoothly.

This suggests a second possible explanation; namely that many migrants employ violence when they are unable to employ alternative strategies. This is not to suggest migrant workers have no knowledge of the existence of labor arbitration or the legal system, but that they lack the specific knowledge that would allow them to actually take advantage of these channels. As one interview respondent who worked in construction in Beijing suggested, he knew many workers who had experienced labor disputes, but violent action was the only strategy with which he had any experience ("Interview Beijing 0111" 2007).

> We first tried to call the labor contractor, and then went to the labor bureau. The bureau went to see if the company was registered, but couldn't find it. As the labor bureau sees it, this was just a small thing. We really didn't know what to do. In that situation, all we could do was to go back to the construction site, and try and find the boss. They knew we had come back to fight. ("Interview Beijing 0111" 2007)

A third explanation may be that workers engage in violent protest when time is short or alternatives are limited, but given the stakes involved, giving up may not be an option. Recall the workers in Shenzhen, described in chapter 2, whose son had fallen ill, yet their employer would not help them return home by agreeing to pay them half their owed wages. Faced with this type of dilemma, violence or unorthodox protest options may be the only choice available.

Some dispute types may also be more likely to end in violence than others. Occupational illness cases for example are extremely difficult to resolve through legal channels. Migrant workers facing wage arrears issues always have the option of simply searching for a new job. An afflicted migrant worker, or one suffering a severe injury may be unable to earn any income. Acting as a financial burden on his or her family, he or she may be willing to go to extremes to receive compensation and avoid throwing the whole family into poverty. Faced with this situation, it is thus unsurprising that many migrant workers suffering from occupational illnesses are willing to go to extremes to resolve their disputes.

Workers with access to urban ties however are better positioned to engage in multiple types of protest options, including informal bargaining with employers, use of the formal legal system, or even nonviolent collective action, rather than being forced to rely on violence alone. By providing access to a number of different protest options, migrant workers with access to urban tie information are able to avoid the negative consequences of engaging in violent protest activities, and are better positioned to take non-violent action. As the data below demonstrates, access to urban ties are positively associated with nonviolent protest such as use of labor arbitration and the courts, and negatively associated with violence.

Table 5.7 provides the correlation coefficients and p-value results of a multinomial logit model, which investigates the likelihood of workers engaging in different types of protests. The model contains each of the variables contained in the logit model described above. Four different types of protest activities are examined, and the dependent variable is a categorical variable consisting of five categories; 0 = no protest activity;[4] 1 = informal bargaining; 2 = use of the legal system; 3 = non-violent strikes and mass protests; and 4 = violence. This coding seeks to capture the escalatory nature of labor protest activity as described in the spectrum of protest escalation laid out in chapter two, with the costs of action generally rising for each successive type of protest behavior (informal bargaining as the least costly activity, and violence as the most costly). Respondents who engaged in multiple protest actions were coded according to the most costly activity in which they engaged.[5]

Table 5.7 provides strong evidence that workers' propensity to use different protest channels varies depending on the social ties available, and the resources they can obtain from those ties. Workers who are able to rely on urban ties for information for example are more likely to employ legal channels of dispute resolution, and far less likely to engage in violent strategies.

Workers attempting to navigate the formal system are aided by having access to someone with direct experience with the legal system guiding them through the process. Being able to consult with someone who has interacted with arbitration personnel in the past can provide migrant workers with advice far more valuable than any information they could glean from local news articles or television programs. As a migrant worker, connecting with a

Table 5.7.   A Multinomial Logit Model of Specific Dispute Activity

Protest Type	Information Source	Coefficient (standard error)
1. Informal Bargaining	Urban Ties	.15 (.78)
	Rural Ties	-1.48 (.30)
2. Legal channels	Urban Ties	1.01** (.40)
	Rural Ties	.09 (.56)
3. Non-violent strikes and demonstrations	Urban Ties	.57 (1.37)
	Rural Ties	.26 (1.40)
3. Violence	Urban Ties	-2.81** (.31)
	Rural Ties	-.85 (.19)

Source: Author's interviews. * $p<.10$; ** $p<.01$; *** $p<.001$.

fellow worker who has experience with the labor arbitration process, who may have been successful in retrieving compensation, and who can provide details on the system and its processes, such as the fact that it is unnecessary to return to one's hometown to apply for arbitration for example, increases one's ability to navigate the system far more effectively than simply hearing the heartwarming tale of a similar migrant workers' success story on the local news. Data in table 5.7 supports this assertion. As shown in table 5.7, migrant workers whose best source of information is derived from urban ties are more likely to use legal channels, compared to individuals whose best source of information is derived from a rural tie.

Moreover, information derived from urban ties is also negatively associated with violence. Having access to the information that helps workers employ alternatives to violence, such as informal negotiation or the legal system, allows them to avoid costly and violent protest. It is unsurprising therefore that workers relying on urban place ties as their best source of information rarely engaged in violent protest activity, and urban tie information was strongly and negatively associated with violent protest (cc. = -2.81).

This is not to suggest that all workers lacking urban ties engage in violence, only that when pressed, workers lacking urban ties are more likely to use violence than workers with other less costly options. Faced with an "all or nothing" choice of violence or inaction, many workers simply give up, as the costs of any available action outweighs any potential benefit. Lacking the intermediate strategies urban ties can provide however, it is unsurprising that workers without urban ties are less likely to take action overall.

The analysis above provides strong evidence that different social ties provide different resources, and that access to these different ties strongly affects the strategies that migrant workers adopt. Previous literature on Chinese migrant labor has aptly demonstrated how migrants rely on rural ties for material support, and the data above supports those conclusions. However, the data also demonstrates that information, rather than material support, derived from urban rather than traditional rural ties, not only supports protest activity, but supports non-violent protest activity.

CONCLUSION — RURAL TIES, URBAN TIES, AND PROTEST

In this chapter, I provide quantitative evidence in support of the argument that different social ties provide different resources, and that these resources critically impact migrant workers' ability to engage in protest activity. The evidence above supports an argument that social ties play a critical role facilitating labor dispute activity among Chinese migrant workers, allowing them to engage in protest activity despite state and market restrictions on their ability to formally organize or obtain information.

Variation in workers' access to different types of social ties significantly influences the shape of their protest behavior. Workers able to obtain information on different protest activities from urban ties are better positioned to utilize nonviolent protest strategies, and less likely to employ violent strategies. Thus, information derived from urban ties is positively correlated with non-violent protest strategies such as use of the legal system, and negatively correlated with violence.

This chapter provides strong quantitative evidence that access to different types of social ties has an important effect on migrant workers' choice of protest strategies. Chapter 6 expands upon this argument by providing evidence in the form of detailed case studies, which explain how different social ties are able to provide these different resources. In the next chapter, I examine the causal logic behind the relationship between social ties and migrant worker dispute behavior, by describing how access to material support from rural ties can help expand migrants' window of opportunity for protest, and how information from urban ties can help migrant workers access new dispute options and strategies, facilitate collective action, navigate the legal system and access alternative sources of support.

NOTES

1. Even this conception of disputes being "large" or "small" is of course subjective, and dependent upon the size of the individual's income.

2. Although interview respondents were given the opportunity to provide written information on their participation in strikes and forms of violent protest, many chose instead to divulge this information through the open ended interview rather than commit that information to writing, given the sensitive and oftentimes illegal nature of the activity.

3. These categories include no education, elementary education, experience in middle school education (non-graduate), middle school graduate, experience with high school education, (non-graduate), high school graduate, university or technical school experience.

4. No protest activity is the referent group. Each of the logit estimates are therefore compared to this base outcome.

5. For example, workers who first engaged in informal bargaining and later went on to engage in violent protest were coded as having engaged in violence, the more costly protest action.

Chapter Six

Social Ties and Labor Protest: Case Study Analysis

The evidence in chapter 5 supports the argument that different types of ties provide different types of resources. Traditional rural ties for example are a critical source of material support for migrant workers. As described below, such material support can help workers sustain themselves while living in the city, and expand the time during which they may engage in protest activity before being forced to return home or find a new job. Rural ties can also help workers pay costs associated with the formal legal system, such as travel or associated court fees, or fees for legal representation.

Yet rural ties can also impede protest activity. Support from family members or hometown associates for example can provide opportunities for "exit," to borrow Albert Hirschman's term, allowing migrant workers to avoid protest activity altogether. Other times, rural ties may pit different local and ethnic groups against each other, undermining worker solidarity and limiting opportunities for broader collective action. In contrast, urban ties, links between individuals with different backgrounds and experiences that develop while operating in the cities, provide information useful for engaging in protest activity. The statistical analysis provided in chapter 5 supports an argument that workers with access to information derived from urban ties are not only more likely to engage in protest, but are more likely to do so through non-violent channels.

This chapter compliments the data presented in chapter 5 by providing a series of qualitative case studies, describing the utility of both rural and urban ties, and the resources they provide. It explains the causal mechanisms behind these relationships, illustrating the ways in which rural ties provide material and financial aid, and how urban ties help workers identify new dispute options and strategies, facilitate collective action, navigate the formal legal system, and identify new sources of support.

RURAL TIES AND MATERIAL SUPPORT

The idea that migrants rely on rural ties for material support goes back to studies of labor migration patterns in the late Qing dynasty and Republican periods (Perry 1994). Much has also been written regarding the importance of traditional rural-based networks in the employment process, and how those networks allow migrants to carry aspects of their informal social safety net with them when travelling to the city. As early as 1996, Chinese Academy of Social Science (CASS) researcher Li Peilin examined rural migrant workers' reliance on "native place relationships," which he refers to as "blood ties" (*xueyuan*) or "native place ties" (*diyuan*). These important informal institutions facilitated rural to urban migration and migrant labor employment (Li 1996). A 2003 study of female migrant workers in Guangdong by Ying Ganpiao found roughly 70% of his 1,039 respondents used hometown friends and family members to find their first urban job; percentages strikingly similar to what Li encountered in his research almost a decade earlier (Li 1996, 45–46).

When available, rural ties can cushion migrant workers against unforeseen financial hardship. Migrant workers with large networks of hometown associates for example are better positioned to manage financial difficulties (Cao 2003). Migrants in construction often choose to work for labor contractors from their hometown, not only because they are a known quantity, but because this increases their ability to find and confront them over any non-payment issues ("Interview 23, Professor Han Junkui, Qinghua University" 2007). In their analysis of two Shenzhen factory strikes in 2004 and 2007, Chris King-Chi Chan and Pun Ngai found that both "exclusive networks" and "strong ties," played key roles in facilitating strike activity, though the authors did not attempt to define the relationships falling into these categories, or identify the causal processes which generate the resources allowing workers to strike (Chan and Ngai 2009, 288).

Table 6.1 records the sources of material support for migrant workers interviewed during this research. Most respondents relied on either friendships established while operating in the cities (30.4%), or family members (29.2%) for material support. Others relied on hometown associates (19.2%) or fellow coworkers (17.2%) with whom the respondent shared no prior connections. In addition, approximately forty percent of the workers I interviewed (39.2%) were unable to obtain any material support, reflecting the reality of the financial hardships that many migrants face.

Material support can be a boon to migrant workers seeking to protest their treatment, expanding the window of opportunity during which they can engage in protest activity by providing the resources to remain in the city and pursue a resolution to their grievance, rather than being forced by economic circumstances to find a new job or return home. When a group of villagers from Jiangge County in Sichuan were not paid after the completion of a construction project, the group tried to retrieve their back wages through direct negotiation, appeals to the labor bureau, the local petition office, and finally by fighting with the security guards on the construction site where they were working. Throughout this time, the group managed to pool together their meager financial resources, sharing money for rent, food, and travel expenses to different government agencies ("Interview Beijing 0110" 2007).

Money from rural ties can also help workers pay costs associated with labor arbitration or the courts. While the *2008 Law of the PRC on Mediation and Arbitration of Labor Disputes* abolished labor arbitration fees, pursuing a labor dispute through arbitration and the courts remains far from costless. Limited financial resources and free time, transportation costs associated with evidence collection, the long procedural process, and opportunity costs associated with lost wages, are all challenges to using legal channels (Ho 2003, 153–54). In addition, many lawyers require their fees be paid up front when taking on remuneration or illegal termination fees, creating an additional expense of 2–10,000 RMB, a sizable amount which can create difficulties for many migrants (Sichuan Migrant Worker Legal Aid Station 2011). In these situations, the material aid that rural ties provide helps bear these costs, and many workers relied heavily on the financial support of relatives or hometown village associates when attempting to use the legal system, including family members living in the same city ("Interview Changzhou 0724" 2008), and fellow villagers ("Interview Beijing 0118" 2007).

In contrast, having no financial resources may limit the number of available protest strategies. One migrant worker for example was recruited by a

Table 6.1.   Migrant Workers' Sources of Material Support

Source (Resource Type)	Source of Material Support (%)*
Family (rural)	29.2%
Hometown Associate (rural)	19.2%
Friend (urban)	30.4%
Co-worker (urban)	17.2%
None	39.2%

N=282 (Source: Author's interviews). * Respondents allowed to select multiple responses, thus percentages do not equal one hundred.

labor contractor in Jiangsu to work construction in Beijing, and was promised a monthly salary and comfortable work hours. After arriving in Beijing however, the contractor refused to pay him as promised, distributing only living expenses (*shenghuofei*), while working the respondent 11 hours a day without overtime pay. Though he wanted to quit, he was alone in Beijing, and given his lack of funds and the shame of returning to his hometown empty handed, he feared he had no choice but to accept whatever the contractor agreed to provide ("Interview Beijing 0130" 2007).

Other times, rural ties can actually minimize protest behavior by providing alternatives to protest. A twenty-six year old woman from outside Bazhong city in Sichuan had been living with her husband in Changzhou since 1997, in an area known for having many Sichuanese residents. After an industrial accident destroyed the use of her left hand, she was given approximately 15,000 RMB by her boss and was dismissed. Jobless and handicapped, the respondent and her husband decided to talk to a lawyer and officials at the local labor bureau, paying for the initial legal expenses by borrowing money from some of the villagers that had come from her hometown living nearby. Despite this financial assistance however, hiring a lawyer was still prohibitively expensive. Moreover, without a labor contract, she believed it would be impossible to prove a labor relationship in court, and none of her coworkers would testify on her behalf for fear of losing their own jobs. Finally, the respondent and her husband borrowed more money to purchase a train ticket home, allowing her to rest and recuperate for half a year while her husband remained working in Changzhou ("Interview Changzhou 0723" 2008).

Rural ties can undermine broader worker solidarity as well. Chinese labor history is rife with examples of different rural tie groups competing for resources, including competition among ethnic lines. In the summer of 2009, after failing to find employment, an ethnic Han Chinese worker began spreading rumors about a group of Uighurs who had recently come to the Xuri (Early Light) Toy Factory in the southern Guangdong city of Shaoguan, blaming them for a rash of recent criminal activity. This helped spark an ethnic riot between the two ethnic groups, killing two workers and injuring 118 others (Pomfret 2009). After the news of the heavy handed treatment which Uighur workers received at the hands of local authorities made its way back to Urumqi, this helped spark another riot which left over 140 dead and 800 injured (Demick 2009).

While material support is important, access to material support does not always translate into action, as many of the obstacles to protest are overcome by information rather than money. Often, migrants are largely unaware of how to pursue different protest strategies, be they legal channels or informal negotiation and bargaining. The next section examines how urban ties help workers pursue these strategies.

URBAN TIES AND INFORMATION

Sitting down over *Yanjing* beer and roast meat at a street-side stall just east of Beijing's East Fifth Road, a group of Sichuanese construction workers described to me how they were recently denied their wages after the completion of a project. After listening to them for a few minutes, I asked one of their members; "when these sorts of things [labor disputes] occur, how do you know what to do?" His answer was telling, "watch other people, watch other situations, watch what they do" ("Interview Beijing 0107" 2007).[1] When these "other people" include individuals with knowledge of and experience with labor dispute activity, access to such practical and relevant information can be of immense help for workers seeking to take action.

Migrant Labor Information Sources

To what extent do migrant workers rely on urban ties as an information resource compared with other potential information resources such as rural ties, newspapers, television, or the internet? Table 6.2 lists the general sources that migrant workers used when first attempting to obtain information on possible actions after their dispute took place. In general, migrant workers cast a broad net, with one third of the respondents accessing traditional mass media such as newspapers (34%) and television (36%). Other forms of mass media, such as radio (3%), were less often utilized. In addition to these traditional media resources, migrant workers' information searches included both urban ties, such as fellow workers (45%) with whom they had no hometown or familial connections, and to a lesser extent, rural ties, such as hometown associates (32%).

Much ink has been spilled discussing the role of information communication technology, including the internet and social media, in promoting social movements in authoritarian states, including social movements and revolutions in Egypt, Tunisia and elsewhere (O'Neil 1998; Cohen 2009; Shino 2007). Such new technologies have been identified as useful tools for disseminating information and for having a multiplier effect on protest activity. When conducting detailed information to prosecute a labor dispute however, the adoption of these new technologies among migrants in China appears to be lagging. As table 6.2 shows, only 16% of respondents interviewed during this research utilized the internet as a general source of information, compared to the third of workers who turned to newspapers or television programs, or almost half of all workers who turned to other fellow workers.

This is not to suggest that QQ instant messaging, text messaging, online discussion boards, or other internet-based tools of mass communication, are irrelevant to migrant labor protests in China. However, their impact on protest activity appears much more nuanced than what is commonly discussed in the western press. Chapter 7 is devoted to examining this issue in detail.

Sources of "New Information" and "Best Information"

Many migrant workers search far and wide when initially seeking information to help them take action. This is not surprising. However, crucial to the argument posited in this book is the extent to which various information sources affected migrant labor dispute behavior. The argument put forth here is that information derived from migrants' urban ties is more useful in helping migrants take advantage of non-violent protest strategies, including informal bargaining and use of the legal system. Indeed, the quality of the information available to migrants varied considerably, and this variation depended largely upon its source. In migrant workers' own evaluation, information derived from urban ties was more likely to be new information, or information they deemed to be more useful for helping them to engage in protest activity, compared with other sources of information.

Table 6.3 lists interview respondents' various sources of information, and the extent to which these information sources provided workers with "new information" or "new strategies" (*xin de xinxi huo fangfa*) helping them to act. Table 6.3 also lists the information sources that, in migrant workers' own opinion, provided them with the "best, most useful" (*zuihao, zui youyong*) information.

As can be seen from table 6.3, most respondents obtained new information from urban ties, with 39% of respondents receiving new information from friends they met while operating in the cities, while 34% were able to obtain new information from coworkers who were not family members or hometown associates (individuals from the same hometown with whom they

Table 6.2. Migrant Labor: Sources of General Information

Information Resource	Percent
Fellow Worker	45%
Television	36%
Newspaper	34%
Hometown Associate	32%
Internet	16%
None	5%
Radio	3%

Source: Author's Interviews. Respondents allowed to select multiple options, thus percentages do not equal 100. N = 282.

Table 6.3.   Sources of New and Best Information

Information Source (Resource Type)	Source of "New Information" (% of Respondents)	"Best" information Source (% of Respondents)
Friends (Urban Ties)	39%	20%
Workers (Urban Ties)	34%	25%
Hometown Associates (Rural Ties)	26%	9%
Family Members (Rural Ties)	15%	12%
Civil Society Organizations (NGOs)	17%	8%
Government Institutions	7%	5%
None	17%	17%

Sources: Author's Interviews.* N = 242

*"Best Source of information," totals do not equal 100% due to omission of "other" categories (media resources, individual lawyers, *tongxianghui* (association), other organizations), which cumulatively account for 4% of the total. Respondents were allowed to select multiple sources of new information.

had a prior connection). Respondents were far less likely to obtain new information from rural ties. For example, although table 6.2 notes that 32% of all respondents reached out to hometown associates as part of their initial information search, as noted on Table 6.3, only 26% of the respondents reported that these same hometown associates were able to provide *new information*. Only 15% of respondents were able to obtain new information directly from family members. These results suggest that although migrants reached out to a broad range of individuals when first seeking information, they were more likely to be successful in obtaining new information from urban ties.

The importance of urban ties as an information source is even clearer when examining where migrant workers were most likely to obtain what they considered to be their *best* information, as workers were more than twice as likely to obtain what they considered their best information from urban ties, such as friends or fellow workers (20–25%), as opposed to rural ties (9–12%). In short, the data above suggests that despite initially investigating a wide range of information sources, which included rural ties, migrant workers were most likely to obtain new or useful information from urban ties.

These findings are consistent with the hypothesis that rural ties are less likely to provide new or useful information for protest activities, given that

rural ties link individuals with common backgrounds and similar work experiences, and individuals sharing rural ties are more likely to possess redun-
dant information. In contrast, one fifth of all migrant workers' best information came from fellow coworkers. This is consistent with the argument that
individuals expanding their information searches to include those outside
their traditional social circles are more likely to obtain practical and useful
labor dispute information, including information regarding relatively scarce
and esoteric knowledge unavailable to many migrants.

The statistics in table 6.3 regarding government and non-government institutions point to the utility of information derived from grassroots migrant
labor NGOs. While 17% of all the workers received new information from
non-governmental institutions such as migrant labor NGOs, *all* of these individuals came from the test sample—respondents selected from migrant labor
NGOs and government legal aid centers—while none came from the control
sample. The test sample includes workers from both NGOs as well as
government affiliated legal aid centers. Of those individuals interviewed at
NGOs, 64.6% obtained new information from these organizations. In
contrast, only 9% of the respondents interviewed at government affiliated
legal aid centers received new information from this source.

A comparison of the information derived from government and non-
government organizations compared to other sources would require a larger
sample selected across a greater number of organizations. These initial findings regarding the utility of migrant labor NGOs do however suggest that
when available, they can be a significant boon to workers. The importance of
these organizations to migrant labor protest is examined in detail in chapter
8.

The Utility of Information in Promoting Labor Dispute Activity

When searching for information that may help resolve a labor dispute, migrant workers initially conducted searches that covered a wide array of
sources, including traditional media such as newspaper and television, as
well as urban and rural ties. Not all information is created equal however.
According to workers own evaluations, information obtained from urban ties
was more likely to provide a new method or a new strategy for engaging in
protest activity, and was more often evaluated as the most useful information
source that they had available. Whether or not this new information helped
workers to take action however is a separate question. To what extent did this
information matter for migrant workers seeking to take action? Table 6.4
examines migrant workers' average number of protest actions based on what
they considered to be their best source of available information.

Not all new information is necessarily helpful for workers seeking to take
action, and while urban ties may be useful for providing new information, the

Table 6.4.   Protest Activity by Best Information

Best Information Source (Resource Type)	Percent age	Avg. No. Protest Actions	Excluding five "most active" respondents
Workers (Urban Tie)	25%	1.98	1.7
Friends (Urban Tie)	20%	1.91	1.6
Family Members (Rural Tie)	12%	1.37	.7
Hometown Associates (Rural Tie)	9%	1.33	.9
Other (media, individual lawyer, etc)	4%	1.08	.7
None	17%	.54	.3
Non-governmental Organization	8%	N/A	N/A
Government Institutions*	5%	N/A	N/A

Sources: Author's Interviews. N = 242

* Respondents within these two categories [non-governmental organization; government institution] were all derived from the test sample, while none came from the control sample. Because the test sample was designed specifically to guarantee variation on the dependent variable by ensuring respondents within the test sample had taken action, these categories tell us little about the relationship between information derived from migrant labor organizations, government institutions, and protest activity. More informative is the fact that *no one* in the control sample listed government institutions as their best source of information. Chapter eight examines the role of migrant labor NGOs in migrant labor protest activity in detail.

extent to which this information facilitates protest activity is a separate question. Table 6.4 shows the average number of protest actions that migrant workers engaged in compared to what they considered to be their best source of information. Table 6.4 also lists the average number of protest actions for each information source after excluding the top five most active respondents in each category, helping to control for their high level of protest activity relative to the other respondents in that category. As is clear from table 6.4, not only did more respondents receive their best source of information from urban ties such as friends and fellow workers, those that did so engaged in more protest actions, even after controlling for the top five most active respondents in each category. Individuals whose most useful information was derived from traditional rural ties, such as family members or hometown associates, engaged in 1.37 and 1.33 average dispute actions respectively. Those with access to urban ties, such as friends or workplace colleagues however, engaged in 1.91 and 1.98 average protest actions per respondent.

After controlling for the top five most active respondents, the average number of dispute actions among those relying on rural ties declined much more rapidly compared to workers who relied on other information sources. After adjusting for these outliers, the difference between the categories expands significantly. Migrant workers who obtained their best source of information from other workers for example engaged in one full additional protest action, taking 1.7 actions on average, compared to only 0.7 for those who obtained their best source of information from family members.

The evidence above supports the argument that migrant workers with access to information derived from urban ties, such as friends or workers with whom they share no previous native place connections, appear better positioned to engage in protest activity when encountering a labor dispute. But how exactly does information derived from urban ties help migrant workers act? Below, I provide a series of examples analyzing the casual link between urban ties, the information they provide, and the way in which this information influences migrant workers' dispute behavior.

Accessing New Dispute Options and Strategies

First, information may help reveal new dispute options that were previously inaccessible. In their study of rightful resistance in rural China, Kevin O'Brien and Lianjiang Li note how protesting peasant groups search for patrons at various levels of government in order to exploit differences in their policy preferences (O'Brien 2006, 27–30). Aggrieved Chinese migrant workers employ similar strategies, searching for patrons within a collection of enterprises or within an industry in order to play different interests against each other.

When facing non-payment issues in the construction industry for example, the complex web of relationships between parent companies, contractors, and subcontractors, often make it difficult for workers to identify an interlocutor. Attempting to negotiate one's case alone may also be intimidating, especially for uneducated, inexperienced migrants. In these cases, access to an experienced negotiator can be helpful, providing aid beyond what is available through traditional information and media channels.

The story of one worker in Changzhou is an excellent example of this process. An eighteen year old from Yucheng in Henan Province, he had come by himself to Changzhou, and was working on a small construction project near Miaoqiao village in the southern suburbs. After the project's completion, the contractor refused to pay him the remainder of his wages, citing faulty work. At first, the respondent simply asked for his money, and was quickly rebuffed ("Interview Changzhou 0710" 2008).

Afterwards however, the respondent had the opportunity to talk to an older worker living in his building. This migrant also worked in construction, and had experience with contractors withholding wages. The older worker, whom the interview respondent referred to as a "fellow worker" (*gongyou*), said that if the refusal to pay was not a result of failing to receive money from higher levels of the contracting process, the respondent could approach the contractor at the next highest level in the hopes of obtaining a written IOU, as an IOU from the "big boss" (*dalaoban*) may provide the necessary pressure allowing the worker to retrieve his wages. The older worker even accompanied the respondent to negotiate with the "big boss," providing the necessary emotional support and negotiating skill. Using this method, the younger worker successfully retrieved his back wages ("Interview Changzhou 0710" 2008).

Having such an experienced advisor working on one's behalf greatly increases the likelihood of action, providing negotiating leverage which was previously unavailable. Without this aid, the younger worker would not have thought to approach the contractor at the next highest level within the project, nor would he have had the savvy to do so on his own. While newspaper articles and television programs touting workers' legal rights are increasingly common in Chinese society, few provide the type of detailed informal negotiating advice available through the respondent's connections with this experienced worker.

Facilitating Collective Action

Second, urban ties allow workers to identify others with similar disputes, promoting a sense of shared grievance that can give rise to collective action. Factory or construction site dormitories often act as mechanisms for labor control. Employing a militaristic factory regime, where workers' time and interactions are strictly monitored and restricted, make it difficult for workers to have the interactions necessary to develop urban ties. When dormitory restrictions are relaxed however, these arrangements can provide opportunities for grievance sharing, coordination, and cooperation (Chan and Ngai 2009, 291). One example of this took place between workers in a Nanjing hotel. A twenty-one year old worker from northern Jiangsu Province had been working in a hotel and karaoke bar six days a week, ten hours per day for two months. At the end of the second month, his manager stopped paying his wages, promising him that the delay was only temporary.

After two months of not receiving his wages however, this worker began talking to coworkers. During these conversations, they discovered that over half of the 72 employees had not been paid for two months or more. After a week of planning in the dormitories, the group of thirty two decided to approach the hotel manager en mass, calculating that the hotel could not afford to lose them all simultaneously. Four workers in the group who had faced similar situations before also suggested waiting until early October to act, when the hotel would be at its busiest, thus providing the group with more leverage. This strategic delay was important, but not something my interview respondent would have considered on his own, having had no prior experience in planning or participating in such activities ("Interview Nanjing 0909" 2008).

While the cooperation described above was aided by the workers' proximity and dormitory lifestyle, grievance sharing is not automatic, as illustrated by a woman from Anhui Province, who also worked in the same Miaoqiao village in the suburbs of Changzhou, and was employed in a local textile factory. Though she signed a contract, she still worked seven days a week and was not paid overtime, both in violation of Chinese labor law. Despite working in a factory of over one thousand workers, she argued no one had any ideas how to resolve her situation, stating that "the knowledge of us migrant workers is all too shallow" ("Interview Changzhou 0712" 2008). During the interview however, she also revealed that she had recently come to the factory alone, and knew only a few individuals working there. This respondent consulted only with her family back in Anhui, who advised her to simply leave her job and avoid trouble.

Navigating the Legal System

Third, urban ties help migrants navigate China's complex legal system. In countries with established legal institutions, one need not be a legal expert if the process of applying for legal redress is clear, and officials can provide coherent direction on how to proceed. As described in chapter 3 however, workers in China seeking to use the formal legal system face numerous obstacles, including complex labor relationships which obscure many companies' legal responsibilities, a lack of documentation and evidence, and overworked and under informed legal personnel.

Urban ties however can be extremely useful in helping migrant workers navigate this system, as can be seen in the case of one of my interview respondents from Baoying County in central Jiangsu Province. Employed in a small textile factory in the northern suburbs of Changzhou, the respondent had first come to the city in 2005 with twelve others from his hometown. At the end of 2006 however, their boss went missing, and the respondent and 45 other workers at the factory went unpaid for roughly two months.

While labor bureau officials eventually agreed to provide compensation to the group, this was only the beginning of the workers' problems. Accessing these funds required large amounts of paperwork, multiple visits and

interactions with different government agencies, and various forms of identification to prove the worker's identity and his work relationship with the
factory. To navigate this process, the respondent relied heavily on the more
experienced workers in his group, who advised him on what materials to
bring to which agency, how to prepare paperwork, interact with labor bureau
personnel, and what to expect more generally during the entire process. In
the respondent's opinion, he would not have successfully navigated this tor-
tuous process if not for the help of these workers and their ability to guide
him through the system ("Interview Changzhou 0721" 2008).

In this example, one may reasonably expect that the interview respondent
would be able to rely on labor bureau officials to help him retrieve his back
wages, particularly after it had been determined by the bureau that he was
rightfully owed compensation. Yet by his own admission, had he relied on
the labor bureau alone, it is doubtful he would have ever been able to successfully retrieve his wages, despite the fact that the courts had already ruled
in his favor. Instead, this respondent was fortunate to have access to other
workers with direct and applicable knowledge and experience in such matters. In these types of situations, such a resource can be critical.

Accessing Alternative Sources of Support

Fourth, urban ties allow workers to access alternatives sources of aid, such as
the growing number of migrant labor organizations or "citizen representatives" (*gongmin dailiren*) operating in China; individuals possessing expertise on workers' legal rights, but often lacking formal legal credentials. Giv-
en the government's prohibitions on their activities, citizen representatives or
migrant labor NGOs do not often advertise their services openly, and informal channels such as word of mouth from friends or coworkers may be the
only source of information connecting migrant workers to this valuable resource.

While interviewing migrant workers in Changzhou, I met an individual
who, as a result of past labor grievances, had turned into a self-taught legal
expert or "barefoot lawyer," developing an immense wealth of knowledge of
the legal system, as well as an extremely impressive collection of labor law
books, documents, and other legal rights materials. A worker from Guizhou
named Mr. Li,[2] he quickly learned through his own experiences as a migrant
worker that without any knowledge of his legal rights, he had no way to
counter employers who he thought made unjust claims. "If he [the employer]
says he is justified, (*youli*) and I say I am justified, but I don't have any legal
knowledge to back me up, then what am I to do" ("Interview Changzhou, 44"
2008)? It was after this insight that legal knowledge could help Mr. Li defend
his own rights against unscrupulous employers that he began to take an
interest in the law. Gradually, he acquired a large collection of labor law

materials, and began to help workers he knew negotiate with employers, providing legal advice and consultation.

While not using the phrase, Mr. Li argued that bargaining within the "shadow of the law" was important, and could help support workers' demands for fair treatment which may otherwise be ignored by employers. "There are some employers here who look down on outsiders, but if you speak clearly about the law, then they quickly know you understand the law, and problems can be resolved" ("Interview Changzhou, 44" 2008, 44).[3] Mr. Li even provided specific advice on how to prepare cases for labor arbitration, and had general guidelines for workers to follow ("Interview Changzhou, 44" 2008, 44).[4]

Mr. Li was not a professional legal advocate however, and did not advertise his services in any way, as doing so without a license to practice could get him into trouble. The only way to reach him therefore was through word of mouth. Interestingly enough however, three days before interviewing Mr. Li, I interviewed another worker less than four hundred yards from Mr. Li's house. A forty year old construction worker from Anhui Province, he had come with ten others from his hometown to work on one of the many building projects in the city, and was promised a monthly salary of 3,000 RMB to be paid upon completion of the project. Upon completion however, the contractor refused to pay the workers their wages. When I asked this worker why the group did not appeal to the local labor bureau, he stated they had no knowledge of the law, and no contacts in Changzhou (*meiyou guanxi*).

The sole resource available to this respondent was his family back in Anhui. He knew no locals in the area, and only interacted with villagers from his work group. Moreover, when asked where he and his group could obtain advice regarding possible dispute options, the respondent replied "nowhere, we just thought about it ourselves" ("Interview Changzhou 0717" 2008). Had these workers been able to expand outside their closely knit Anhui village circle, they may have been able to obtain advice on additional dispute strategies, such as how to approach the labor bureau, what evidence to collect, or how to leverage their specific knowledge of the worksite or their employers' business practices to negotiate more effectively. They might also have been able to interact with someone who could have connected them to Mr. Li and his services. Instead, these workers were completely shut off from this resource.

In contrast to the examples above, many other workers lacked the knowledge to act. This was a common theme that many returned to throughout the interview, especially when workers relied primarily upon family members or hometown associates as their primary source of information. In these cases, respondents often used similar language to describe their frustrations, complaining that they and their fellow workers were all in similar situations, yet no one within their group seemed to know what to do.

One thirty-four year old worker, who had just recently arrived in Changzhou from Hubei, had been fired along with four others he had arrived with after not being paid for two months. When asked why he had not decided to pursue this case, the worker responded, "I'm all on my own here away from home, and I don't know anyone" (*gushenyiren zaiwai meiyou shouren*) ("Interview Changzhou 0701" 2008).

A lack of information limits the number of protest options available to workers, and may even encourage workers to engage in unsanctioned or violent activity if desperate enough. Another respondent from Sichuan was part of a small group of three construction workers, all from the same hometown, working in Beijing. They had been recruited by a local labor contractor back in Sichuan to work on a renovation project. During the course of their work however, the respondent's younger brother, who was part of the group, had been injured on the job, falling from a ladder and injuring his back ("Interview Beijing 0111" 2007). After taking his brother to the hospital, the respondent was contacted by the labor contractor, who fired the two workers, offering only one month's salary to each and refusing to pay hospital fees or injury compensation, all in violation of the law.

All three of the workers were inexperienced, having never previously gone out of their home county to work. The first step these workers took was to negotiate with the labor contractor directly, yet they were quickly rebuffed. In contrast to the successful young construction worker in Changzhou described above, these workers lacked any strategic knowledge that might provide them leverage in the negotiations. Despite being a larger group of workers, they were all from the same village, and no one in the group had any prior knowledge of how the construction industry is structured, how different contractors on the project interacted with each other, or what levels of the contracting process might be played off against each other. This lack of knowledge limited their ability to take advantage of any potential cleavages within the loosely affiliated collection of contractors and enterprises, thus limiting their opportunities for action.

When direct negotiations failed, the respondent and his group next went to the local labor bureau, expecting to obtain the necessary information there. Yet as a group, they "didn't know the procedures," lacked the relevant paperwork or evidence, and failed to obtain necessary advice regarding the next steps in the process. In contrast to the Changzhou factory worker described above, who relied on his colleagues' information to make successful appeals to the local Labor Bureau, the workers in this case were hindered not by a lack of financial or material support, but by their lack of understanding regarding how to even begin the formal legal process. Being from the same village and sharing similar work experiences, none of the workers in this insolated group had any experience taking action in a labor dispute before.

Labor injury cases are complex, even in comparison to most migrant labor dispute cases. Unlike remuneration cases which can be relatively straight forward, injury cases involve a number of steps such as medical diagnosis, obtaining a worker injury certificate, and having the extent of the injury evaluated. While this group of workers were clearly motivated, sometime motivation is not enough. In this case, being able to navigate the various legal and administrative procedures involved were beyond their capacity. It is not surprising therefore that these three migrant workers from Sichuan, connected by their hometown ties and lacking input from other individuals that may have previous experience or involvement in a similar dispute process, were unable to take legal action.

Unable to take legal action or engage in any serious informal negotiations, the three workers relied on the only option remaining, returning to the construction site as a group to attack the labor contractor. When the security guards (*baoan*) attempted to bar them from the construction site, a fight broke out which drew the attention of some local police, who then mediated the dispute informally, arbitrarily awarding the group 10,000 RMB. Escalating labor disputes to the point of violence is a risky option, opening workers to retaliation by their employer or criminal punishment by the local authorities. This is especially true in this scenario, given the small number of workers involved. Moreover, it was clear from the interview that the respondent's first choice was to appeal to the legal system, as he feared the legal and physical consequences of fighting ("Interview Beijing 0111" 2007).

Use of the legal system is highly problematic, and the above example is not meant to suggest that limited information is all that stands in the way. However, when migrant workers have limited information regarding how to navigate the legal system, this surely contributes to its ineffectiveness.

CONCLUSION: SOCIAL NETWORKS AND RESOURCES FOR PROTEST

This chapter has sought to illustrate the causal mechanisms by which different ties provide different resources through a series of detailed examples. Like previous research on Chinese migrant labor, the examples above illustrate how migrant workers often draw on traditional rural ties for material support. While such ties can help expand workers' window of opportunities for protest, they are not well positioned to provide information, which is vital for migrants seeking to engage in protest. To obtain information, migrants often rely on urban ties to supply relevant and case specific knowledge. Such knowledge can facilitate use of labor arbitration or the courts, or informal bargaining.

Such information may help workers take action by providing a better understanding of the enterprise in question, providing them with access to new negotiation strategies or better leverage when negotiating. They may be able to identify others with similar disputes, developing a sense of shared grievances which can lead to collective action, or obtain expert help in using the legal system. Workers with access to these sources of information may also be able to acquire the aid of someone with legal expertise, such as a "barefoot" or "citizen surrogate" lawyer, and are also better positioned to avoid more violent, costly strategies.

One important factor that has yet to be fully addressed in this book is the role of new information communication technology (ICT) in Chinese migrant labor protests. The past decade has witnessed a remarkable rise in the use of ICT in China, to the extent that most migrant workers now own a cell phone and communicate regularly through SMS and instant messaging services such as QQ. What impact have these new technologies had on migrant labor's likelihood and capacity for protest, either through legal channels such as labor arbitration and the courts, or through other means? The next chapter takes up this topic, examining the ways social media interact with social ties, and its impact on migrant labor protest activity.

NOTES

1. "*kan bieren, kan biede shiqing, kan bieren zenmeban.*"
2. Individual's name changed to maintain confidentiality.
3. "*Haiyou youxie laoban kanbuqi waidiren, ni ba falv shuo qingchu zhihou, ta jiu zhidao ni dongfa, wenti jiu jiejue.*"
4. For example, "If the dispute is under 3,000 RMB" he said, "we could manage the dispute ourselves, and I would go talk to the boss. However, if the dispute is over 3,000 RMB, I would suggest that we find a lawyer."

Chapter Seven

Technology and Migrant Labor Protest

In the summer of 2011, a violent clash between migrant workers and police in the southern Guangdong city of Zengcheng was touched off by migrant workers spreading information online about police abuse of a pregnant fruit vendor from Sichuan. Workers in the area later used internet message boards to call for a one month general strike ("Chinese Police Restore Order to Restive Town" 2011; Chan 2011). A year earlier, workers participating in the Honda automobile strikes were sharing information through cell phone, text messages, and online message boards, while uploading videos of the strikes, and communicating through QQ, a Chinese instant messaging service (Barboza and Bradsher 2010).

Many organizations providing services to migrant workers, including migrant labor NGOs, as well as government and union affiliated legal aid centers, maintain websites, which provide contact information, copies of relevant labor laws and regulations, and dedicated message boards and email addresses for sending and receiving legal advice. Some Chinese labor activists are even active on Chinese micro blogs (*weibo*), a twitter style Chinese online communications tool. By the fall of 2011, some labor rights activists, were even using *weibo* to launch their own campaigns for local peoples congress positions, albeit with little success (Richburg 2011; Zhang 2011).

The role of the Internet, SMS text messaging services, *weibo*, and other information communication technologies (ICT) in shaping the frequency and form of popular protest in China has received significant attention in recent years (Yang 2011; Sullivan and Xie 2009). This attention to online protest in China has only increased since the Arab Spring, as online social networking tools such as Facebook, Twitter, and YouTube were heralded as important resources, helping activists to organize under authoritarianism.

137

Chinese migrant workers are not without access to online communication technology. Many migrant workers now have access to cell phones, while the younger generations of migrant workers increasingly communicate with friends and family through cheaper SMS text messaging, rather than phone calls. Yet just as workers adopt new technology to facilitate strikes and protest, the government adopts new methods and strategies to limit their use. Clearly ICT such as cell phones, text messaging, and online communication tools have impacted workers' lives, but how has this new technology influenced their capacity to engage in labor protest? This chapter explores the precise nature of technology's role, examining the benefits and limitations of ICT to protests in an authoritarian state.

ICT AND MIGRANT LABOR PROTEST: OBSTACLES AND ADVANTAGES

One of ICT's greatest advantages is its capacity to rapidly disseminate information to many people across long distances. While much has been made of the benefit of ICT to protest in authoritarian states, ICT users in China face three challenges. These challenges are particularly acute when seeking to promote what social movement theorists refer to as *behavioral diffusion;* the dissemination of specific protest plans, tactics, or repertoires for protest activity (Givan, Roberts, and Soule 2011, 4).

First, ICT channels are often blocked or closely monitored by government security organizations. This government oversight only increases during times of political sensitivity, such as political anniversaries like June 4 (Tiananmen) or during events that could be used as a rallying point for protest. Thus, using these channels to distribute actionable information, such as the details of a planned protest action during that time, or specific tactics protesters should employ, becomes both difficult and dangerous. Meanwhile, efforts to mitigate those dangers, through the use of coded messages for example, necessarily makes the dissemination process more complicated, limiting the ability to reach large audiences at once, a key advantage of ICT.

Second, the type of information necessary to facilitate behavioral diffusion is often very context specific, which may require multiple rounds of interaction between the sender and receiver(s). While protest entrepreneurs may be able to provide advice on the best way to organize a protest, that advice is likely contingent upon the specific circumstances of the group, and understanding those circumstances may require additional back and forth communication. Given the uncertain legal status of many purveyors of labor protest strategies in China—grassroots migrant labor organizations, *tiaolou* entrepreneurs, or citizen legal representatives for example—frequent back and forth communication via ICT can become both practically difficult and politically dangerous.

Third, even when both sides of the information transaction can identify a safe distribution method, the transaction is still likely to be rooted in the personal relationships and social networks which exists both prior to and independent of the method of communication. Information can be sent between workers via text messages and cell phones, but these workers must first know who to contact, and trust that the individual receiving that information will not report the sender. Thus, despite ICT's numerous benefits, particularly its ability to rapidly spread information, its ability to distribute detailed, time sensitive and actionable information to large groups of individuals in China is highly constrained.

This is not to suggest that the revolution in social networking and communications have had no impact on migrant labor protests in China. Far from it. Yet rather than promote behavioral diffusion, this new technology's impact on Chinese migrant labor has perhaps been most strongly felt in its ability to promote *ideational diffusion*, defined as the dissemination of larger frameworks through which migrant workers interpret everyday events, such as their treatment at the workplace, their position and influence within the party-state, and their place in Chinese society more broadly.

While opportunities to disseminate detailed protest tactics or plans of action through ICT may be constrained, other information, such as the working conditions in other areas compared to one's own, is far easier to convey. Though not related to any one specific protest activity, such information can motivate workers by drawing attention to unjust or unfair treatment similar to their own conditions, or by fostering a sense that their conditions are unfairly lacking by comparison. Such information may also modify workers' calculations regarding the likelihood of their own success at taking action, or expand worker solidarity to include a wider range of migrant workers with whom they come to empathize. In this last sense, ICT's capacity to promote migrant workers' ability to "feel and articulate the identity of their interests as between themselves, and as against other men whose interests are different from (and usually opposed to) theirs" (Thompson 1964, 9) can, in a very real sense, be seen as promoting a traditional form of working class consciousness.

Migrant Workers as "Netizens"?

Like much of the Chinese population, migrant workers' access to ICT has expanded rapidly in recent years. Cell phone and internet usage in China for example has grown at an astonishing rate over the past decade. By 2010, roughly 75% of Chinese phone lines were cell phones. In 2010 alone, the number of households with cell phones increased by over 111 million, reaching approximately 859 million (Ministry of Industry and Information Technology 2011). By October 2013, the Ministry of Industry and Information Technology (MIIT) reported Chinese mobile phone users had surpassed 1.22 billion (Xinhua 2013).

Internet usage has grown at a strikingly similar pace. By 2013, the number of internet users reached 618 million, over twice as many as recorded just five years prior in 2008. However, unlike most Americans, whose first interaction with the World Wide Web came through desktop or laptop computers, many in China have grown up using mobile phones and other mobile devices. By 2013, roughly 80%, or 494 million of those going online in China, did so using their cell phones (Ministry of Industry and Information Technology 2014).

This rapid growth in internet users has given rise to an online culture of mostly affluent, educated, middle class Chinese citizens; active online and known to discuss popular social, economic, and political issues. Collectively referred to as "Netizens," this new social group has influenced both local and national issues (Richburg 2009). To what extent are migrant workers joining the ranks of China Netizens? Like the rest of the population, ICT usage among migrant workers is expanding rapidly. Cell phone usage among migrants for example is common, with all but the most impoverished migrants having some access to a mobile device to make phone calls and text messages. Migrant workers' internet usage has increased as well, often as a source of entertainment. Migrant workers in the Pearl River Delta interviewed as part of a Peking University study for example visited internet cafes at least once every five days on average, spending about 68 RMB, equal to approximately 20% of their total monthly consumption (Ngan and Ma 2008).

Despite this common view of migrant workers in China having access to ICT, there are reasons to believe that migrants are lagging behind many other social groups in terms of their access to ICT. According to the China Internet Network Information Center's (CNNIC) *23rd Report on Internet Development in China* published in 2011, migrant workers were the least active and least represented of the major Chinese social groups, comprising only 2.6% of all online usage (China Internet Network Information Center 2010, 22). Moreover, compared with other groups in the study such as university students, professional white collar office workers, and the general population, migrant workers in the CNNIC study scored the lowest in their use of online media, online communications such as email and instant messaging, and use of online social networking tools such as blogs, internet forums and BBS, or social networking websites such as *Weibo* (China Internet Network Information Center 2010, 42).

Migrant workers also used fewer internet applications, and spent less time online overall compared to these other groups as well (China Internet Network Information Center 2010, 44). This suggests that although Chinese society as a whole is becoming increasingly conversant with ICT, these skills are not necessarily being distributed equally throughout the population, and groups such as migrant workers are falling behind other groups in Chinese society.

CHALLENGES TO BEHAVIORAL DIFFUSION

Clearly the use of ICT, including internet and cell phone usage, is growing among the migrant labor population. But what does this new technology enable them to do? Following the Iranian "twitter revolution" of 2009, and the summer 2010 political revolutions in Egypt, Tunisia, and elsewhere, there has been a growing debate over the extent to which social media can act as a tool for protests, with some arguing that this new technology can provide access to new, specific protest tactics and strategies previously unavailable (Shirky 2011). For Chinese migrant workers however, using ICT to facilitate *behavioral diffusion*, or the spread of new strategies or tactics for protest, is fraught with challenges, arising from government regulation and control of ICT environments, as well as migrant workers' own position in Chinese society. The following section examines these obstacles.

Government Regulation and Monitoring of ICT

The Chinese state imposes a wide-ranging system of monitoring and restrictions on citizens seeking to use ICT. The PRC government already allocates massive amounts of resources to this task, limiting access to information online, monitoring cell phone conversations, text messaging, and SMS instant messaging services, and acting directly to influence the online discussion of politically sensitive issues.

During the March 2011 National People's Congress sessions in Beijing, a report released by the Ministry of Finance revealed that 2010 annual spending on internal security issues, including new technology spending related to ICT control and management, surpassed spending on national defense for the first time. Chinese internal security spending in 2010 grew 15.6% to 549 billion ($84 billion), compared to spending on national security, which grew 7.8% to 533.4 billion (Hook 2011; Buckley 2011). Of course, no amount of spending will allow the Chinese government to keep an eye on every online discussion board or an ear to every cell phone conversation in the country, nor is that likely the government's intent. However, the expenditure of such massive amounts of resources, combined with conscious efforts to develop a system of ICT management and control, have allowed the Chinese government to become increasingly sophisticated over time, targeting the transmission of more sensitive information, the exact information required to facilitate behavioral diffusion.

Historically, responsibility for government oversight of online usage and content has been shared by multiple organizations. One organization key to those efforts has been the Computer Management and Supervision Bureau (CMSB) within the Public Security Bureau (PSB). The CMSB oversees all registered internet service providers, as well as individual and commercial entities operating online (State Council of the People's Republic of China 1997). The Ministry of State Security takes an interest in online security issues as well, particularly as they pertain to foreign security threats such as the activities of dissidents overseas ("Review of China's Internet Regulations").

Other government agencies play a role as well, leading to a confusing web of overlapping bureaucratic authority. The State Council Information Office (SCIO) for example has the power to restrict which organizations post online news content. As part of its responsibilities for regulating the telecommunications and software industries, MIIT controls the licensing of internet content providers, while the State Administration of Radio, Film and Television is responsible for internet streaming and other internet broadcasts ("Agencies Responsible for Censorship in China" 2014).

Over the past few years, the Chinese government has begun streamlining this system, consolidating government oversight into the hands of fewer agencies. In the summer of 2011, the SCIO announced the creation of a new agency, the State Internet Information Office (SIIO), which would absorb personnel previously under the SCIO, and take responsibility for oversight of online content management, online gaming, video, publications, and also play a role in managing government propaganda online. Perhaps most importantly, under this revised organizational structure, the new office would oversee the telecommunications companies that provide access for internet users, as well as online content providers, thus consolidating the current system of management and control (Wines 2011a).

This collection of institutions is supported by a host of regulations, shaping the online and telecommunications environment in ways that hinder the ability of Chinese citizens, including migrant labor, to disseminate sensitive information via ICT. The promulgation of Chinese ICT regulations began in earnest in the late 1990s, with the 1997 *Computer Information Network and Internet Security, Protection, and Management Regulations*, which places the responsibility for monitoring online activity, and curtailing anti-regime activity, directly on internet providers. The 1997 *Computer Regulations* in particular provide opportunities for the state to limit online activity, identifying and barring a wide range of loosely defined and proscribed activities, prohibiting individuals from engaging in any activities that "harm national security, disclose state secrets, harm the interests of the state, of society or of a group, the legal rights of citizens, or to take part in criminal activities" (Mulvenon and Chase 2002, 57).

The promulgation of ICT regulation accelerated throughout the 2000s in an attempt to get ahead of newly emerging technology. The 2000 *Regulations on the Management of Internet Electronic Bulletin Services* for example sought to regulate the use of online discussion boards, chat rooms, message boards, and similar methods of online communications (Ministry of Information Industry 2010). In 2005, the *Non-Commercial Web Site Registration Regulations* required all noncommercial websites to register with MIIT or face financial penalties ("Analysis of China's Non-Commercial Web Site Registration Regulation" 2006). These regulations also give the PSB authority to request information from ISP customer databases, and demand their assistance in any investigation regarding any activity originating from their networks, creating an environment of self-censorship, and engendering disincentives to disseminate information deemed sensitive by the state.

That same year, in an effort to control and monitor the growing use of Bulletin Board System (BBS) communications on university campuses, the Ministry of Education began requiring students to use their real names and other personnel information before connecting to the forum. Before the regulations, such boards served both as a forum for interaction within the university, while also connecting students to alumni, friends, and other non-university students who commonly used the boards as a platform for communication and interaction. After the implementations of the new rules however, use of university affiliated discussion boards declined dramatically, while use of the boards by individuals outside the university system dried up ("The Impact of the Real Name System in University BBS's" 2005).

One milestone in the government's attempt to control the ICT environment was the PSB's 2003 launch of the *Golden Shield Project*, also known colloquially as the "Great Firewall," a policy program designed to limit internet user's ability to find information, particularly information deriving from outside the country, using politically sensitive search terms. As part of this program, western social media sites such as Facebook, YouTube, and Twitter were banned, and search engines such as Google and its Chinese counterpart Baidu restricted. As a result, Chinese websites, discussion boards, and twitter-style "micro-blogs" (*weibo*) are often suspended or shut down for posting politically sensitive materials (Wines 2011b).

Other government programs have sought to be more assertive. In May 2008, in conjunction with multiple Chinese software companies, the PRC unveiled its ambitious "Green Dam Youth Escort" project; content-controlling software designed to be preinstalled within every computer sold within the PRC. The program quickly ran into a number of issues however. Limited financial support, problems with foreign copyright violations, and extreme opposition to the program on the part of the Chinese online community, all proved to be significant challenges. By 2009 MIIT officials announced that new computers were no longer obligated to have the software preinstalled (EastWestNorthSouth 2010).

The government policies and regulations described above have eroded the sense of anonymity that is considered part and parcel to online communication, making it increasingly difficult for individuals to take advantage of ICT's ability to coordinate large scale activities without attracting the attention of the state. In 2009 for example, Ning Wenzhong, an unemployed worker in Henan, was arrested for posting an online message encouraging others to bring flowers to Tiananmen in memory for the 1989 crackdown ("CECC Political Prisoner Database" 2014). In 2010, Xue Mingkai, a 20 year old factory security guard in the Baoan district of Shenzhen, was imprisoned for planning to organize a "China Democratic Workers Party" online ("Implications of the Strike in Honda Auto Parts Manufacturing Co Ltd (CHAM)" 2010, 11). In neither case were the individuals involved actually able to take any action offline, but were instead jailed for disseminating these ideas online. While both Ning and Xue could have hidden their online calls to remember Tiananmen, or coded their calls to organize an independent labor party, helping to mitigate the personal risk, doing so would have limited the reach of their message, defeating the overall purpose. By seeking to avoid government surveillance, the larger audience is lost.

To be sure, Chinese Netizins have devised multiple strategies for circumventing internet restrictions, while also improvising methods to share information while avoiding unwanted government attention. However, mastering such techniques for government avoidance requires significant levels of technological sophistication; a challenge for the vast majority of migrant workers who have less experience with new communication technologies than many other social groups in China.

The PRC has employed low tech strategies to control the use of ICT as well, such as hiring large numbers of pro-government online commentators and monitors to watch and influence the discussion of sensitive topics on politically active message boards. Often referred to as the "Fifty Cent Party" (*wu mao dang*), which comes from the small payments members receive for each post, the group consists largely of college students, SOE employees, civil servants, and retirees. These individuals support party and state policies by writing pro-government postings on online message boards, helping, in the words of the Gansu Provincial Government, to "guide public opinion on controversial issues" ("China Pays Internet Users to Flood Web Forums with pro-Government Propaganda" 2011).

Begun in the early 2000s, initial Fifty Cent Party activities largely consisted of writing pro-government slogans and posting them online. More recent activity however has become increasingly sophisticated. Rather than simply rehash old slogans and propaganda, members now focus on nuanced, pro-government arguments, while sometimes spreading misinformation on individuals or groups considered in opposition to the state. Online fifty cent posters for example were vocal in protesting the 2011 attacks on Libya by US and European forces, and have been vocal in their criticism of artist Ai Weiwei, noble laureate Liu Xiaobo, and other prominent dissident figures.

Finally, the Chinese government seeks to control the dissemination of online information through its traditional controls over media and journalistic activities, often administered through many of the same institutions tasked with controlling ICT. For example, the government's desire to control the flow of information clearly played a role in the experiences of one CCTV reporter in Foshan at the time of the Honda strike in the spring of 2010. According to this reporter, even at the initial stages of the strike, journalists were subject to significant restrictions, both at the local level as well from the Party Central Publicity Department (*xuanchuanbu*).

For example, both local and national level restrictions during the strike limited the use of certain key words and phrases when describing the Foshan event, including "strike" (*bagong*) or "mobilize" (*dongyuan*). Government policies limited their ability to report on strikes taking place in other areas at the same time, while reporters had to submit any interview notes to the local Public Security Bureau for review. By the end of May, the Central Publicity Department had, in this reporter's words, "gone crazy" (*zhongxuanburen deyou kuangduo ya!*) submitting orders to each journalist department three times per day on average, and requiring reporters covering the strike to use only official Xinhua News Agency wire copy ("Interview with Foshan CCTV Reporter" 2010).

Despite these restrictions however, this reporter noted how journalists were sometime able to circumvent these severe restrictions by reprinting print media sources online, helping promote the spread of information despite the government's best efforts to control it.

> However, the reporting restrictions place on this strike and the strike wave by the central media (the Central Publicity Department) were numerous. The local government had a lot of restrictions as well, especially the Guangdong Provincial Government. Conversely, much of the reporting about the strike was based on print media, which we were able to reprint online, thus disseminating the news of the strike. ("Interview with Foshan CCTV Reporter" 2010)

Information on the Honda strikes clearly remained available online despite the government's best efforts. However, the Chinese ICT monitoring and regulatory framework was relatively successful in limiting the ability of workers to disseminate specific, actionable information, useful for employing certain protest actions or tactics. Consisting primarily of general descriptions of the conditions of the strikers and workers' demands, most available information seemed to lack detail such as an analysis of the strikers' protest tactics and how they were implemented, or a discussion of other protest options within the migrant workers' repertoire of contention.

Social and Economic Challenges to Migrant Worker ICT Use

In addition to government monitoring and regulation, access to ICT is limited by migrant workers' social and economic circumstances. While much ink has been spilled describing the technological sophistication of China's younger generation of migrant workers, migrant workers as a whole still lag behind in their use of social media, online communication applications, and other social networking tools. As discussed in chapter 6, only 16% of migrant workers in my own research stated that they used the internet as a source of useful news or information when their dispute took place. As graph 7.1 below illustrates, most of these that did so were below the age of 30, with the majority of older migrants relying on other sources of information.

Nor does ICT usage necessarily lead to a capacity to use the internet as a tool to conduct information searches and gather data relevant to engaging in protest activity. For many migrants; those working on the shop floor or on the construction site, ICT can provide a welcome relief from a life of hard, often dangerous work for little pay. Younger migrants, who may be alone and away from their home town for the first time can find entertainment playing games at a local internet café, or cheaply texting friends back home.

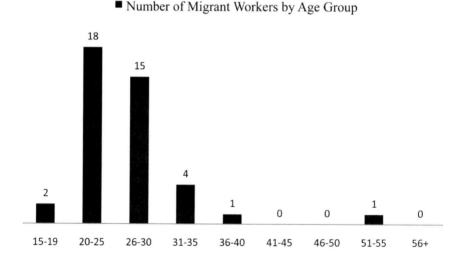

Graph 7.1. Use of the Internet as an Information Source by Age Groups. Source: Author's Interviews

Studies on Internet usage among Chinese migrant workers have found education and employment to be important factors in determining how individuals use this resource. Migrant workers at the level of clerical staff and junior management for example are more likely to use the internet for work related activities and information searches. One foreman in an electronics factory described his internet usage:

> I feel the Internet is very useful. If I want to get some data that are related to my work, I can use the Internet to search them. Without the Internet, it would be very hard to get these data....And I often use the Internet to get job information.

Contrast this with the words of a shop floor worker who stated, "I believe the main function of the internet is relaxation and entertainment," or another who stated "If I feel bored, I will go to the Internet café" (Peng 2008).

This is not to suggest that for migrants on the shop floor, the internet and other forms of ICT are useful only as recreation. However, much like the migrant workers in chapter 6, who were unaware that their fellow workers shared similar disputes, despite working twelve hour shifts together and sharing a dormitory room, we should not assume frequent internet usage automatically translates into the capacity to conduct specific research on esoteric legal topics or protest strategies.

In addition, many tactics for social protest, such as the strategic use of *tiaolou*, manhunts, or the selective use of industry or company specific information, are highly context specific, making their dissemination and application to other situations more challenging. *Tiaolou* entrepreneurs for example, individuals that have experience organizing and executing *tiaolou* protests, need to have specific, localized details for their advice to have the most impact. For example, the timing and location for a *tiaolou* event, the organization and division of the respective duties of participants, and the interaction with local media, are likely to require a level of interactive back and forth that, while perhaps conducted in part via cell phone, would be difficult to support via ICT alone.

Finally, even if workers can identify a migrant labor NGO or "public interest representatives" solely through their online presence, absent a referral from a trusted source, it can be difficult for migrants to differentiate between these potentially useful resources and the multitudes of actors seeking to exploit them. One organization representative I spoke with from Shandong Province for example discussed the migrant worker training classes his organization conducted, which provided free training on migrant workers' legal rights, as well as some free job skills training.

As we drove through his neighborhood however, I noticed a number of signs offering similar job training services. When I asked him about this he noted that many companies did offer job training, although they often charged for this service. While there is nothing wrong about charging for such services, he went on to explain that many organizations claim to provide free job training, but begin charging workers only after they attend a certain number of classes. Needless to say, this business model made it extremely difficult for him to convince workers that his organization was not designed that way as well.

Behavioral diffusion is difficult to achieve in authoritarian states via ICT alone. Government monitoring and restriction of the ICT environment increases the costs of disseminating protest information, particularly information which can facilitate protest activity directly, such as an analysis of protest tactics and their implementation. In China, this is achieved through a wide array of government institutions, supported by an ever increasing budget, and armed with a host of regulations which provide wide authority and discretion. While individuals can take action to avoid government monitoring, those efforts necessarily limit the capacity of their audience to obtain and translate the sender's message, making broad dissemination of information more difficult. Migrant workers' social and economic conditions pose challenges to behavioral diffusion as well, as the limited education or ICT experiences of many migrant workers, particularly older workers, create difficulties to using ICT as a research tool for gathering information on protest activity.

Behavioral diffusion may be difficult to achieve, but it is not the only type of activity that ICT information may promote. The following examines how other forms of information may be used to promote *ideational diffusion*, influencing the ways migrant workers view themselves and other migrants within Chinese society.

ICT AND IDEATIONAL DIFFUSION

The examples below show how ICT can facilitate *ideational diffusion*, or the spread of common frameworks for interpreting and defining workers' key issues, goals or targets for protest. Through the dissemination of more general information, such as the conditions of workers in other areas for example, ICT can help workers reframe issues in ways more amenable to protest. By helping workers learn of and empathize with the struggles of others, and by generating a shared understanding of the nature of those activities, the information spread through ICT can have a substantial impact on migrant labor protest activity without necessarily spreading specific and actionable information, strategies, or tactics (Givan, Roberts, and Soule 2011, 4).

ICT Technical Legal Advice

One of the most straightforward ways ICT can help migrant workers is simply by increasing their access to technical legal information. Workers facing complex disputes, such as workers with occupational illness or labor injuries for example, may go online to obtain copies of relevant labor law legislation. Government and union affiliated legal aid centers often respond to workers' requests for information on their websites, while many migrant labor NGOs maintain an online presence as well, operating online blogs, posting labor law legislation, and even answering specific questions from workers who submit them via email and instant messaging. Between 2010 and 2011 for example, one labor rights organization located in the Baoan district of Shenzhen handled roughly 1,200 requests from workers asking for help in resolving labor disputes, the majority of which, 54% arrived via QQ instant messaging, while 42% were received via cell phone. [1]

This increasing use of technology, such as cell phones or QQ messaging, in connection with migrant labor organizations or legal aid centers, does not suggest that traditional social networks are unimportant however. While some organizations maintain a robust online presence, others do not. As described in chapter 6, many sources of support for migrant workers, such as local public interest representatives, are available only through word of mouth.

ICT and Issue Framing

ICT can also facilitate ideational diffusion by helping workers reframe issues in ways that garner broader support from the general public. The online public outcry after the Sun Zhigang incident in 2003 for example, when a young migrant worker was beaten to death while in police custody, is a good example of how ICT can play an important role in the framing process. Although migrant workers are more often subjects of scorn rather than sympathy, individuals sharing information about the incident online, posting eulogies and creating online petitions, were able to reframe the issue in such a way as to evoke sympathy for the victim, creating a groundswell of online support for reform of the 1982 Regulations which provided the legal basis to detain persons lacking identification. As word of the Foxconn suicides in the spring of 2010 spread, Foxconn employees began posting copies of their pay stubs online to show how their hours violated China's overtime regulations, gaining the attention and sympathy of Chinese society both online and offline. This discussion helped reframe the Foxconn issue from a mental health story involving a few troubled workers, to a social justice issue involving workers' legal rights in general.

ICT can also encourage workers to act by reshaping their calculations regarding the likelihood of success. Some of the workers involved in the spring 2010 Nanhai Honda strikes in Foshan for example cited their knowledge of labor conditions abroad as a motivational factor. One worker explicitly cited his knowledge of labor unrest in the United States and Europe, culled from online news sources, as a source of encouragement.

> We were ordinarily on the internet a lot, and were after 2008 when our overtime was cut. All my fellow workers and I could do was get on the internet to pass the time. Prices were rising rapidly, and it was not easy to save money. On the internet we saw the financial crisis. US, England, Greece, everywhere workers were striking. Workers struck and employers didn't dare to reduce salary or lay off workers. Many of us workers were influenced by this encouraging news ("Interview with Nanhai Honda Strike Participant #1" 2010).

Clearly this worker's analysis of labor's position in the US and Europe after the financial crisis was not completely accurate. While workers in Europe, and to a lesser extent the United States, did strike from 2008 to 2010, the idea that employers were unable to cut salary or workforce during this time was decidedly untrue. More important than the accuracy of his analysis however was how having a sense of the broader international context modified his perception of workers' conditions in his location, providing a motivation to act.

Just as workers in Foshan were motivated by what they heard online about workers' conditions abroad, workers in other locations were motivated by the knowledge of what was going on in Foshan. A worker involved in one of the many strikes in the automobile industry at this time, this one in Beijing, identified the Foshan strike as a source of motivation. To be clear, this worker had no specific information regarding how the Foshan workers acted; how they were able to organize, or how they settled upon the specific protest tactics in use. But just hearing about the striking workers in Foshan in general made him and his fellow workers in Beijing think of their own situation. "A few of us section heads (*zuchang*) got together and said the whole country and Honda are on strike everywhere, we should strike too."

> The Honda strike was earlier, the internet and newspapers reported [it] in great detail. After seeing this, we felt very familiar with the situation, and our lives were pretty much the same. They were on strike, we should do the same. Online we saw the conditions that the strikers [in Foshan] raised, and then you knew what to do. According to the issues raised by the Honda strikes, [the way] they were changing the factory to their conditions, me and [worker's name] went to a friend's apartment after work, printed out copies of our own demands, and after going on strike immediately posted them to the factory gates. ("Interview with Beijing Strike Participant" 2010)

The interview respondent in this case stated that he and his fellow workers were able to obtain specific information from online sources discussing what was occurring in Foshan, such as the content of their strike demands. However, while these workers were able to learn about strike demands as part of the Foshan workers' strategy for protest, they mentioned nothing about how workers in Foshan were convincing their fellow workers to organize, participate, or how they conducted the strike itself. In fact, the worker in Beijing acknowledged that specific information was often hard to come by.

> You want me to evaluate the car industry strike [including the Nanhai Honda strike]? Well I think there really isn't anything special about it. This country has strikes everywhere; it's only that no one reports them. ("Interview with Beijing Strike Participant" 2010)

Contrast this with the experience of another strike participant in Nanhai, who explicitly cited the importance of first hand advice obtained from the urban ties he developed while working at the factory, or as he put it, "a few older workers, who had experience in strikes." According to this worker, during the course of the Nanhai Honda strike, there was some consideration about whether the workers should expand the strike to occupy the area outside the factory gates and block traffic. This is a common protest tactic in China, although some workers with previous strike experience cautioned against it, arguing that it would only create more enemies and damage the group's solidarity.[2] In the end, the workers decided to heed the advice of those with first-hand experience. "There were a few older workers who had participated in strikes before. We talked with them and decided to proceed based on their previous experiences" ("Interview with Nanhai Honda Strike Participant #1" 2010).

ICT and Motivation

Finally, once protests begin, ICT can support them by connecting protesters with others who can provide motivational support, improving group morale. As information about the Nanhai Honda strike in Foshan began to appear online, strike participants started communicating with friends and colleagues located in other areas via cell phones and text messaging, receiving requests for information and words of encouragement from their friends and family back home.

One worker, a twenty-two year old from Hebei who was employed as a section manager at the Foshan factory during the time of the strike, was unhappy with his stagnant wages and the lack of advancement opportunities. According to this worker, what made the Honda strike different was the extent to which society took an interest in their plight. Throughout the strike, this worker felt that others were paying attention to their actions online, as striking workers uploaded pictures and provided descriptions of the situation through discussion board posts. This sense of importance grew when some of his former classmates and hometown associates (*laoxiang*) began sending him text messages, asking him about the strikes and if he was taking part.

> Frankly speaking, I never thought the influence of our strike would be so great. Seeing news from cell phones and the internet, everywhere they were reporting about the Nanhai strike. This gave me a lot of encouragement. The first time I looked at my cell phone and saw that someone had sent me some news reports on the strike, and asked me if we were striking, I felt extremely proud. 'You're really hardcore!' [*lihai*] my schoolmates from my hometown would say. ("Interview with Nanhai Honda Strike Participant #2" 2010)

Not all such motivation is based on positive reinforcement however. ICT can just as easily motivate workers to act by fostering demands for revenge. Online rumors that police had beaten a migrant worker to death in the Guangzhou suburb of Zengcheng, Guangdong Province, for example helped spark violent clashes between migrants and police in the summer of 2011. In 2010, rumors of ethnic Uyghur workers in South China attacking Han Chinese women resulted in violent confrontations between the two groups in Guangdong, which in part led to the Xinjiang riots later that year.

CONCLUSION: ICT AND MIGRANT LABOR PROTEST

Information communication technology such as cell phones, text messaging, SMS instant messaging, and internet communications have played a key role in recent protest activities in authoritarian states, and China is no different. While some argue that this new technology can dramatically remake the protest environment, allowing individuals to organize in ways never seen before, questions remain regarding the extent to which ICT can replace traditional organizing.

The spring 2010 automobile strikes which began in the Nanhai Honda plant in Foshan provide a useful case study to examine the utility of ICT to protest activity in China, and the record appears mixed. While ICT can and did facilitate the rapid diffusion of information across long distances, not all information is readily and equally transferable through such channels. Government monitoring and restrictions of the ICT environment, and migrants' social and economic conditions, both pose challenges for migrant workers seeking to use ICT to facilitate behavioral diffusion by distributing information regarding specific protests tactics and strategies.

The interactive and context specific nature of such information can make ICT an awkward channel as well, as limited interactions between senders and receivers make it difficult to place the information within the appropriate context. Such difficulties can be seen in the actions of the striking Honda workers, who, despite their access to ICT information, still relied on the experiences of older workers within their group to formulate their tactics.

Perhaps more useful to migrant workers is ICT's ability to promote ideational diffusion, helping workers reframe protest issues, provide moral support, or reevaluate the likelihood of success based on the situation of events occurring elsewhere. ICT's role in promoting ideational diffusion during the Honda protests was clear, as workers in Foshan received words of encouragement from their friends and family during the strike, while workers in other parts of China were encouraged to act as well, not necessarily by obtaining specific tactical information on how protests should be conducted, but simply by hearing of workers similar to themselves taking action, and reevaluating their ability to act based on this new information.

ICT is not a replacement for traditional social networks. The general knowledge and information often available through these channels can certainly provide the motivation to act, but there remains significant difficulty in obtaining "how to" information regarding specific protest tactics. However, when combined with the traditional social networks more suited to disseminating that type of information, ICT can be a powerful supporting tool in workers' arsenal.

NOTES

1. Information and Statistics provided by migrant labor NGO Representative via email, 7 January 2012.

2. As one of these older workers argued, "the day we went outside the factory gates would be the day we would break up" (*yidan chuqu women jiu fensanle*).

Chapter Eight

Social Sources of Support: Migrant Organizations and Labor Activism

Just as state and market forces have changed the urban landscape for migrant workers, creating space for greater protest activity, these same forces have influenced migrants' organizational capacity as well. Over the past decade, the number of self-described "worker's service bureaus" (*fuwubu*), "consultation centers" (*zixun zhongxin*), "worker hotlines" (*dagong rexian*), "legal aid centers" (*falu yuanzhu zhongxin*), and other similarly named entities have mushroomed in areas with large migrant populations. As their numbers have grown, they have become increasingly active, causing some Chinese scholars to refer to these new social organizations as "resource mobilizing machine[s]" (Huang 2007).

Migrant labor organizations and activists are defined here as civil society organizations or individuals, whose primarily objective is to support migrant workers seeking to protest their exploitation or resolve a labor dispute. For many reasons, migrant labor activists can often provide better aid and support than what is available from government affiliated organizations or professional lawyers. First, the aid they provide is often free, or substantially cheaper than what migrant workers would pay to a licensed lawyer, provided they could find one willing to take their case. Second, many are flexible in the type of aid they provide, helping workers to use the legal system, or engage in other activities, including strikes or informal bargaining. Third, organization personnel are often more ideologically motivated, having previously experienced exploitation themselves, and are thus more likely to invest the time and the resources to help workers fight their case to the end. Fourth, because they specialize in the labor law as it relates to migrant workers, many organizations can provide better advice than lawyers in government legal aid centers, who are rarely labor law specialists, much less in the labor law as it pertains to migrant workers, given that this branch of the law promises little financial returns for Chinese law students.

Different types of migrant organizations provide workers with different types of support, but government restrictions on their activities influences both the type of services they provide, and migrants' ability to access those services. The fact that many of these organizations offer both legal advice and support for extra-legal activities such as strikes and collective action is one reason they have been a concern for the Chinese government (The Politics and Law Committee of Guangdong Province 2009). However, limited opportunities to publicize their work in the local media, tenuous or even hostile relations with local government agencies, and the general sense of distrust within the migrant labor community, all create challenges for migrant labor organizations that seek to build a base of support.

For some, these problems can be mitigated. Organizations that possess journalist contacts for example may have activities publicized in the local media. Moreover, just as the CCP has co-opted other elements of society, such as private entrepreneurs, local governments and union branches have developed lines of communication with larger, more active migrant labor organizations in their areas. In turn, organizations with government ties may have cases referred to them, or even act as informal labor representatives for workers, with the government's consent.

For the vast majority of smaller migrant labor organizations, citizen representatives, or labor activists, however, opportunities to reach out to migrants through the media are scarce. Instead, these smaller organizations take their message directly to the migrant labor community, distributing information in migrant neighborhoods or outside factory gates, or holding information sessions in areas with large migrant populations. Many obtain clients through referrals from migrant workers they previously aided, relying on word of mouth to develop a trusted name for their organization.

Such direct marketing strategies place a premium on personal, face to face contact in order to develop trust over time, and unless they are lucky enough to be approached directly by organization personnel, many migrant workers rely on informal social networks to learn of these organizations. Relying on personal referrals to develop trust however is a slow and tedious process, as organizations can only connect with a small number of individuals at one time. As discussed in chapter 7, a growing number of organizations maintain an online presence, distributing information and advice through email, text, and instant messaging services. However, the problem of linking migrant workers to these organizations, and developing bonds of trust between these organizations and the migrant labor community, remains, even in the internet age. Thus, government commitments to maintain a monopoly on labor's capacity to organize presents migrant labor organizations with a difficult trade-off; grow too large and risk being co-opted or repressed, or stay small and possess only limited influence.

EARLY MIGRANT LABOR ORGANIZATIONS

According to official estimates by the Chinese Ministry of Civil Affairs, the number of registered NGOs in China reached almost half a million by 2012, including both non-profit *social organizations* (*shehui tuanti*), and income generating *non-governmental, non-corporate entities* (*minban fei qiye*) (Ministry of Civil Affairs of the People's Republic of China 2012; Ma 2009). These statistics however only report officially registered organizations. There is, in addition, a growing number of domestic organizations that operate as NGOs but do not register, unregistered foreign organizations, and organizations registered as businesses that provide social services. Different scholars have provided estimates of these unregistered organizations, with roughly 1.5 million operating in urban areas nation-wide (Deng 2010). Most migrant labor organizations fall into this second category of Chinese civil society organizations.

Migrant labor organizations began to appear in the late 1990s, partly as a result of the economic policies of the Jiang Zemin regime, which focused on generating growth at the expense of social equality. This period also witnessed a rise in the number of organizations concerned with problems of poverty and income inequality more generally. Migrant labor organizations began to appear in regions where migrants were highly concentrated, such as the Pearl River Delta cities of Shenzhen and Guangzhou, and other major urban areas such as Beijing. Often established by former migrant workers, these organizations grew in response to the rise in labor disputes, and demands for help fighting unfair and exploitative labor practices.

This growth in migrant support organizations was aided by the government's general policy of "small state large society" (*zhengfuxiao, shehuida*), which aimed at shifting the burden of providing social services away from the state. As the provision of pubic goods in China continued to erode into the 1990s, local government agencies realized that the demand for services, including the demand for various worker and legal training programs, could partly be provided by these burgeoning new social organizations, without adding to local governments' financial burdens (Howell 2008; The Politics and Law Committee of Guangdong Province 2009, 2).

Early migrant labor organizations were heavily tied to the state, providing education and health services to the most sympathetic subsets of migrant labor such as women and children. *Migrant Women's Home* (*Dagongmei zhi Jia*) for example was established in Beijing in 1996 in connection with the All China Women's Federation. In Shenzhen that same year, the *Nanshan*

District Women Worker Consulting Center, (*Nanshanqu Nugong Fuwu Zhongxin*) was established through cooperation between the Hong Kong based *Chinese Working Women Network* (*Nuxing Lianwang*) and the local district trade union.

By the end of the 1990s however, a new class of migrant labor organization began to appear, focused on providing a broader level of aid and support to the migrant labor population at large. New, more independent organizations were established by former migrant workers, including the *Panyu Migrant Document Handling Service Center* in Guangdong (*Guangdong Panyu Dagongzu Wenshu Chuli Zhongxin*) in 1998, and *Little Bird* (*Xiaoxiaoniao*) in Beijing in 1999. Others were founded by professionals interested in the plight of migrant labor, such as the *Institute for Contemporary Observation* in 2001 (*Shenzhen Dangdai Shehui Guancha Yanjiusuo*) which was established by Liu Kaiming, a former journalist for the *Legal Daily*. In September 2005, Tong Lihua, a former head of the Legal Aid Committee of the China Bar Association, founded the *Beijing Migrant Worker Legal Aid Workstation* (*Beijing Falu Yuanzhu Gongzuozhan*), which has since expanded to include branches in over twenty provinces and provincial level municipalities ("Beijing Migrant Labor Legal Aid Work Station Website").

The above are just a few of the more well known organizations. In addition, the past decade has seen dramatic growth in the number of smaller, less well established migrant labor organizations, as well as an explosion of "citizen representatives" that provide low cost legal services. The growth of these smaller, more independent organizations and individual activists has been aided by the central government's changing approach towards migrant workers which, while not altering its official prohibition on independent organizing, has created a more tolerant environment, where local governments have been willing to experiment with non-governmental initiatives to help manage labor disputes and curb social unrest.

Because of government restrictions on non-profit registration, the vast majority of migrant labor organizations register either as commercial entities, or remain unregistered, making it difficult to estimate their numbers. At the low end of these estimates, some researchers have argued that only 30–50 total organizations existed nationwide by the end of 2007 (Zhan and Han). and that migrant labor organizations were still in the "newborn stage" of development (*chusheng jieduan*) (Tao and Sun). Estimates from the Guangdong provincial government however suggest otherwise. According to a widely circulated research report by the Guangdong Provincial Party Committee of Politics and Law, by the end of 2008, there were over 50 citizen representative organizations and 500 citizen representatives operating within Guangdong Province alone (The Politics and Law Committee of Guangdong Province 2009; Zhang 2007). ACFTU research places the number of "grassroots lawyers" even higher, estimating approximately 10,000 such individuals operating solely in the Pearl River Delta (Wang 2009).

CHALLENGES TO MIGRANT LABOR ORGANIZATIONS

Market forces, such as labor's increasing mobility and flexibility, created a demand for the services that migrant labor organizations and activists provide, while relaxed state policies toward migrants during the Hu Jintao regime created the space necessary for them to multiply. However, migrant labor organizations continue to face a host of government restrictions. While the central government has recognized that certain organizations can benefit one party rule by providing needed social services, the potential for independent, organized labor to act as a political force requires that any sanctioned organizations be apolitical, closely monitored, and embedded within a state corporatist structure. Any attempt to establish migrant labor organizations for the expressed purpose of bargaining on behalf of migrant labor rights for example, rather than providing social services, remains prohibited. Onerous registration processes, restrictions on organizations' ability to raise funds, and an uncertain legal status, have all limited the development of migrant labor organizations compared to the growth and maturation of organizations in other areas of Chinese civil society (Simon 2013). Yet such government policies have not stopped the growth of migrant labor organizations as much as they have influenced the shape and direction of that growth.

Government Registration and State Control

The Chinese government continues to maintain strict controls on NGO development through a system of "dual registration status" (*shuangchong guanli tizhi*) under which social organizations and non-governmental, non-corporate entities (*minban fei qiye*) must register with the Ministry of Civil Affairs (MoCA). NGOs must also find a sponsor organization within their administrative level and professional field, being re-registered and vetted annually. In addition, regulations for registration and management of Chinese social organizations also require NGOs to maintain what amounts to reserve requirements, forcing them to retain a minimum number of personnel and operating funds (State Council of the People's Republic of China 2014).

Many migrant labor organizations are also legally restricted in their ability to raise funds. Government restrictions regarding fund-raising have relaxed in recent years, and some organizations, such as Jet Li's *One Foundation*, have been allowed to engage in expanded charitable giving activities (Wu and Wu 2011). Only those organizations that can legally register as NGOs however are allowed to participate in domestic fund-raising activities, thus excluding the vast majority of migrant labor organizations (State Coun-

cil of the People's Republic of China 2004 Article 3, 25, 40; Standing Committee of the National People's Congress 1999 Article 3,10; Congressional
Executive Commission on China 2008). As a result, most remain heavily
reliant on financial support from foreign donors or the government (The
Politics and Law Committee of Guangdong Province 2009).

Well established organizations may supplement this income through prof-
it making activities—conducting worker safety training exercises for example—or by serving as auditors for companies' voluntary corporate social
responsibility (CSR) programs. *The Institute for Contemporary Observation*
conducted many such training programs, while also working with multinational organizations on voluntary CSR audits in the Pearl River Delta.[1] Organizations affiliated with *China Labor Watch* occasionally conduct audits,
evaluations, and worker training programs for multinational corporations
such as Wal-Mart or Nike. For smaller organizations that lack these revenue
options however, financial resources remain a constant concern.

Organizational Responses to Government Controls

Government policies which place migrant labor organizations on unstable
financial and legal footing have had profound yet unintended consequences
on their growth and development. Restrictive regulations have made formal
registration practically impossible, but this has not stopped migrant labor
organizations from proliferating at a rapid pace. Instead, groups have responded in a variety of imaginative ways. First, rather than registering as a
formal NGO, many migrant labor organizations register as for-profit organization with the Ministry of Commerce. *Dagongzhe*, a migrant labor NGO
based in Shenzhen for example, had originally planned to register as an
NGO. Knowing that providing legal advice and representation to migrants
would make organization personnel subject to employer retaliation, it was
hoped that formally registering as a nonprofit would provide greater protection. When told by the relevant departments that it would be impossible to
gain government approval however, they were left with little choice but to
register as a commercial enterprise (Fu 2007).

Others have cultivated government and social ties by affiliating themselves with established organizations, or setting up research institutions
under academic universities. Some have formed informal social networks
and have organized through projects funded from international organizations
(Howell 2004, 149). Still others have chosen not to register at all, arguing
that it provides little actual protection, either from the government, or from
vengeful employers ("Interview 51, Migrant Labor Organization Representative, South China" 2008, 51). One individual in Shenzhen attempted to formally register his organization as an NGO, but was soundly rebuffed by local
Civil Affairs officials. Rather than register at the Ministry of Commerce like

Dagongzhe however, he established what he calls a "migrant worker association" (*wailaigong xiehui*) which amounted to an unregistered institution
("Interview 37, Migrant Labor Organization Representative, Shenzhen"
2008, 15). While providing legal aid to workers, he is sometimes harassed by
labor bureau officials as an illegal organization or "black lawyer," particularly when providing assistance to workers involved in collective cases.

   Migrant labor organization's registration status, either as a for-profit business or as an NGO, is no guarantee against government interference, given
the sensitive nature of their work. Yet the government's system of regulation
clearly influences their behavior. For some organizations, the best strategy is
to develop close government contacts. For others, a strategy of misrepresent-
ing their activities by registering as a commercial business is an option. Some
avoid registration all together, seeking instead simply to keep a low profile.
While each strategy has its own merits, as I describe below, each impacts the
support and services that the organization can provide.

MIGRANT LABOR ORGANIZATIONS—SUPPORT AND SERVICES

Migrant labor organizations and labor activists provide a variety of services
to Chinese migrant workers. This includes passive aid, such as disseminating
information by distributing legal pamphlets and guidebooks, conducting legal training classes, and providing space for worker interaction, to help when
negotiating with employers, navigating the legal system, and providing aid
and advice on strikes and other forms of unsanctioned protest activity. Yet
the ability and types of services migrant labor organizations can provide
varies in part depending upon the organizations' size, their formal status, and
the nature of their relationship with the local government.

   While larger, more formal organizations possessing good relations with
the local media and government are better positioned to negotiate directly
with employers, these same connections often make the organization leery of
helping migrant workers take actions that might be seen as politically sensitive, for fear of damaging those relations. In contrast, smaller organizations
and individual activists have less capacity to connect with a large numbers of
workers at any one time, but are less constrained when it comes to providing
politically sensitive support, such as advice on strikes and mass protest. If
their reputation and impact grows, however, once unknown organizations
quickly become the object of local government scrutiny, and their actions
become similarly limited. One organization representative described this
challenge to me quite succinctly; "if we hold activities (*huodong*) that are too
small, or get too little press, we get no results, but if we hold activities that
are too large, the government may get nervous" ("Interview 32, Migrant
Labor Organization Representative, Shenzhen" 2008).

At a basic level, many organizations provide legal advice and consultation, regardless of their size or the nature of their government contacts. While consulting with a lawyer would be costly, many organizations provide free or low cost legal advice, and this is often a key reason why workers seek them out. Of the 47 workers interviewed at one migrant labor organization in Guangzhou for example, over one third of them mentioned, without prompting, the importance of obtaining free legal aid in their decision to come to the organization. As one worker put it plainly, "I came here [to the *Guangzhou Organization*],[2] because they could provide free legal advice on what to do" ("Interview Guangzhou 0604" 2007).

Most migrant labor NGOs also provide reference materials and copies of relevant laws and regulations, while others organize legal rights training classes. The value of both varies widely, as some significantly improve workers' knowledge and understanding of the law, while others simply reprint relevant clauses and statutes, or provide incomprehensible lectures on the content of the laws without providing any practical context.

Some organizations provide published materials and training classes with more context specific information, such as how to negotiate with your employer, how to collect evidence, and what to anticipate when appealing to the local labor bureau or the courts. For example, between April 2010 and April 2011, one unregistered migrant labor organization operating in multiple cities in the Pearl River Delta, gave a total of 87 free classes, teaching roughly 1,800 migrant workers what should be included in a labor contract, or how to calculate monthly wages and overtime payments based on that area's local regulations. According to the organization's representative, workers attending these classes often became angry and resentful after comparing their actual wages with what they should have been paid according to the law.[3]

Others publish gazettes containing migrant workers' firsthand accounts of their exploitation, and what other can do to avoid it. "In these past few years of work" (*chulai gongzuo*) one worker writes, "I've experienced all types of people and things. I'm writing this because I believe some of those fellow migrants who have just started working can learn from my experiences. Don't be cheated by black hearted bosses. Make sure to protect your rights." The author then recounts his past troubles and how they could have been avoided (Zi 2007; Anonymous, 14). By moving beyond simple legal recitation, and providing examples of the applicability of the law to workers' lives, these materials improve workers' legal rights consciousness and encourage action.

Many organizations also provide space for workers of different backgrounds to meet and share their experiences and ideas. Organizations such as Beijing's *On Action* (*Zai Xingdong*) or *Migrant Women's Home* not only provide legal aid services, but access to reading rooms and libraries, holding social activities and cultural exchanges. This social space can expand the size of migrant workers' social networks, and also add to the variation within that network. They can also mitigate the isolation and helplessness felt by many aggrieved migrants, while providing access to new dispute options and ideas (Gallagher 2007, 219–220; Chen 2004, 36–37). In a study of migrant labor NGOs in Qingdao, Shenzhen, and Dongguan, Zhong Zhangbao and Li Fei found that migrants in neighborhoods with a migrant labor organization were more likely to have connections to individuals outside their traditional rural ties, more likely to have a greater number of friends within their social circle, and more likely to possess a higher self-assessment regarding their place in local society, compared to migrants in neighborhoods lacking such organizations (Zhong and Fei 2008, 41–44).

These new social spaces give migrant workers opportunities to learn directly from others, obtaining new ideas about what employers to avoid, how to ensure they are not being underpaid, or who to contact if they encounter a labor dispute (Fu 2007). As one worker participating in some social activities arranged by an organization in Shenzhen said, "I don't have any problems at the moment but now I know where to go if I do!"[4]

Direct Intervention

Migrant labor NGOs intervene directly on behalf of migrant workers in a number of ways; through direct negotiations with employers, legal representation, and by providing advice on the use of alternative protest strategies. First, legal representation from organization staff, whether in the form of informal negotiations with employers or more formally in conjunction with appeals to labor arbitration and the courts, is an important resource for those migrant workers who can obtain it, improving their ability to take action and attain greater compensation. In an analysis of 588 labor law cases brought to the *Sichuan Province Migrant Worker Legal Aid Work Station* in Chengdu between 2009 and 2010, the work station found that roughly 75% of cases were resolved only after initiating formal legal proceedings. Furthermore, migrant workers with access to legal representation were able to retrieve all the compensation that they requested 79% of the time, compared to those workers who attempted to go forward without representation, who were similarly successful only 23% of the time (Sichuan Migrant Worker Legal Aid Station 2011).

Government and union institutions engage in direct negotiations on behalf of migrants workers as well. While many private enterprises still lack a union presence, regional based unions, such as those at the municipal level for example, may engage in mediation between the workers and management at the enterprise level ("Interview Chinese Academy of Social Science" 2007). In addition, People's Mediation Committees connected with the local Justice Bureau, or Labor Mediation Committees associated with Resident's Committees, may intervene to resolve disputes before they escalate (Halegua 2008, 136–38).

Informal government negotiation on behalf of labor however is highly problematic.[5] At a fundamental level, government and party affiliated organizations often have different interests from the workers they represent, seeking first to avoid adversely impacting social stability and the local investment climate rather than obtaining compensation for workers. Government agents also frequently lack specialized knowledge of the labor law, and the motivation necessary to handle long and complex cases. In fact, where migrant labor organizations possess good government relations, government agencies often refer their migrant labor cases to these organizations, rather than handle them in house ("Interview 1, Migrant Labor Organization Representative, Beijing" 2007). In contrast, migrant organization personnel often have more knowledge of the labor law as it relates to migrants specifically, (Gallagher 2007, 202) and possess the motivation to take on the type of complex, time-consuming cases that migrants face.

Even during informal negotiations, migrant labor organization representatives often use their legal knowledge as leverage when trying to win workers compensation by negotiating within the "shadow of the law," using the law in unorthodox and creative ways. When working on a wage arrears case, one lawyer from the Beijing workstation needed to first prove a labor relationship between the worker and the employer, as the worker had no labor contract. During negotiations, she argued that arbitration would be onerous for both parties, regardless of who won, and suggested they negotiate an agreement acceptable to all parties. The employer agreed, signing a statement indicating the worker's length of service and the agreed upon settlement. The lawyer then used this document as proof of a labor relationship, allowing the worker to obtain his remaining wages through labor arbitration ("Interview 1, Migrant Labor Organization Representative, Beijing" 2007).

Two well-known Beijing organizations, the *Beijing Migrant Worker Legal Aid Station* (Beijing Workstation) and *Little Bird*, both provide excellent examples of established migrant labor organizations with strong media, government, and legal bureaucratic contacts. First, both organizations commonly use their close government contacts to influence employers' perceptions into believing they are negotiating with government or government affiliated institutions (Halegua 2008). In September 2004, *Little Bird* was given the official title of "Little Bird People's Mediation Committee" (*Xiaoxiaoniao Renmin Tiaojie Weiyuanhui*) of the Donghuamen sub district in Beijing, which according to the organization's founder, provides them with an air of government legitimacy when engaging in employer negotiations ("Interview 5, Weiwei, Director, Little Bird" 2007). Although this official title does not provide any actual legal jurisdiction outside Donghuamen, a small affluent tourist area near the center of Beijing, the title itself often makes employers more hesitant to simply ignore their mediation attempts ("The Awkward Strides of Little Bird: Subordinate to the Donghuamen Sub-District Justice Office [Xiaoxiaoniaode Qugangga: Lishu Donghuamen Sifasuo Quezai Quan Beijing Weiquan] 北京：四区劳动部门回应农民工讨薪" 2005; Halegua 2008, 145).

The head of the Beijing Workstation, Tong Lihua, was formerly the head of the Legal Aid Committee of the China Bar Association, and founder of the "Beijing Youth Legal Aid and Research Center." Mr. Tong has cultivated many useful ties within the Beijing government, legal community, and the media ("Tong Lihua and His Migrant Worker Legal Aid Workstation [Tong Lihua he Ta Chuangban de Jincheng Wugong Nongmingong Falv Yuanzhu Gongzuozhan] 佟丽华和他创办的进城务工农民法律援助工作站" 2005). The Beijing Workstation's reputation and relationships with other local legal aid centers are strong enough that the Fengtai District legal aid center routinely forwards the workstation their migrant labor cases ("Interview 1, Migrant Labor Organization Representative, Beijing" 2007).

Well established organizations such as these also rely on strong media connections and the legal bureaucracy to provide workers with negotiating leverage. One strategy both organizations use is to provide information about their cases to media contacts, or to invite media personnel to accompany them on trips to factories or work sites ("Interview 1, Migrant Labor Organization Representative, Beijing" 2007; Halegua 2008, 153). The Beijing Workstation's contacts within the legal bureaucracy also afford it some leeway when taking cases to arbitration or the courts. Shi Fumao, a lawyer at the Workstation, boasts that his teams of lawyers have never lost a case (Halegua 2008, 155).[6] Another Workstation lawyer stated that even if a case is weak, many arbitration officials are sympathetic to migrants' plight, familiar with the activities of the Workstation, and therefore tend to look favorably upon their cases ("Interview 1, Migrant Labor Organization Representative, Beijing" 2007).

In contrast, smaller organizations that lack government or media connections often find it more difficult to negotiate directly with employers, lacking the leverage to pressure them to settle. One organization in Shenzhen who occasionally runs into difficulties with local government officials as a result of its work, rarely engages in direct negotiations. A key reason for this, according to a representative, is because they lack the sympathetic government and media contacts that can influence negotiations. This is not to suggest institutional contacts are the only determinate in successful legal representation for migrant workers. Companies with larger workforces who engage in systematic labor exploitation for example may fear that settlements of any kind might open a floodgate of other workers with similar demands. However, organizations with strong government or media connections are often better positioned to force employers to the table.

Navigating the Legal System

Navigating the legal system can be costly and time consuming for migrant workers, as barriers to access such as time and monetary expenses can be excessive. Workers who obtain help from labor rights organizations however are better positioned to overcome these obstacles, increasing their likelihood of engaging with the legal process and pressuring government institutions to implement the laws as they are written.

Many migrant labor organizations can help workers obtain evidence for use during the dispute process, such as evidence proving a labor relationship or wrongdoing on the part of the employer. Organization representatives can also help convince fellow workers to provide testimony and act as witnesses. For migrant workers with limited education, entering a formal government building to apply for labor arbitration can be an intimidating experience, and workers often receive poor treatment from government employees (Michelson 2006). Many of my own interview respondents expressed anger at their treatment at the hands of government bureaucrats, while those bureaucrats in turn expressed frustration with their lack of resources, large caseloads, and migrant workers' lack of understanding of the legal process and unreasonable expectations ("Interview 36, Labor Arbitration Official, Shenzhen" 2008). Having a migrant labor organization representative active in this process can aid both sides; ensuring the worker receives fair treatment, while at the same time helping to manage migrant workers' expectations.

The utility of having an organization representative on hand was illustrated in the case of a group of 45 construction workers in Beijing, working for a labor contractor who refused to pay their wages upon the project's completion. Like many migrants in their situation, the group selected a spokesman from their group, who sought to open a case on the group's behalf in multiple labor bureaus and petition offices, only to be told time and again he was in the wrong office. When the group attempted to file a lawsuit, they were told by the court they would first have to pay 3,000 RMB in procedural fees. It was only through the intercession of a local migrant labor organization representative that the group convinced the court to accept the case, and to allow each worker to pay only the 50 RMB "economic hardship fee" (*jingjin pin-kun*), in place at the time (Beijing Migrant Worker Legal Aid Station 2007).

Another organization, the Yuandian Workers Service Department (*yuandian gongyou fuwubu*), based in Shenzhen, was able to provide advice and consultation to roughly 300 workers during the first quarter of 2012, returning over RMB 280,000 in compensation. Intersession on behalf of workers can be a dangerous task however, as the organization was shut down in the spring of that year ("Yuandian Worker Service Blog"). Other organizations have also been known to be harassed or threatened with physical violence when pressuring government officials to follow the law. As one organization's representative in Shenzhen recalled, "On February 4th I was handling a case for a worker, and the official I was dealing with was really poor [quality]. He looked like he was going to hit me or something, but he didn't know I was videotaping the whole thing" ("Interview 37, Migrant Labor Organization Representative, Shenzhen" 2008).

Informal Strategies—Encouraging Collective Action

While organizations with government connections may be better positioned to negotiate with employers, their size and status often constrains the advice and aid they provide. Smaller organizations or unregistered activists however, are unconstrained by government ties or government patronage, and may encourage collective action among workers, providing help in coordinating strikes, walkouts, traffic disruptions, or other types of protest activities. Acting as focal points for migrant labor cooperation, these organizations connect workers within the same factory, or even help them connect with others in different factories sharing similar disputes, such as workers suffering from the same occupational illness. Shortly after the promulgation of the *Labor Contract Law* in 2008 for example, activists in Shenzhen encouraged workers within different factories to take advantage of their new legal rights to demand back wages collectively.

Other organizations have advocated developing links with low and mid-level factory management, whose interests are more aligned with shop floor workers, and are better positioned to coordinate collective actions ("Interview 53, Migrant Labor Organization Representative, South China" 2007). One small organization in Guangdong expressed disdain for the legal system, arguing it was more important for workers to protect their rights through collective action, rather than relying on legal representatives to protect those rights for them ("Interview 52, Migrant Labor Organization Representative, South China," 2008). Another argued he *always* advised workers to confront management directly and collectively before appealing to the law, believing that even if workers win their court case, they will most likely be forced to find another job, and thus the cycle of exploitation simply begins anew. If workers bargain collectively with their employers however, they can not only resolve immediate problems, but can also safeguard their future interests. It was for this reason he urged workers to strike (*bagong*), even over small issues, as a week's lost wages in strike activity would be made up by developing the precedent that workers cannot be so easily taken advantage of in the future ("Interview 52, Migrant Labor Organization Representative, South China," 2008).

Still other, more radical organizations help connect migrant workers with disaffected white collar workers, academics, and members of other social groups. One such organization for example provides opportunities for low income migrant labor and white collar workers to come together, arguing that as members of China's working class, both groups share mutual concerns and interests that can bridge the differences between traditionally discon-nected social classes ("Interview 51, Migrant Labor Organization Represen-tative, South China" 2008).

Like individual migrant workers who stand up to their employers, organ-izations who attempt to provide support to migrant workers, even through the legal system, also face the risk of violent reprisal. In Shenzhen in the fall of 2007 for example, *Dagongzhe*, a migrant labor organization operating in the city's Longgan district, came under attack by armed thugs allegedly hired by local factory owner Zhong Weiqi (Fu 2007). In one such attack, the head of *Dagongzhe*, Huang Qingnan, was critically injured by a group of men wield-ing knives (Fu 2007). During a different instance in the same Longgan dis-trict, Li Jinxin, a labor rights activist with a *Guangdong Labor Rights Center*, was kidnapped outside his center and beaten so severely he had to be hospi-talized. Other activists routinely receive death threats for helping workers to act (Civil Rights and Livelihood Watch 2007).

THE PROVISION OF SERVICES AND THE ROLE OF INFORMATION

When available, migrant labor organizations can be extremely useful re-sources, providing basic legal information or formal legal advice, informal representation in negotiations, and even advice on unsanctioned dispute ac-tions and strategies. Yet gaining access to such organizations is often proble-matic for the vast majority of migrant workers, and urban ties can be crucial in helping them connect with migrant labor activists and organizations.

Migrant Labor Organizations, Labor Activists, and Problems of Publicity

Although larger organizations, such as *Little Bird* or the *Beijing Workstation*, receive significant media coverage, similar coverage is minimal to non-exis-tent for the vast majority of smaller organizations. Many lack the finances to run advertising campaigns, or the media contacts to have their organizations featured in local publications. To get their organization's name out to the migrant community, many instead rely heavily on direct marketing tech-niques, distributing flyers, leaflets and pamphlets, and holding information sessions in industrial worksites or outside factories. While these activities are a natural response to the problem of information dissemination, direct mar-keting activities do not have the capacity to reach as many individuals as traditional media. Thus, for migrant workers searching for sources of support, the lack of publicity for the majority of migrant labor organizations or labor activists makes finding them even more of a challenge.

This problem is even more acute for China's citizen representatives or individual activists, whose use of unorthodox or unsanctioned strategies, such as *tiaolou* for example, make them a target of local authorities. In these cases, media attention is not even particularly desired. As *tiaolou* protests have become more common in the past decade, press reports in newspapers and television have become more frequent, making it easier for migrants to learn of and copy this strategy, further promoting its use. This might suggest that urban ties are unnecessary for *tiaolou* protesters, but there is more that goes into threatening to jump off a building than first meets the eye. Like many protest strategies, even simple ones can benefit from solid organization and leadership, and some migrants have taken it upon themselves to become *tiaolou* entrepreneurs, helping other workers use this strategy more effectively.

The story of Zhang Jun is one such example. A worker from Wuhan, Zhang first employed *tiaolou* as a protest strategy when resolving his own dispute. After this initial success, he began helping some of his friends to engage in *tiaolou* protests as well. During the record snowstorms which blanketed much of China in the Winter of 2008, Zhang counseled his friends to stage their "*tiaolou* performance" (*tiaolouxiu*) at Wuhan's Fujiapo long distance train station, in front of the large audiences that would be making their way home for spring festival. This way they would have a captive audience, and be able to leverage their actions to achieve maximum exposure.

Zhang Jun worked to coordinate the event, dividing up the workers so that some would climb with him while others would stay on the ground and attract public attention. Through previous experiences, Zhang had also developed a relationship with Shen Yourong, a reporter for the Wuhan newspaper the *Changjiang Times*, and had developed ties with other local media as well. Zhang had also become quite adept at keeping the others in the group calm while sitting on the top of a building in the middle of a snowstorm threatening to jump to their deaths.

Zhang's story was actually featured in the well-known publication, *China Newsweek*, and while the basic information provided in that article would be useful to other workers seeking to replicate Zhang's successes, it is no substitute for the personal help of a *tiaolou* entrepreneur like Zhang Jun. The event at Fujiapo turned Zhang into something of a celebrity among the local migrant population, and he is now considered a "director of *tiaolou* performances" (*diaoyan tiaolouxiu*), helping others coordinate and orchestrate their own protests; choosing the right location, helping them contact the appropriate authorities and media, and cautioning them in terms of what to expect during the process (Hui 2009). Finding a grassroots activist like Zhang can greatly help workers take action, whether through the legal system, or by using other unorthodox measures such as *tiaolou*. Yet locating these entrepreneurs is difficult. Most activists do not receive this level of media attention, and it may even be dangerous to do so. Even in the case of the *China Newsweek* story, no contact information was provided, suggesting a level of difficulty in connecting with one of China's most well-known *tiaolou* entrepreneurs.

Problems of Access and Fear of Exploitation

Many smaller migrant organizations and activists are established in working class suburbs with large concentrations of migrant labor. While this facilitates the direct marketing strategy that many employ, it also brings with it additional challenges. Unregistered migrant labor organizations often face difficulties renting office space. Thus many organizations lack a noticeable physical presence, operating out of an apartment residence on a poorly marked street for example, making the simple act of locating them far from straight forward.

Lest one believe locating such organizations is a problem solely for American researchers, newly arrived migrants who are unfamiliar with the city face similar difficulties. Throughout the course of this research project, there were a number of interview respondents that took more than one attempt to locate the specific migrant labor organization they were searching for. Others said they would not have been able to locate their target organization, or be aware of the organization's existence at all, if not for the help of some of their coworkers who had visited there previously ("Interview Beijing 0256" 2008).

An organization's location can be dangerous for staff as well, as many personnel fear being the target of disgruntled employers who may physically intimidate the organization into giving up its work (Fu 2007). The well-known organization *Little Bird* for example established their Beijing office in Wangfujing, a popular tourist area in the heart of the city. The founder of the organization, Weiwei, noted that operating from such a high profile location can help maintain the safety of his staff (Dagongzhe and Little Bird 2007). While this may not be as problematic for an organization like *Little Bird*, others have no choice but to place themselves in working class neighborhoods. The head of *On Action*, a migrant labor organization in Beijing, felt it necessary to situate his organization adjacent to the Beijing West Train station, an area with significant migrant labor foot traffic.

It is also common for migrant labor organizations and activists to run into conflict with local government agencies, which may shut them down or force them to relocate. For some organizations, this happens multiple times per year, making them even more difficult to locate. One labor organization in

Guangzhou for example was forced to relocate four times within one year ("Interview 53, Migrant Labor Organization Representative, South China" 2007), while another was forced to move his offices outside the city permanently ("Interview 51, Migrant Labor Organization Representative, South China" 2008). A third was forced out of his Dongguan offices after local authorities pressured his landlord into refusing to renew their lease, a commonly used tactic. While organizations can mitigate some of these problems by relying on cell phones, text messaging, and QQ for communication, very often cell phone numbers must be changed as well, creating additional obstacles for migrants seeking to locate these organizations.

Finally, many migrants discount potentially useful sources of information for fear of exploitation, and are often weary of approaching unknown organizations unless they are first referred by a trusted source. Even organizations that are well known in the migrant labor community often find it difficult to convince workers they are not trying to take advantage of them (Shenzhen Spring Wind Representative 2007). According to the head of *Spring Wind*, a migrant labor organization located in Shenzhen, even after the organization had organized a free event for workers from one particular factory, no one showed, for fear they were being cheated (Shenzhen Spring Wind Representative 2007). Limited media coverage, constant relocation, and the general distrust among the migrant community suggests that information helping workers locate trusted migrant labor organizations is extremely valuable. Moreover, given the difficulties in obtaining such information from traditional media sources, informal ties are often the best, if not the only, source of information allowing workers to contact migrant organizations, citizen surrogate lawyer, or grass root activist such as the *tiaolou* entrepreneurs described above.

The importance of information derived from informal ties is reflected in table 8.1, which compares the general information sources workers interrogated depending on whether they were selected randomly or interviewed through cooperation with migrant labor organizations. While workers selected randomly relied heavily on traditional information sources such as newspapers and television, over half the workers interviewed at migrant labor organizations relied on their personnel connections, such as fellow workers (51.6%), and to a lesser extent hometown associates (37.3%). Moreover, workers who were able to access a migrant labor organization were less likely to believe that they had no information sources to rely on at all, compared to respondents selected through random sample. Given the importance of informal information, it is unsurprising that workers who were successful in gaining help from these groups would have greater access to such resources.

The importance of informal information to institutional access was echoed in interviews with many labor organization representatives, who

Table 8.1.   Workers' Information Searches (Percentage)

	Newspaper	Television	Hometown Associates	Fellow Workers	None
Workers interviewed at migrant labor organizations	32.9	31.7	37.3	51.6	0.0
Workers selected through random sample	36.1	41.2	22.7	32.0	12.4
Total	34.1	35.3	31.8	44.2	4.7

Source: Author's Interviews. Totals do not sum to one hundred.

argued that referrals were crucial to their work. Many migrants who walked through their doors were brought there by workers the organization had helped in the past. The founder of the Beijing migrant labor organization *On Action* for example argued that informal connections between workers were key to their success. "Because we helped them [migrant workers] in the past, we can [later] give them a call, and through them, we can connect to their fellow workers [*lianxi tamen de gongyou guolai*] and then those workers tell others, and this way we can contact more and more workers" (OnAction Representative 2007).

Han Huimin, a representative from *Migrant Women's Home* in Beijing, argued that even for this well known organization, word of mouth and local community activities, rather than traditional media, were critical. According to Han, traditional media such as newspapers and television are of little use to migrants, particularly the female migrant domestic workers (*baomu*), or those in the restaurant and service industries (*fuwuyuan*), which are the focus of their work. These workers lack the time and money to spend on traditional media sources, and so direct marketing and referrals are essential to connecting with this branch of the migrant worker community.

> Because of the situation and environment they [migrants] are in (*shenghuo huanjing tiaojian*), they don't have opportunities to go out every day and buy newspapers, buy magazines, watch TV or go on the internet, and so we have to go out to where they live and where they work to disseminate information (*zuo xuanchuan*). We talk to their acquaintances (*shouren*) or their fellow villagers (*laoxiang*), and friends will bring their friends to the event. Interviewer: Okay—so you use that sort of social circle? (*shehui quanzi*). Han: Yes, and so we get more and more people this way (*ren yuelai yueduo*). (Han Huimin 2007)

Mr. Tang,[7] the director of an unregistered organization who provides legal aid and other services to migrants in Shenzhen, believes the media is playing an increasingly important role in publicizing egregious cases of labor exploitation, such as the Shaanxi brick kiln slave labor scandal which broke during the summer of 2007. These sources however are not likely to report on the most common types of labor disputes, which Mr. Tang believes are so common as to no longer be newsworthy. According to Mr. Tang, the best way to educate migrants and inform them of his organization's work is through direct introductions, with "friends introducing friends or others being introduced by those involved in the case (*pengyou jieshao pengyou huo dangshiren jieshao de*)," which breaks down barriers of distrust (Tang 2008).

> People really believe those few media sources that report the real news, like the *Southern Metropolitan Daily* and *First Scene* in Shenzhen. People like to watch and see their reports because they dare to speak the truth. But for the most common labor dispute cases—how can [we] get reporters to report on those cases? (Tang 2008)

For many organizations, bringing information directly to the migrant community, and developing trust within that community, is vital. Many recruit former clients either as volunteers or full time workers. Such trusted spokesmen are extremely helpful in overcoming initial distrust, and helping promote the organization among the local migrant community. According to a representative at *Spring Wind* in Shenzhen, because migrants are inherently distrustful of anything labeled as a free service, it is often difficult to recruit workers. For this reason, workers with successful cases are often asked to bring their friends and fellow workers along whenever the organization holds information sessions or workshops (Shenzhen Spring Wind Representative 2007).

Another smaller organization in the Pearl River Delta spends a significant amount of time distributing informational materials at train and bus stations, worksites, and factories. However, because this advertising strategy is also practiced by unscrupulous social actors seeking to cheat migrants as well, nothing is as useful as getting a former successful clients to act as a spokesman on the organization's behalf ("Interview 53, Migrant Labor Organization Representative, South China" 2007).

Even the *Beijing Migrant Workstation*, one of the most well-known migrant labor organizations in Beijing, relies heavily on referrals and word of mouth. According to statistics provided by that organization, of the 108 individuals requesting aid between mid-September to mid-October of 2007, approximately 30% learned of the organization via referrals, by far the most common of any information source (see table 8.2).[8] Since 2007, the Workstation has actively pursued a growth strategy, establishing branch offices in over twenty provinces, something the vast majority of migrant worker organizations are unable to do. Yet even the *Beijing Migrant Workstation* continues to rely on personal referrals to promote their activities.

CONCLUSION: MIGRANT LABOR NGOS AS ALTERNATIVE
SOURCES OF SUPPORT

Since the mid-1990s and partially as a result of the growth of civil society and social organizations within China more broadly, there has been a marked increase in the number and types of "migrant labor organizations," and resources available to migrant workers, including Chinese labor NGOs, unregistered "citizen representatives," and individual labor rights activists. While government policies designed to regulate these more contentious components of civil society have not stopped their numbers from increasing, they have certainly influenced their growth trajectory, as well as the nature of the services they provide.

Migrant labor organizations in large metropolitan areas such as Beijing, Shenzhen, or Guangzhou for example provide workers with a number of different services, ranging from simple information dissemination, representation in informal negotiations with employers, or advice on how to navigate the legal system. Citizen representatives can help migrants take legal action, while labor activists, as well as smaller labor NGOs, may help workers employ collective action.

Yet not all of these sources of support are equally accessible. Limited media coverage, an often tenuous relationship with local governments, and a general sense of distrust among the migrant labor community, all make connecting with many labor organizations or labor activists highly problematic. For some of the better established organizations with strong local government and media contacts, these problems can be mitigated. For workers seeking to locate smaller, less well established organizations that lack such contacts, the sources of support most likely to provide help engaging in unsanctioned protest activities such as strikes or *tiaolou* protests, doing so

Table 8.2.   How Did You Hear About Our Organization? (the Beijing Migrant Worker Legal Aid Workstation)

Source	Percentage
Friend	30%
Television	18%
Labor Department	16%
Internet	13%
Direct Organization Activities	10%
Newspapers	8%
Other Government Institutions	5%

Source: Beijing Migrant Worker Legal Aid Workstation

may be difficult. The problem is even more severe for individual citizen representatives or labor activists, whose activities are unlikely to be publicized in the local media at all, and who often avoid the limelight for fear of drawing attention to their activities.

In light of these restrictions, many migrant labor organizations promote their activities through direct marketing strategies; holding information sessions or distributing fliers and pamphlets within the community to make their presence known. As a result, informal ties between migrants have become important conduits of information, and referrals from migrants that have been helped in the past become invaluable. Thus, it is not surprising that almost every organization interviewed during the course of this research stated that a large proportion of the individuals seeking their aid did so through referrals from other workers, demonstrating the importance of informal information to migrant labor protest activity.

NOTES

1. See Institute for Contemporary Observation Website, http://www.ico-china.org/guwm1/Einglish/Ewmdsy.asp.
2. Name of the organization withheld to protect anonymity.
3. Email communication with migrant labor organization, 29 October 2010.
4. Interview notes provided by South China Migrant Labor Organization, 15 May 2006.
5. See Halegua, "Getting Paid," for a positive assessment. For a more negative assessment, see Gallagher, "Help for Protection and Helpless Choice."
6. "Losing a case" however may be open to definition, as other lawyers at the center during interviews stated they were able to retrieve *some* compensation for workers in at least 95% of the cases.
7. Name changed to preserve anonymity.
8. My thanks to the Beijing Migrant Worker Legal Aid Work Station for providing me with this data.

Chapter Nine

Conclusion: Labor Protest in Authoritarian States

This book has sought to explain when and how migrant workers in China protest their exploitation, and to shed light on how workers in authoritarian states engage in collective action more broadly. In the preceding chapters, I demonstrate how China's migrant workers engage in protest activity despite constraints on formal organizing, relying on urban and rural ties to obtain the necessary material and informational resources. While migrants' traditional rural ties may provide them with material support, access to urban ties help migrant workers take action by providing them with access to new dispute options and strategies, facilitating collective action, helping workers navigate the legal system, and identify alternative sources of support, such as migrant labor organizations and citizen representatives. In chapters 5 and 6, I demonstrated how migrant workers with access to urban ties were both more likely to engage in labor protest, and more likely to employ nonviolent protest strategies, such as use of labor arbitration or the courts.

By the early 1980s, the dismantling of the rural commune system provided Chinese peasants opportunities to leave the land and engage in nonagricultural production. Yet considered neither members of the working class nor members of urban society, migrant workers were provided little if any access to the rudimentary yet growing number of social or legal protections available to urban workers at the time. Freedom of movement and mobility remained officially restricted, while this new, emerging segment of the working class was blamed for many of urban society's ills.

As the migrant labor population continued to grow throughout the 1990s, and into the 2000s, policy changes under the Hu Jintao regime slowly began integrating migrant workers into urban life. Although still considered second class citizens and denied many of the rights and benefits afforded urban citizens, migrant workers have increasingly come to be seen as a permanent facet of modern, urban Chinese society. As the government expanded the legal and administrative protections available to migrant workers, while also changing the political rhetoric used to describe migrant workers' place in Chinese society, this provided them with the opportunities to engage in the level of migrant labor protest activity seen in China today.

Despite the significant changes which have occurred over the past two decades however, Chinese migrant workers continue to face challenges to engaging in labor protest activities, such as state prohibitions on formal organization, and restrictions on the ability to obtain and disseminate information. The chapters presented above provide an argument that access to urban ties can help migrant workers overcome these obstacles. Urban ties developed while living and working in the cities help workers take action in new and previously unforeseen ways, allowing them to connect with migrant labor organizations, citizen representatives, or other labor activists. While new information communication technologies, such as online message boards or instant messaging services, have certainly affected migrant labor protest activities, as I demonstrate in chapter 7, these new tools have only augmented the effects of urban ties, rather than replacing them altogether.

In this concluding chapter, I examine the implications of these findings regarding the importance of urban ties to migrant labor protest, both for China as well as other authoritarian states.

URBAN TIES AND LABOR PROTEST: IMPLICATIONS FOR THE DEVELOPING WORLD

The creation of urban ties among migrants in China is largely a function of changing social structures that have emerged from the migration process itself. This finding has important implications for other countries experiencing similar rural to urban migration, urbanization, and the accompanying pressures of social dislocation. Vietnam is one such case where urban place ties may prove to be an important factor influencing labor dispute activity. Like the CCP, the Communist Party of Vietnam (CPV) maintains a monopoly on political organization. Like China's ACFTU, the Vietnam General Confederation of Labor (VGCL) is the sole organization allowed to represent workers' interests. Vietnam also has a household registration system that, like China's, limits rural migrants' access to housing, employment, and education, making Vietnamese migrant labor similar to Chinese migrants in a number of respects.

Also like China, Vietnam is experiencing a wave of rural to urban migration, with approximately 25–30% of the country's largest cities comprised of internal rural migrants. Like China's migrant workers, these Vietnamese migrants come to the cities in search of higher wages and a better life (Marshall 2000). Unlike the ACFTU however, the VGCL has been afforded more political space to defend the rights and interests of workers (Chan and Nor-lund 1998; Chan and Wang 2004). Yet workers in Vietnam are still officially denied the right to form independent unions, and while strikes and protests in Vietnam are common, they are rarely if ever organized or led by the official trade union. As Vietnamese society continues to undergo significant demo-graphic change and urbanization, the CPV's continued restriction on labor's access to alternative channels for organization and interest representation will likely force Vietnamese migrant workers to rely on informal links, such as those currently facilitating protest in China's migrant labor community. Thus, as urbanization and demographic changes continue in Vietnam, we should expect to see newly created urban ties playing an increasingly impor-tant role in Vietnamese labor protest activity.

Cambodia is another country where urban ties will likely play a role in future labor protest activity. Since the end of the Khumer Rouge and the introduction of market reforms in the late 1990s, Cambodian peasant farmers have faced many of the same push and pull factors that Chinese peasants did in the early years of China's economic reforms. With the retreat of the state from the economy, Cambodia has been experiencing a growth in the con-struction, textile, and garment sectors, as well as the service industry. Tour-ism has increased more than sevenfold since 2000, rising from 466,000 thou-sand in 2000 to approximately 3.5 million by 2012, while the number of workers in the service, construction, and garment industries has also risen dramatically (Cambodia Ministry of Tourism 2012).

Like Vietnam, the nature of the Cambodian rural to urban migration process is reminiscent of what we have witnessed in China, with Cambodian migrants relying heavily on informal social connections from their home-towns. One report produced by the Cambodia Development Resource Insti-tute for example describes a migration process extremely similar to those found in the early years of China's economic development and reform.

> A construction foreman in one studied village would phone to his home village when he needed more labour; as a result, most of his unskilled workers were young men from this village. In the same vein, a vast majority of waiters and waitresses in a particular restaurant came from the same or a nearby village of the restaurant owner. Cases of siblings or friends from the same village work-ing in the same factory, restaurant or car-washing garage are very common. (CDRI 2007)

While Cambodian workers formally have the right to strike, poor working conditions, minimum wage violations, and violence against labor organizers are common, particularly in the garment and construction industries (Interna-tional Labor Organization 2010). Many workers for example have to pay

bribes to employers to secure their positions, similar to the *yajin* payments
many Chinese migrant workers are forced to pay upon beginning a job.
However, just like in China, the integration of rural migrants into urban
society has been limited. Again, quoting the Cambodia Development Resource Institute:

> The new friends they make are from other parts of rural Cambodia, rather than
> from the cities they reside in. They are either too busy or too scared to go out
> or unwilling to spend money to explore the city. Waiters and waitresses virtu-
> ally confine themselves in their workplaces and rarely venture out; car washers
> are similar. Construction workers mostly stay in their makeshift huts in or
> around construction sites. Garment workers know only the road on which they
> shuttle to work. Only a minority were making new friends, who were them-
> selves migrant workers from rural areas rather than urban adults. (CDRI 2007)

Cambodian workers experience restrictions on their ability to organize to
protect their interests similar to those experienced by workers in Vietnam
and China. Yet like China's migrant workers, Cambodian migrants are beginning to experience a growth in labor protest activity following a period of
urbanization and subsequent changes to traditional social ties and interactions. As the construction, service and garment sectors have expanded, workers in these sectors have participated in a growing number of labor strikes
and protests. In the fall of 2010 for example, tens of thousands of garment
workers walked out of their factories in Phnom Penh to protest low wages
(Brady 2010).

Rapid urbanization, such as that currently being experienced by Vietnam
and Cambodia, is a common facet of development for many emerging economies. However, in the wake of these rapid demographic changes, and the
changes in the structure of social interactions that follow, governments in
Vietnam, China, Cambodia, and elsewhere have failed to fully integrate recent rural to urban domestic migrants with their longtime urban counterparts,
and have continued to restrict the organizational and informational capacities
of these recently emerging members of the working class. Yet as the examples of countries such as Vietnam, Cambodia, and China demonstrate, massive demographic changes often unleash social forces which can reorder
social relations in ways that empower emerging social groups to take action
despite restrictions imposed by the state.

URBAN TIES IN CHINA: FOCAL POINTS FOR MIGRANT LABOR INTERACTION

China's urban areas continue to undergo a transformation as profound as any
in the nation's modern history. Migrants already constitute the majority in

metropolitan areas such Shenzhen, and Guangzhou. Moreover, these urban areas are expected to continue adding to their populations despite the fact that more migrants are remaining closer to home, lured by the prospect of lower living costs and higher relative wages. A well publicized 2008 report by the consulting firm McKinsey predicted that by 2025, China will add approximately 350 million to its urban population, 70% from rural to urban migration (Woetzel et al. 2009, 13).

Nor is China's household registration (*hukou*) system likely to undergo any modifications which would limit labor mobility or undermine this growth. The central government is increasingly placing decisions regarding *hukou* reform in the hands of local municipalities, providing them with opportunities to essentially use the sale of urban registration permits as a source of income, thus adding to the challenges of obtaining urban citizenship for the majority of the country's migrant labor, who are increasingly priced out of the urban *hukou* market (Wing Chan and Buckingham 2008). However, this selective discrimination between rural migrants based on their ability to afford an urban residence permit differs greatly from a return to the strict controls on internal movement which existed in the early 1980s. Given the Chinese economy's reliance on migrant labor for continued growth, labor market flexibility and mobility is likely to continue.

This continued urban growth, fueled largely by continued rural migration, suggests that opportunities for migrant workers to develop urban ties will continue as well. Yet as illustrated in the preceding chapters, the creation of urban ties is not automatic. It is no coincidence that the vast majority of literature on migrant labor in China has focused on the importance of traditional family, kinship, and native place ties, and the manner in which those ties help migrant workers transition to urban life. Indeed, the majority of workers interviewed during the course of this research relied heavily on such ties. Yet those workers who were able to cultivate ties outside these traditional networks were better positioned to engage in protest activity.

So how do urban ties between migrant workers develop? Many develop through their workplace, and this was reflected in many of the examples provided in chapter 6. Connections that emerge between individuals with different backgrounds and experiences on constructions sites, or in factory dormitories, can become useful resources when attempting to engage in dispute activity. Other locales may provide similar opportunities. Grassroots migrant labor organizations for example have acknowledged the importance of informal referrals to their work. As these organizations develop connections within the larger migrant labor community, they can provide a location for workers to interact, exchange ideas and strategies, and develop urban ties similar to those cultivated at the workplace. Other social spaces can provide opportunities for interaction between workers sharing similar grievances across employers or industries. Workers that may have different employers for example may still develop connections while receiving medical treatment at hospitals.

Some organizations have even helped connect Chinese workers and activists in the mainland with similarly aggrieved workers abroad. In the fall of 2006, the Asia Monitor Resource Center organized a "victim exchange," taking Chinese migrant workers suffering from silicosis, an occupational illness and respiratory disease common among workers in the gemstone and jewelry industries, (China Labour Bulletin 2005) to Gujarat India, to connect with other workers also suffering from the disease (George 2007). Chinese workers met with members of the Indian People's Training and Research Center (PTRC), a grassroots organization active in organizing victims of silicosis related occupational illness in India. Through these interactions, Chinese workers were able to learn how Indian workers attempt to resolve occupational illness issues, gaining insight into new strategies for organizing silicosis victims that may be of use in Guangdong and other Chinese provinces.

While international exchanges of this type are rare, they appear to be growing, and provide another example of how worker interactions outside the workplace may promote urban tie development. Opportunities to share information and experiences with others, whether in the context of hospital wards, grassroots migrant labor organizations, the workplace, or through grievance specific organizations and activities, can all foster the urban tie relationships that facilitate protest activity.

AN EMERGING MIGRANT LABOR CLASS?

To what extent will migrant workers' interests and identities converge, such that scholars can begin to identify a truly conscious and coherent migrant labor class in China? While earlier research into the development of working class consciousness focused on the creation of a broadly based working class, complete with "identity and interests between working men of the most diverse occupations and levels of attainment" (Thompson 1964, 807), scholars have more recently sought to explain why labor as a class remains divided along various ethnic, regional, and occupational lines (Perry 1994; Blecher 2002).

Nowhere are these divisions more apparent than in Asia, where factors such as gender, family, and native place origin have been critical to shaping the political behavior of the working class (Perry 1996, 3). Indeed, within the Chinese historical context, it has only been when labor's various social circles could be made to cooperate; be they native place associations, kinship networks, industrial sectors, or other social gatherings, that large scale labor action has been possible (Perry 1994, 251). While a unified labor movement in China may be unlikely, the growing number of opportunities for migrant workers to expand their social networks may provide a means for them to expand these areas of cooperation and solidarity. The development of urban ties linking victims of similar labor exploitations from various occupations or regions for example may provide the foundation for a broader movement, expanding the interest and identity formation of Chinese migrant workers beyond their traditional family and hometown associations.

CHINESE MIGRANT LABOR AND THE PARTY-STATE

Any development in the formation of a more inclusive migrant labor identity will of course be influenced by the state, particularly the extent to which the PRC attempts to provide labor with a greater voice in the policy making process, or continues to exclude it from that process. What role will migrant labor play in China's political future?

Popular protest involving not only migrant labor but other groups; Chinese peasants or the middle class for example, over issues as varied as corruption, environmental degradation, and social inequality, pose a significant problem of governance for the PRC. Absent channels for interest articulation and interaction with the party-state, the PRC government could face growing intensity of conflict between entitled business interests in conflict with exploited groups, including migrant labor, creating a situation not unlike that experienced by governments in Latin America (Gilboy and Heginbotham 2004).

Yet the "Latin Americanization" of China is not the only possible scenario. Other authoritarian states such as Vietnam have been successful providing greater voice for institutions representing labor within the political process, providing the space for the Vietnamese trade union to represent the rights and interests of labor at the level of elite politics, while permitting labor associations, loosely tied to the VGCL, to represent workers at the shop floor. Moreover, this has been done without significant political reform.

China's citizens also appear to have widely accepted the free market, and its associated inequalities (Whyte 2010). The party-state has become adept at managing social issues in part by selectively providing opportunities for some groups in society to make demands on the state, while simultaneously excluding other groups who may demand too much in terms of economic redistribution or political reform. Private entrepreneurs and the urban middle class for example have successfully formed business associations and civil society groups, which have helped articulate their interests to the state.

In contrast, migrant workers appear to be limited to pre-reform methods of interest articulation. Confined to mass organizations such as the ACFTU, labor in China, including migrant labor, lacks alternative channels to articulate its demands and defend its interests. The extent to which the party leadership provides labor a larger say in the political process might play a key role in shaping the future of labor as a political force in China. This might take the form of providing labor with a voice in the party comparable to that given to business over the past few decades, granting the ACFTU more autonomy to better articulate labor's demands, or allowing for the maturation of other channels of interest articulation similar to the growth of business associations.

Cooptation and Repression

Changes in relations between the CCP and Chinese labor aside, the likelihood of labor leading a broad based, polish style solidarity revolution in China remains highly unlikely in the near term. The CCP has continuously proven highly adept at managing the dramatic social and economic changes that have taken place since the beginning of economic reform, and has largely done so through the adoption of a two pronged strategy; engaging in both the cooptation of certain important domestic groups, while simultaneously defending against "reform from within." In regards to migrant labor, this general strategy manifests itself in two distinct policies, cooptation and coercion.

The party's efforts at maintaining a monopoly on political power throughout the economic reform period have provided it with ample experience in managing the introduction of new social groups into the political process. The CCP has to date successfully managed the integration of private entrepreneurs into the political system, a group whose loyalty to traditional party ideals may be questionable, but whose importance to continued economic growth made their integration into the Party a political necessity (Dickson 2008). While migrant labor has unquestionably played a key role in China's economic development, as a social class, individual migrants do not possess the high concentrations of economic resources which make China's capitalists such a formidable social class. Ironically however, China's migrant workers have much more in common with the Party's traditional base of support, which historically has consisted of workers, peasants and soldiers.

This is not to suggest however that migrant labor is inconsequential to either future party building or government policy making. As described in chapter 8, the ACFTU, the party, and the state have worked to develop close links with "model" migrant labor organizations, offering selected organizations opportunities to align themselves more closely to the state in exchange for political protection and legitimacy. In exchange, local governments obtain valuable information regarding potential hot spots for social unrest, providing them with an "early warning system" to monitor possible protest activity.

The CCP has even begun to reform its strategy on migrant labor recruitment as well. Migrant labor has not traditionally been a focus of party recruitment, reflected by the fact that only 2.5% of all migrant workers are party members, compared with approximately 5.5% of the population nationwide (Qi 2008). Just as migrant workers' high level of mobility makes it difficult for many migrant labor organizations to establish a base of support within the migrant labor community in any one area, migrant mobility makes party recruitment difficult as well. Those migrant workers who do not formally register in their place of work for example, face difficulty joining a party branch in their new area (Yang 2007). In addition, while private entrepreneurs may join the party for financial opportunities, many migrants do not view party membership the same way, with the phrase "whether or not you join the party is only the difference of a few mao," common among peasants and migrants. [1]

Certain regions however have been more active than others in their attempts to recruit migrant labor into the party. Since the mid-2000s for example, Xinyang City in Henan Province has instituted the "Golden Bridge Project" (*Jinqiao*), an initiative designed to attract migrant workers with Xinyang residency status working outside their home region into the party, helping to establish party branches specifically designed to organize and provide services to Xinyang migrants in the cities, while providing incentives to entice successful migrants to return home.

Under this initiative, Xinyang party officials have dispatched cadres to other cities to organize Xinyang migrants; as few as 3 Xinyang migrant party members in one city for example can establish a township level party branch, while 50 can establish a county level branch (Yang 2007). Through this process, the city has been able to organize party branches among Xinyang migrant workers in major cities such as Beijing, Shanghai, Shenzhen, Wuhan and Hangzhou, cooperating with local unions to help migrants resolve labor disputes, establish boarding schools back home for children whose parents have gone to work in other cities, and negotiate with specific regions on behalf of migrant workers to obtain more affordable health care (Yang 2007).

Migrant labor is increasingly taken into account at the level of national policymaking as well, as the central government continues to promulgate migrant labor focused legislation, and has begun to incorporate migrants into political institutions. The 2008 *Labor Contract Law*, *Labor Dispute Mediation and Arbitration Law*, and *Employment Promotion Law* were all undertaken at least partially to provide greater protection for migrant labor. The 2008 *Employment Promotion Law* for example expressly prohibits discrimination against migrant labor, stating, "Rural workers who move to urban areas to seek employment shall enjoy equal labor rights to urban workers and shall not be subject to discriminatory restrictions" (10th National People's Congress 2007 Article 31). More symbolically, in 2008, three migrant workers were selected for the first time to be delegates to the National People's Congress (NPC). Indeed, after being named a delegate, one factory worker in Guangdong, who was originally from Sichuan, became inundated with requests for help from other migrant workers in dealing with their labor grievances (Bristow 2009).

As a compliment to these cooptation strategies, the Party has also sought to divide those migrants and migrant labor organizations that may usefully be included in the political process from those that lack sufficient party loyalty or threaten to reform the party from the inside (Dickson 2000, 520). Cognizant of the dangers of "reform from within," the party has studied carefully the demise of the Soviet Union and other one party communist regimes of Eastern Europe, and has learned to be watchful of factors leading to "peaceful transition" (Shambaugh 2009). In CCP academic studies of the solidarity movement in Poland for example, the development of autonomous labor organizations, and the rise of contacts with the west, were credited with dividing the labor class, enticing Polish labor organizations to abandon their working class base in exchange for western ties (Shambaugh 2009, 50).

While this danger of reform from within relates to political change more broadly, it also has implications for the ACFTU, and the party-state's relationship with migrant labor specifically. One implication of the Party's increasing concern with migrant labor issues is the way in which the ACFTU views foreign influence in migrant labor activities. As the growth of migrant labor organizations within Chinese civil society continues, the ACFTU has been suspicious of increasing contact between these organizations and western donors. This suspicion is reflected in a February 2008 quote from ACFTU vice Chair Sun Chunlan:

> We need to keep a close lookout for foreign and domestic hostile forces using the difficulties encountered by some companies to infiltrate and undermine the ranks of migrant workers. ("Protecting Workers' Rights or Serving the Party: The Way Forward for China's Trade Unions" 2009, 7)

Through its analysis of the fall of communism in Europe, the ACFTU is well aware of its need to develop union organizations that can "act as a bridge (*qiao*) between the party and the working class" (Shambaugh 2009, 50), while at the same time avoid the rise of any independent labor organizations which may seek to challenge the ACFTU's monopoly as the representative of migrant labors' interests. As the party continues to focus on its core goals of economic modernization and social stability, the extent to which the CCP, and by extension the ACFTU, are able to include migrant labor into the current political system, relying on a balance of cooptation and repression, will be crucial in shaping the relationship between the Party, labor, and the state in China's future.

NOTE

1. "*dangyuan budangyuan jiu cha jimaoqian*," quoted from Research Office of the Ningxia Central Party Committee Party and Government Office, "Attaching a High Degree of Importance to the Question of Youth Farmers Joining the Party" [Gaodu Zhongshi Qingnian Nongmingong Rudang Wenti], *Communist Party Member Journal*, vol. 19 (2006).

Appendix A. Interview Questionnaire

LABOR DISPUTE RESEARCH QUESTIONNAIRE

Sir/Madam: Hello!

We have designed this questionnaire in order to make a theoretical review of the reforms of our country's labor system, with the aim of hearing the ideas and opinions of a wide range of workers. During your time as a migrant worker (either now or previously), if you've experienced a labor dispute or issue with your employer (for example: nonpayment of wages, worker injury compensation, a work related illness, etc.), then you may participate in this questionnaire. This questionnaire is anonymous, and we are committed to maintaining the strict confidentiality of all information collected. The questionnaire touches upon a number of issues, and will be used solely for academic purposes.

Thank you for your support and cooperation:

Labor Dispute Research Organization Group

Explanatory Note: Please mark the choice that best fits your own personal experience with a√。

1. Sex: Male ☐   Female ☐

2. Year of Birth: _____

3. Place of Registered Permanent Residence:

            _____Province   _____County
4. The first time you came to this location to work _____(year)

5. How many other workers did you come with? _____ (individuals)

6. How many times on average do you return home? _____ (times)

7. You have an:

            Urban household registration   ☐
            Rural household registration   ☐

8. What is your educational level?
            A. No formal education   ☐   B. Primary School   ☐
            C. Junior Middle School ☐   D. Junior Middle School Graduate ☐
            E. High School   ☐   F. High School Graduate   ☐
            G. University   ☐

9. Are you: CCP Member ☐   CYL Member ☐   Neither   ☐

10. Your dispute began: _____Year   _____Month
11. Your dispute involved approximately: _____RMB

12. What type of work were you engaged in when your dispute took place?

    A. Construction □   B. Manufacturing □

    C. Wholesale □   D. Hotel restaurant □

    E. Service □   F. Transportation □

    G. Other_____

13. When your dispute took place, how long had you worked at this location?

    _____

14. What was your monthly income when your dispute took place? (average)

    _____RMB / month

15. At this time, you worked (average)_____days per week, _____hours per day

16. At the time your dispute took place, did you have a labor contract?

    Yes □   No □   Unsure □

17. What was the nature of the dispute you experienced?

    A. Nonpayment of wages □   B. Work injury □

    C. Illegal dismissal □   D. Sexual harassment □

    E. Unsafe work conditions □   F. Work related illness □

    G. Nonpayment of overtime pay □

    Other (Please describe)

    _____

18. When your dispute took place, how many workers shared this dispute with you?
_____(individuals).

19. When your dispute took place, where did you go to obtain useful information to help resolve the dispute? (**Choose all applicable**)

    A. Newspaper □   B.   Television □   C. Radio   □

    D. Internet   □   E.   Hometown associates   □

    F. Fellow Workers □   G.   Local association (*tongxianghui*) □

    H. Religious organization □

    I. Other media source, social organization, or individual (Please Describe)

    _____

20. When your dispute took place, did anyone provide you with monetary support or other material support? For example, did anyone pay for your medical expenses? If you experienced a nonpayment of wages dispute, did anyone or any organization within that time period provide you with financial aid or any other type of material support?

    (**Select all appropriate**)

    A. Family member   □   B. Friend   □

    C. Hometown Associates □   D. Fellow Worker □

    E. Local association (*tongxianghui*) □

    F. Religious organization □

    G. None □

    Other social organization or individual(s) (Please Describe)

    _____

21. When your dispute took place were you able to obtain new information or new methods to use to help you take action to resolve your dispute? If so, where did it come from? (please check all appropriate)

    A. Family member   □   B. Friend   □

    C. Hometown Associates   □   D. Fellow Worker   □

    E. Local association (*tongxianghui*)   □   F. Religious organization   □

    G. None   □

Other media source, social organization or individual(s) (Please Describe)

_____

22. Where do you think you were able to obtain the best, most useful, information to help you take action to resolve your dispute?

(Please select only one)

    A. Family member   □   B. Friend   □

    C. Hometown Associates   □   D. Fellow Worker   □

    E. local association (*tongxianghui*)   □   F. Religious organization   □

    G. None (no useful source of information)   □

Other media source, social organization, or individual(s) (Please Describe)

_____

What is your opinion on the following statements? (Please mark the option you feel most appropriate with a √. **Please select only one option.**)

23. "I see examples of labor disputes in the media (television, newspapers or radio) that are very similar to my own experiences"

1.	Strongly Agree	□	2. Agree	□
3.	Disagree	□	4. Strongly Disagree	□

24. Seeing examples of labor disputes in the traditional media (television, newspapers, or radio) can help me resolve my own labor dispute.

1. Strongly Agree	□	2. Agree	□
3. Disagree	□	4. Strongly Disagree	□

25. When your dispute took place, did your place of work have a union representative?

Yes □   No   □

26. Have you joined the union?   Yes □   No   □

27. Have you participated in union activities?   Yes □   No   □

28. When your dispute took place, what method(s) did you try to attempt to resolve it? **(select all appropriate).** Please arrange according to the order in which the actions were taken (for example, 1 is the first action you attempted, 2 is the second action you attempted, etc.)

    Also, please tell us what you thought of each method (1 = extremely satisfied, 2 = satisfied, 3 = not too satisfied, 4 = extremely unsatisfied).

Method	For each method adopted, please note with a√	Order (example: 1,2,3)	Level of Satisfaction
Leave work			
Talk directly to the boss			
Appeal for mediation			
Go to the local labor bureau for advice			
Apply for labor arbitration			
Petition Office			
Appeal to the police			
Talk with a union representative			
Sue in court			
Government legal aid center			
Consult with a village association (*tongxianghui*)			
Consult with a religious organization			
Any Other Action (Please describe)			

29. Why did you select the above mentioned actions?

    _____

    _____

    _____

30. Were you satisfied with the final outcome of your dispute?

    Yes ☐ No ☐

What is your opinion on the following statements? (Please mark the option you feel most appropriate with a √. **Please select only one option**.)

31. Most of the time, the union can help workers and migrants resolve his (her)   problems

      1. Strongly Agree   ☐   2. Agree   ☐

      3. Disagree   ☐   4. Strongly Disagree ☐

32. Most of the time, the labor bureau can help workers and migrants resolve his (her) problems

      1. Strongly Agree   ☐   2. Agree   ☐

      3. Disagree   ☐   4. Strongly Disagree ☐

Again, a heartfelt thank you for your enthusiastic support and cooperation!!

Appendix B. List of Interviews

Interview Number	Interview Code	Date	Province	Site
1	BJ 0101	6/15/2007	Beijing	Beijing
2	BJ 0102	6/22/2007	Beijing	Beijing
3	BJ 0103	7/7/2007	Beijing	Beijing
4	BJ 0104	7/9/2007	Beijing	Beijing
5	BJ 0105	7/16/2007	Beijing	Beijing
6	BJ 0106	7/21/2007	Beijing	Beijing
7	BJ 0107	7/28/2007	Beijing	Beijing
8	BJ 0108	7/28/2007	Beijing	Beijing
9	BJ 0109	8/6/2007	Beijing	Beijing
10	BJ 0110	8/13/2007	Beijing	Beijing
11	BJ 0111	8/22/2007	Beijing	Beijing
12	BJ 0112	8/27/2007	Beijing	Beijing
13	BJ 0113	8/30/2007	Beijing	Beijing
14	BJ 0114	9/15/2007	Beijing	Beijing
15	BJ 0115	9/18/2007	Beijing	Beijing
16	BJ 0116	9/27/2007	Beijing	Beijing
17	BJ 0117	9/29/2007	Beijing	Beijing
18	BJ 0118	10/2/2007	Beijing	Beijing
19	BJ 0119	10/3/2007	Beijing	Beijing
20	BJ 0120	10/5/2007	Beijing	Beijing
21	BJ 0121	10/5/2007	Beijing	Beijing
22	BJ 0122	10/8/2007	Beijing	Beijing
23	BJ 0123	10/8/2007	Beijing	Beijing
24	BJ 0124	10/17/2007	Beijing	Beijing
25	BJ 0125	10/17/2007	Beijing	Beijing
26	BJ 0126	10/22/2007	Beijing	Beijing
27	BJ 0127	10/22/2007	Beijing	Beijing
28	BJ 0128	10/29/2007	Beijing	Beijing
29	BJ 0129	11/12/2007	Beijing	Beijing
30	BJ 0130	11/14/2007	Beijing	Beijing
31	BJ 0204	2/2008 - 5/2008	Beijing	Beijing
32	BJ 0205	2/2008 - 5/2008	Beijing	Beijing
33	BJ 0206	2/2008 - 5/2008	Beijing	Beijing
34	BJ 0207	2/2008 - 5/2008	Beijing	Beijing

35	BJ 0208	2/2008 - 5/2008	Beijing	Beijing
36	BJ 0213	2/2008 - 5/2008	Beijing	Beijing
37	BJ 0216	2/2008 - 5/2008	Beijing	Beijing
38	BJ 0225	2/2008 - 5/2008	Beijing	Beijing
39	BJ 0228	2/2008 - 5/2008	Beijing	Beijing
40	BJ 0233	2/2008 - 5/2008	Beijing	Beijing
41	BJ 0234	2/2008 - 5/2008	Beijing	Beijing
42	BJ 0235	2/2008 - 5/2008	Beijing	Beijing
43	BJ 0236	2/2008 - 5/2008	Beijing	Beijing
44	BJ 0237	2/2008 - 5/2008	Beijing	Beijing
45	BJ 0248	2/2008 - 5/2008	Beijing	Beijing
46	BJ 0249	2/2008 - 5/2008	Beijing	Beijing
47	BJ 0250	2/2008 - 5/2008	Beijing	Beijing
48	BJ 0251	2/2008 - 5/2008	Beijing	Beijing
49	BJ 0254	2/2008 - 5/2008	Beijing	Beijing
50	BJ 0255	2/2008 - 5/2008	Beijing	Beijing
51	BJ 0256	2/2008 - 5/2008	Beijing	Beijing
52	SZ 0301	12/4/2007	Guangdong	Shenzhen
53	SZ 0302	12/6/2007	Guangdong	Shenzhen
54	SZ 0303	12/14/2007	Guangdong	Shenzhen
55	SZ 0304	1/14/2008	Guangdong	Shenzhen
56	SZ 0305	1/18/2008	Guangdong	Shenzhen
57	SZ 0306	1/18/2008	Guangdong	Shenzhen
58	SZ 0307	1/26/2008	Guangdong	Shenzhen
59	SZ 0308	2/3/2008	Guangdong	Shenzhen
60	SZ 0309	2/3/2008	Guangdong	Shenzhen
61	SZ 0310	2/3/2008	Guangdong	Shenzhen
62	SZ 0311	2/3/2008	Guangdong	Shenzhen
63	SZ 0312	2/4/2008	Guangdong	Shenzhen
64	SZ 0313	2/4/2008	Guangdong	Shenzhen
65	SZ 0314	2/4/2008	Guangdong	Shenzhen
66	SZ 0315	2/5/2008	Guangdong	Shenzhen
67	SZ 0316	2/5/2008	Guangdong	Shenzhen
68	SZ 0317	2/5/2008	Guangdong	Shenzhen
69	SZ 0318	2/5/2008	Guangdong	Shenzhen
70	SZ 0319	2/9/2008	Guangdong	Shenzhen

71	SZ 0320	2/9/2008	Guangdong	Shenzhen
72	SZ 0321	2/9/2008	Guangdong	Shenzhen
73	SZ 0322	2/21/2008	Guangdong	Shenzhen
74	SZ 0323	2/21/2008	Guangdong	Shenzhen
75	SZ 0324	2/21/2008	Guangdong	Shenzhen
76	SZ 0401	1/1/2008-3/2008	Guangdong	Shenzhen
77	SZ 0402	1/1/2008-3/2008	Guangdong	Shenzhen
78	SZ 0404	1/1/2008-3/2008	Guangdong	Shenzhen
79	SZ 0408	1/1/2008-3/2008	Guangdong	Shenzhen
80	SZ 0410	1/1/2008-3/2008	Guangdong	Shenzhen
81	SZ 0411	1/1/2008-3/2008	Guangdong	Shenzhen
82	SZ 0412	1/1/2008-3/2008	Guangdong	Shenzhen
83	SZ 0414	1/1/2008-3/2008	Guangdong	Shenzhen
84	SZ 0415	1/1/2008-3/2008	Guangdong	Shenzhen
85	SZ 0416	1/1/2008-3/2008	Guangdong	Shenzhen
86	SZ 0417	1/1/2008-3/2008	Guangdong	Shenzhen
87	SZ 0419	1/1/2008-3/2008	Guangdong	Shenzhen
88	SZ 0420	1/1/2008-3/2008	Guangdong	Shenzhen
89	SZ 0421	1/1/2008-3/2008	Guangdong	Shenzhen
90	SZ 0424	1/1/2008-3/2008	Guangdong	Shenzhen
91	SZ 0426	1/1/2008-3/2008	Guangdong	Shenzhen
92	SZ 0427	1/1/2008-3/2008	Guangdong	Shenzhen
93	SZ 0428	1/1/2008-3/2008	Guangdong	Shenzhen
94	SZ 0429	1/1/2008-3/2008	Guangdong	Shenzhen
95	SZ 0431	1/1/2008-3/2008	Guangdong	Shenzhen
96	SZ 0432	1/1/2008-3/2008	Guangdong	Shenzhen
97	SZ 0433	1/1/2008-3/2008	Guangdong	Shenzhen
98	SZ 0437	1/1/2008-3/2008	Guangdong	Shenzhen
99	SZ 0438	1/1/2008-3/2008	Guangdong	Shenzhen
100	SZ 0439	1/1/2008-3/2008	Guangdong	Shenzhen
101	SZ 0440	1/1/2008-3/2008	Guangdong	Shenzhen
102	SZ 0441	1/1/2008-3/2008	Guangdong	Shenzhen
103	SZ 0442	1/1/2008-3/2008	Guangdong	Shenzhen
104	SZ 0443	1/1/2008-3/2008	Guangdong	Shenzhen
105	SZ 0444	1/1/2008-3/2008	Guangdong	Shenzhen
106	SZ 0445	1/1/2008-3/2008	Guangdong	Shenzhen

107	SZ 0446	1/1/2008-3/2008	Guangdong	Shenzhen
108	SZ 0447	1/1/2008-3/2008	Guangdong	Shenzhen
109	SZ 0448	1/1/2008-3/2008	Guangdong	Shenzhen
110	SZ 0449	1/1/2008-3/2008	Guangdong	Shenzhen
111	SZ 0450	1/1/2008-3/2008	Guangdong	Shenzhen
112	SZ 0451	1/1/2008-3/2008	Guangdong	Shenzhen
113	SZ 0452	1/1/2008-3/2008	Guangdong	Shenzhen
114	SZ 0453	1/1/2008-3/2008	Guangdong	Shenzhen
115	SZ 0454	1/1/2008-3/2008	Guangdong	Shenzhen
116	SZ 0455	1/1/2008-3/2008	Guangdong	Shenzhen
117	SZ 0456	1/1/2008-3/2008	Guangdong	Shenzhen
118	SZ 0457	1/1/2008-3/2008	Guangdong	Shenzhen
119	SZ 0458	1/1/2008-3/2008	Guangdong	Shenzhen
120	SZ 0459	1/1/2008-3/2008	Guangdong	Shenzhen
121	SZ 0460	1/1/2008-3/2008	Guangdong	Shenzhen
122	SZ 0461	1/1/2008-3/2008	Guangdong	Shenzhen
123	SZ 0462	1/1/2008-3/2008	Guangdong	Shenzhen
124	SZ 0463	1/1/2008-3/2008	Guangdong	Shenzhen
125	SZ 0464	1/1/2008-3/2008	Guangdong	Shenzhen
126	SZ 0465	1/1/2008-3/2008	Guangdong	Shenzhen
127	SZ 0466	1/1/2008-3/2008	Guangdong	Shenzhen
128	SZ 0467	1/1/2008-3/2008	Guangdong	Shenzhen
129	SZ 0468	1/1/2008-3/2008	Guangdong	Shenzhen
130	GZ 0501	3/4/2008	Guangdong	Guangzhou
131	GZ 0502	3/4/2008	Guangdong	Guangzhou
132	GZ 0503	3/4/2008	Guangdong	Guangzhou
133	GZ 0504	3/6/2008	Guangdong	Guangzhou
134	GZ 0505	3/6/2008	Guangdong	Guangzhou
135	GZ 0506	3/6/2008	Guangdong	Guangzhou
136	GZ 0601	3/7/2008	Guangdong	Guangzhou
137	GZ 0602	3/7/2008	Guangdong	Guangzhou
138	GZ 0603	3/7/2008	Guangdong	Guangzhou
139	GZ 0604	3/8/2008	Guangdong	Guangzhou
140	GZ 0605	3/8/2008	Guangdong	Guangzhou
141	GZ 0606	3/8/2008	Guangdong	Guangzhou
142	GZ 0607	3/8/2008	Guangdong	Guangzhou

143	GZ 0608	3/9/2008	Guangdong	Guangzhou
144	GZ 0609	3/9/2008	Guangdong	Guangzhou
145	GZ 0610	3/10/2008	Guangdong	Guangzhou
146	GZ 0611	3/10/2008	Guangdong	Guangzhou
147	GZ 0612	3/10/2008	Guangdong	Guangzhou
148	GZ 0613	3/11/2008	Guangdong	Guangzhou
149	GZ 0614	3/11/2008	Guangdong	Guangzhou
150	GZ 0615	3/12/2008	Guangdong	Guangzhou
151	GZ 0616	3/12/2008	Guangdong	Guangzhou
152	GZ 0617	3/12/2008	Guangdong	Guangzhou
153	GZ 0618	3/14/2008	Guangdong	Guangzhou
154	GZ 0619	3/15/2008	Guangdong	Guangzhou
155	GZ 0621	3/15/2008	Guangdong	Guangzhou
156	GZ 0622	3/15/2008	Guangdong	Guangzhou
157	GZ 0623	3/16/2008 - 3/20/2008	Guangdong	Guangzhou
158	GZ 0624	3/16/2008 - 3/20/2008	Guangdong	Guangzhou
159	GZ 0625	3/16/2008 - 3/20/2008	Guangdong	Guangzhou
160	GZ 0626	3/16/2008 - 3/20/2008	Guangdong	Guangzhou
161	GZ 0627	3/16/2008 - 3/20/2008	Guangdong	Guangzhou
162	GZ 0628	3/16/2008 - 3/20/2008	Guangdong	Guangzhou
163	GZ 0629	3/16/2008 - 3/20/2008	Guangdong	Guangzhou
164	GZ 0630	3/16/2008 - 3/20/2008	Guangdong	Guangzhou
165	GZ 0631	3/16/2008 - 3/20/2008	Guangdong	Guangzhou
166	GZ 0632	3/16/2008 - 3/20/2008	Guangdong	Guangzhou
167	GZ 0633	3/16/2008 - 3/20/2008	Guangdong	Guangzhou
168	GZ 0634	3/16/2008 - 3/20/2008	Guangdong	Guangzhou
169	GZ 0635	3/16/2008 - 3/20/2008	Guangdong	Guangzhou
170	GZ 0636	3/16/2008 - 3/20/2008	Guangdong	Guangzhou
171	GZ 0637	3/16/2008 - 3/20/2008	Guangdong	Guangzhou
172	GZ 0638	3/16/2008 - 3/20/2008	Guangdong	Guangzhou
173	GZ 0639	3/16/2008 - 3/20/2008	Guangdong	Guangzhou
174	GZ 0640	3/16/2008 - 3/20/2008	Guangdong	Guangzhou
175	GZ 0641	3/16/2008 - 3/20/2008	Guangdong	Guangzhou
176	GZ 0642	3/16/2008 - 3/20/2008	Guangdong	Guangzhou
177	GZ 0643	3/16/2008 - 3/20/2008	Guangdong	Guangzhou
178	GZ 0644	3/16/2008 - 3/20/2008	Guangdong	Guangzhou

179	GZ 0645	3/16/2008 - 3/20/2008	Guangdong	Guangzhou
180	GZ 0646	3/16/2008 - 3/20/2008	Guangdong	Guangzhou
181	GZ 0647	3/16/2008 - 3/20/2008	Guangdong	Guangzhou
182	GZ 0648	3/16/2008 - 3/20/2008	Guangdong	Guangzhou
183	GZ 0649	3/16/2008 - 3/20/2008	Guangdong	Guangzhou
184	CZ 0701	3/21/2008	Jiangsu	Changzhou
185	CZ 0702	3/21/2008	Jiangsu	Changzhou
186	CZ 0703	3/21/2008	Jiangsu	Changzhou
187	CZ 0704	3/23/2008	Jiangsu	Changzhou
188	CZ 0705	3/28/2008	Jiangsu	Changzhou
189	CZ 0706	3/28/2008	Jiangsu	Changzhou
190	CZ 0707	3/29/2008	Jiangsu	Changzhou
191	CZ 0708	3/29/2008	Jiangsu	Changzhou
192	CZ 0709	3/30/2008	Jiangsu	Changzhou
193	CZ 0710	3/30/2008	Jiangsu	Changzhou
194	CZ 0711	4/2/2008	Jiangsu	Changzhou
195	CZ 0712	4/2/2008	Jiangsu	Changzhou
196	CZ 0713	4/2/2008	Jiangsu	Changzhou
197	CZ 0714	4/4/2008	Jiangsu	Changzhou
198	CZ 0715	4/10/2008	Jiangsu	Changzhou
199	CZ 0716	4/11/2008	Jiangsu	Changzhou
200	CZ 0717	4/11/2008	Jiangsu	Changzhou
201	CZ 0718	4/11/2008	Jiangsu	Changzhou
202	CZ 0719	4/13/2008	Jiangsu	Changzhou
203	CZ 0720	4/18/2008	Jiangsu	Changzhou
204	CZ 0721	4/18/2008	Jiangsu	Changzhou
205	CZ 0722	4/23/2008	Jiangsu	Changzhou
206	CZ 0723	4/23/2008	Jiangsu	Changzhou
207	CZ 0724	4/25/2008	Jiangsu	Changzhou
208	CZ 0725	4/25/2008	Jiangsu	Changzhou
209	CZ 0801	4/2/08 to 5/18/08	Jiangsu	Changzhou
210	CZ 0802	4/2/08 to 5/18/08	Jiangsu	Changzhou
211	CZ 0803	4/2/08 to 5/18/08	Jiangsu	Changzhou
212	CZ 0804	4/2/08 to 5/18/08	Jiangsu	Changzhou
213	CZ 0805	4/2/08 to 5/18/08	Jiangsu	Changzhou
214	CZ 0806	4/2/08 to 5/18/08	Jiangsu	Changzhou

215	NJ 0901	4/17/2008	Jiangsu	Nanjing
216	NJ 0902	4/17/2008	Jiangsu	Nanjing
217	NJ 0903	4/17/2008	Jiangsu	Nanjing
218	NJ 0904	4/17/2008	Jiangsu	Nanjing
219	NJ 0905	4/24/2008	Jiangsu	Nanjing
220	NJ 0906	4/24/2008	Jiangsu	Nanjing
221	NJ 0907	4/24/2008	Jiangsu	Nanjing
222	NJ 0908	4/27/2008	Jiangsu	Nanjing
223	NJ 0909	4/27/2008	Jiangsu	Nanjing
224	NJ 0910	4/27/2008	Jiangsu	Nanjing
225	NJ 1001	9/2007 - 11/2007	Jiangsu	Nanjing
226	NJ 1002	9/2007 - 11/2007	Jiangsu	Nanjing
227	NJ 1003	9/2007 - 11/2007	Jiangsu	Nanjing
228	NJ 1004	9/2007 - 11/2007	Jiangsu	Nanjing
229	NJ 1005	9/2007 - 11/2007	Jiangsu	Nanjing
230	NJ 1006	9/2007 - 11/2007	Jiangsu	Nanjing
231	NJ 1007	9/2007 - 11/2007	Jiangsu	Nanjing
232	NJ 1008	9/2007 - 11/2007	Jiangsu	Nanjing
233	NJ 1009	9/2007 - 11/2007	Jiangsu	Nanjing
234	NJ 1010	9/2007 - 11/2007	Jiangsu	Nanjing
235	NJ 1011	9/2007 - 11/2007	Jiangsu	Nanjing
236	NJ 1013	9/2007 - 11/2007	Jiangsu	Nanjing
237	NJ 1014	9/2007 - 11/2007	Jiangsu	Nanjing
238	NJ 1015	9/2007 - 11/2007	Jiangsu	Nanjing
239	NJ 1016	9/2007 - 11/2007	Jiangsu	Nanjing
240	NJ 1017	9/2007 - 11/2007	Jiangsu	Nanjing
241	NJ 1018	9/2007 - 11/2007	Jiangsu	Nanjing
242	NJ 1019	9/2007 - 11/2007	Jiangsu	Nanjing
243	NJ 1020	9/2007 - 11/2007	Jiangsu	Nanjing
244	NJ 1021	9/2007 - 11/2007	Jiangsu	Nanjing
245	NJ 1022	9/2007 - 11/2007	Jiangsu	Nanjing
246	NJ 1023	9/2007 - 11/2007	Jiangsu	Nanjing
247	NJ 1025	9/2007 - 11/2007	Jiangsu	Nanjing
248	NJ 1026	9/2007 - 11/2007	Jiangsu	Nanjing
249	NJ 1027	9/2007 - 11/2007	Jiangsu	Nanjing
250	NJ 1028	9/2007 - 11/2007	Jiangsu	Nanjing

251	NJ 1029	9/2007 - 11/2007	Jiangsu	Nanjing
252	NJ 1030	9/2007 - 11/2007	Jiangsu	Nanjing
253	NJ 1031	9/2007 - 11/2007	Jiangsu	Nanjing
254	NJ 1032	9/2007 - 11/2007	Jiangsu	Nanjing
255	NJ 1033	9/2007 - 11/2007	Jiangsu	Nanjing
256	NJ 1034	9/2007 - 11/2007	Jiangsu	Nanjing
257	NJ 1035	9/2007 - 11/2007	Jiangsu	Nanjing
258	NJ 1036	9/2007 - 11/2007	Jiangsu	Nanjing
259	NJ 1037	9/2007 - 11/2007	Jiangsu	Nanjing
260	NJ 1038	9/2007 - 11/2007	Jiangsu	Nanjing
261	NJ 1039	9/2007 - 11/2007	Jiangsu	Nanjing
262	NJ 1040	9/2007 - 11/2007	Jiangsu	Nanjing
263	NJ 1041	9/2007 - 11/2007	Jiangsu	Nanjing
264	NJ 1042	9/2007 - 11/2007	Jiangsu	Nanjing
265	NJ 1043	9/2007 - 11/2007	Jiangsu	Nanjing
266	NJ 1044	9/2007 - 11/2007	Jiangsu	Nanjing
267	NJ 1045	9/2007 - 11/2007	Jiangsu	Nanjing
268	NJ 1046	9/2007 - 11/2007	Jiangsu	Nanjing
269	NJ 1047	9/2007 - 11/2007	Jiangsu	Nanjing
270	NJ 1048	9/2007 - 11/2007	Jiangsu	Nanjing
271	NJ 1049	9/2007 - 11/2007	Jiangsu	Nanjing
272	NJ 1050	9/2007 - 11/2007	Jiangsu	Nanjing
273	NJ 1051	9/2007 - 11/2007	Jiangsu	Nanjing
274	NJ 1052	9/2007 - 11/2007	Jiangsu	Nanjing
275	NJ 1053	9/2007 - 11/2007	Jiangsu	Nanjing
276	DG 1101	2/28/2008	Guangdong	Dongguan
277	DG 1102	2/28/2008	Guangdong	Dongguan
278	DG 1103	2/28/2008	Guangdong	Dongguan
279	DG 1104	2/28/2008	Guangdong	Dongguan
280	DG 1105	2/28/2008	Guangdong	Dongguan
281	DG 1106	3/1/2008	Guangdong	Dongguan
282	DG 1107	4/2/2008	Guangdong	Dongguan

No	Date	Institution Type	Position	Province	City
1	7/25/2007	Legal Aid Center	Staff Lawyer	Beijing	Beijing
2	8/29/2007	Private Enterprise	Director, Human Resources (Shenzhen)	Beijing	Beijing
3	9/18/2007	University Legal Aid Center	Student Volunteer	Beijing	Beijing
4	9/21/2007	Migrant Labor Organization	Organization Founder	Beijing	Beijing
5	9/21/2007	Migrant Labor Organization	Full Time Staff Member	Beijing	Beijing
6	9/22/2007	Migrant Labor Organization	Organization Founder	Beijing	Beijing
7	9/24/2007	People's University	Academic	Beijing	Beijing
8	9/28/2007	China Institute of Industrial Relations	Academic	Beijing	Beijing
9	10/1/2007	Media Institution	Journalist	Beijing	Beijing
10	10/5/2007	Migrant Labor Organization	Full Time Staff Member	Beijing	Beijing
11	10/10/ 2007	People's University	Academic	Beijing	Beijing
12	10/14/ 2007	University Legal Aid Center	Student Volunteers	Beijing	Beijing
13	10/15/ 2007	Migrant Labor Organization	Full Time Staff Member	Beijing	Beijing
14	10/20/ 2007	Beijing Jiaotong University	Academic	Beijing	Beijing
15	10/24/ 2007	Migrant Labor Organization	Organization Founder	Beijing	Beijing
16	10/31/ 2007	Qinghua University	Academic	Beijing	Beijing
17	11/6/2007	Chinese Academy of Social Sciences	Academic	Beijing	Beijing

18	11/8/2007	Unirule Institute of Economics	Academic	Beijing	Beijing
19	11/10/2007	Migrant Labor Organization	Full Time Staff Member	Beijing	Beijing
20	11/10/2007	Migrant Labor Organization	Organization Founder	Beijing	Beijing
21	11/17/2007	Registered Law Firm	Registered Lawyer	Beijing	Beijing
22	12/13/2007	Migrant Labor Organization	Organization Founder	Guangdong	Guangzhou
23	12/14/2007	International NGO#	NGO Representative	China (PRC)	Hong Kong
24	12/19/2007	International NGO	NGO Representative	United States	District of Columbia
25	1/12/2008	Migrant Labor Organization	Organization Founder	Guangdong	Shenzhen
26	1/13/2008	Private Enterprise	Owner	Guangdong	Shenzhen
27	1/13/2008	Migrant Labor Organization	Full Time Staff Member	Guangdong	Shenzhen
28	1/29/2008	Migrant Labor Organization	Organization Founder	Guangdong	Shenzhen
29	2/12/2008	Shenzhen Municipal Labor Arbitration	Arbitration Official	Guangdong	Shenzhen
30	2/15/2008	Public Interest Rep.	Grassroots organization	Guangdong	Shenzhen
31	2/19/2008	Registered Law Firm	Registered Lawyer	Guangdong	Shenzhen
32	2/26/2008	Registered Law Firm	Registered Lawyer	Guangdong	Shenzhen
33	3/25/2008	People's University	Academic	Guangdong	Guangzhou
34	4/1/2008	Government Legal Aid Center	Lawyer	Jiangsu	Changzhou
35	4/14/2008	Public Interest Rep.	Grassroots organization	Jiangsu	Changzhou
36	4/19/2008	Private Enterprise	Director, Human Resources (Changzhou)	Jiangsu	Changzhou

37	4/22/2008	Jiangsu Province Migrant Labor Office	Office Head	Jiangsu	Nanjing
38	5/4/2008	Migrant Labor Organization	Organization Founder	Guangdong	Shenzhen
39	5/7/2008	Government Legal Aid Center	Lawyer	Jiangsu	Nanjing
40	8/12/2008	Migrant Labor Organization*	Organization Founder	Beijing	Beijing
41	12/13/2008	Migrant Labor Organization	Organization Founder	Guangdong	Guangzhou
42	12/14/2008	Migrant Labor Organization	Organization Founder	Guangdong	Zhuhai

* = Interview conducted in Washington, DC. # = Interview conducted in Shenzhen, Guangdong.

Appendix C. Migrant Labor's Use of Traditional Media Sources

Question 1. I see examples of labor disputes in the media (television, newspapers, or radio) that are very similar to my own experiences.

Question 2. Seeing examples of labor disputes in the traditional media (television, newspapers, or radio) can help me resolve my own labor dispute.

Q.1 Completely Agree	Q.2 Completely Agree	5%
Q.1 Completely Agree	Q.2 Agree	4%
Q.1 Agree	Q.2 Completely Agree	2%
Q.1 Agree	Q.2 Agree	49%
Total		**60%**
Q.1 Completely Agree	Q.2 Disagree	3%
Q.1 Completely Agree	Q.2 Completely Disagree	2%
Q.1 Agree	Q.2 Disagree	15%
Q.1 Agree	Q.2 Completely Disagree	3%
Q.1 Disagree	Q.2 Completely Agree	1%
Q.1 Disagree	Q.2 Agree	3%
Q.1 Disagree	Q.2 Disagree	8%
Q.1 Disagree	Q.2 Completely Disagree	1%
Q.1 Completely Disagree	Q.2 Completely Agree	0%
Q.1 Completely Disagree	Q.2 Agree	1%
Q.1 Completely Disagree	Q.2 Disagree	0%
Q.1 Completely Disagree	Q.2 Completely Disagree	2%
Total		**40%**

Bibliography

10th National People's Congress. 2007. *Law of the People's Republic of China on Promotion of Employment*. http://www.npc.gov.cn/englishnpc/Law/2009-02/20/content_1471590.htm.

"2005 National Social Order and Public Stability Criminal Records Fall for First Time After Rising, [2005 Quanguo Shehuizhian Wending Xingshi Lian Shouci Huiluo] 2005全国社会治安稳定 刑事立案首次回落." 2006. *Xinhuanet*. January 19. http://news.xinhuanet.com/legal/2006-01/19/content_4072115.htm.

"45% of Migrant Workers Protect their Rights Through Mass Incidents." 2011. *Henan Business Daily*. September 17. http://ztc.heshan.gov.cn/2011/201109/20110917233112.html.

"5.8% of Workers Returning Home Have Wages in Arrears [Fanxiang Nongmingong 5.8% Bei Tuoqian Gongzi] 国家统计局：返乡农民工中5.8%被拖欠工资." 2009. *China Economy Net [Zhongguo Jingjiwang]*. March 25. http://news.aweb.com.cn/2009/3/25/11720090325142060.html.

"A Journalist's Investigation in Beijing: The Procedures for the Application of a Temporary Residency Permit Is Chaotic; Types of Application Fee Are Confusing." 2002. *Lifestyles*, October.

Agence France Presse. 2012. "Foxconn Shuts Plant after 2,000-Person Brawl." *Mother Nature Network*. September 24. http://www.mnn.com/money/sustainable-business-practices/stories/foxconn-shuts-plant-after-2000-person-brawl#.

"Agencies Responsible for Censorship in China." 2014. *Congressional-Executive Commission on China*. Accessed February 16. http://www.cecc.gov/agencies-responsible-for-censorship-in-china.

All-China Federation of Trade Unions Editorial Department. 2003. "2003 Notice on Better Protection for the Legal Rights of Migrant Workers [Guanyu Qieshi Zuohao Weihu Jincheng Wugong Renyuan Hefa Quanyi Gongzuo de Tongzhi] 中华全国总工会:关于切实做好维护进城务工人员合法权益工作的通知." August 4. http://www.people.com.cn/GB/guandian/8213/8309/28296/2078168.html.

———. 2010. "ACFTU: Regarding Research Report on New Generation of Migrant Workers [Quanguo Zonggonghui: Guanyu Xinshengdai Nongmingong Wenti Yanjiu Baogao] 全国总工会：关于新生代农民工问题的研究报告." *Worker Daily*, June 21. http://acftu.people.com.cn/GB/67560/11923670.html.

———. 2012. *2010 Chinese Trade Unions Yearbook*. Beijing: China Statistics Press.

Al-mahmood Syed Zain. 2013. "Bangladesh Urges Raise in Garment Industry's Minimum Wage." *The Wall Street Journal*. November 5. http://online.wsj.com/news/articles/SB10001424052702303936904579177779284719936.

"Analysis of China's Non-Commercial Web Site Registration Regulation." 2006. Bulletin 011. https://opennet.net/bulletins/011/#3.

211

"Annual Data 1996-2013." 2014. *National Bureau of Statistics*. Accessed February 27. http://www.stats.gov.cn/english/statisticaldata/AnnualData/.

Anonymous. "My Friend [Wode Pengyou]." *Fellow Worker*.

Bannister, Judith. 1993. "China: Population Changes and the Economy." In *China's Economic Dilemmas in the 1990s*. New York: M.E. Sharpe.

Barboza, David, and Keith Bradsher. 2010. "In China, a Labor Movement Aided by Modern Technology." *The New York Times*. June 16. http://www.nytimes.com/2010/06/17/business/global/17strike.html?pagewanted=1&_r=1&.

———. 2012. "Foxconn Plant in China Closed After Worker Riot." *The New York Times*. September 24. http://www.nytimes.com/2012/09/25/technology/foxconn-plant-in-china-closed-after-worker-riot.html?_r=1&.

Becker, Jeffrey. 2012. "The Knowledge to Act: Chinese Migrant Labor Protests in Comparative Perspective." *Comparative Political Studies* 45 (11): 1379–1404.

Beijing Investigation Team of the National Bureau of Statistics. 2014. "Beijing 2009 National Economy and Social Development Statistics Report [Beijingshi 2009 Nian Guomin Jingji he Shehui Fazhan Tongji Gongbao] 北京市2009年国民经济和社会发展统计公报." Annual Report. Beijing: Beijing Bureau of Statistics. Accessed February 16. http://www.bjstats.gov.cn/xwgb/tjgb/ndgb/201002/t20100202_165217.htm.

"Beijing Migrant Labor Legal Aid Work Station Website." *Beijing Migrant Labor Legal Aid Work Station Website*. http://www.zgnmg.org/zhi/about/index.asp.

Beijing Migrant Worker Legal Aid Station. 2007. "Protecting Migrant Labor Rights, The Road Is Long - The Wage Arrears Case of Yang Jiang and 47 Workers Mingong Weiquan – Lu You Duoyuan – Yang Jiang Deng 47 Bei Tuoqian Gongzi An]." Beijing. http://www.zxd.org.cn.

———. "Labor Contractor Flees with the Money, What Do Migrant Workers Do? The Non-payment of Wages Case of Geng Shijing and 66 Other Migrant Workers [Baogongtou Juanqian Taopaole Nongmingong Zenmeban? Geng Shijing Deng 66 Ming Nongmingong Bei Tuoqian Gongzi]." Beijing Migrant Worker Legal Aid Station: Safeguarding Rights Case Examples. Beijing: Beijing Migrant Worker Legal Aid Station. http://www.zgnmg.org/zhi/wqal/3txt.asp?id=31.

Beijing Municipal Statistics Bureau. 2007. *Beijing Statistical Yearbook*. Beijing: China Statistics Press.

Bellin, Eva. 2000. "Contingent Democrats." *World Politics* 52 (2): 175–205.

———. 2002. *Stalled Democracies*. Ithaca, NY: Cornell University Press.

Bergquist, Charles. 1984. *Labor in the Capitalist World Economy*. Beverley Hills: Sage.

Bernstein, Thomas P., and Xiaobo Lu. 2003. *Taxation Without Representation in Contemporary China*. Cambridge: Cambridge University Press.

Bian, Yanjie. 1997. "Bringing Strong Ties Back In: Indirect Ties, Network Bridges, and Job Searches in China." *American Sociology Review* 62 (June): 366–85.

Blecher, Marc J. 2002. "Hegemony and Workers' Politics in China." *The China Quarterly* 170 (June). doi:10.1017/S0009443902000190. http://www.journals.cambridge.org/abstract_S0009443902000190.

Brady, Brendan. 2010. "Cambodia Garment Workers Protest Low Pay." *Los Angeles Times*. September 19. http://articles.latimes.com/2010/sep/19/world/la-fg-cambodia-garment-strike-20100919.

Brandt, Loren, and Thomas G. Rawski, ed. 2008. *China's Great Economic Transformation*. Cambridge; New York: Cambridge University Press.

"Breaking the Impasse: Promoting Worker Involvement in the Collective Bargaining and Contracts Process." 2007. China Labor Bulletin Research Reports. China Labor Bulletin. http://www.clb.org.hk/en/node/50693.

Bristow, Michael. 2009. "Chinese Delegate Has 'No Power.'" *BBC News, Asia-Pacific*. March 4. http://news.bbc.co.uk/2/hi/asia-pacific/7922720.stm.

Brown, Ronald C. 2010. *Understanding Labor and Employment Law in China*. Cambridge; New York: Cambridge University Press.

Bu, Kitty. 2008. "Beijing Olympic Clean up Sweeps out Migrant Workers." *Reuters*. July 21. http://www.reuters.com/article/2008/07/21/us-olympics-migrants-idUSSP26521520080721.

Buckley, Chris. 2011. "China Internal Security Spending Jumps Past Army Budget." *Reuters*. March 5. http://in.reuters.com/article/2011/03/05/industry-us-china-unrest-idIN-TRE7222RA20110305.

Bueno de Mesquita, Bruce, and George W. Downs. 2005. "Development and Democracy." *Foreign Affairs* 84 (5): 77–86.

"Bureau of Statistics: Chinese Migrant Workers Totaled 225.42 Million at the End of 2008." 2009. *Chinanews.com*. March 25. http://www.chinanews.com/cj/kong/news/2009/03-25/1616960.shtml.

Cai, Fang. 2007a. "Demographic Analysis of Surplus Labor in Rural China [Nongcun Shengyu Laodongli de Renkouxue Fenxi]." In *Green Book of Population and Labor*. Beijing: Social Science Academic Press.

———. , ed. 2007b. *Green Book of Population and Labor*. Beijing: Social Science Academic Press.

Cai, Fang, Yang Du, and Meiyan Wang. 2009. "Migration and Labor Mobility in China." United Nations Human Development Research Paper.

Cai, Fang, Albert Park, and Yaohui Zhao. 2008. "The Chinese Labor Market in the Reform Era." In *China's Great Economic Transformation*. New York: Cambridge University Press.

Cai, Fang, Du Yang, and Meiyan Wang. 2001. "Household Registration System and Employment Protection." *Journal of Economic Research [Jingji Yanjiu]*, no. 12: 41–49.

Cambodia Ministry of Tourism. 2012. "Tourism Statistics Annual Report 2012". Phnom Penh, Cambodia. http://www.tourismcambodia.org/images/mot/statistic_reports/tourism_statistics_annual_report_2012.pdf.

Cao, Zewei. 2003. "Migrant Workers' Reestablished Social Networks and Inner Network Resources [Nongmingong de Zaijiangou Shihuiwang Yu Wangnei Ziyuan Liuxiang]." *Sociological Research*, no. 3: 99–110.

Card, David. 1990. "Strikes and Bargaining: A Survey of the Recent Empirical Literature." *American Economic Review* 80 (2).

Carothers, Thomas, ed. 2006. *Promoting the Rule of Law Abroad: In Search of Knowledge*. Washington, DC: Carnegie Endowment for International Peace.

Carrillo, Beatriz, and David S. G. Goodman. 2012. *Peasants and Workers in the Transformation of Urban China*. Cheltenham: Edward Elgar.

CDRI. 2007. "Youth Migration and Urbanisation in Cambodia." 36. Phnom Penh, Cambodia. http://www.cdri.org.kh/webdata/download/wp/wp36e.pdf.

"CECC Political Prisoner Database." 2014. *Congressional Executive Commission on China*. Accessed February 16. http://ppdcecc.gov/QueryResultsDetail.aspx?PrisonerNum=7682.

Chan, Anita. 2001. *China's Workers under Assult: The Exploitation of Labor in a Globalizing Economy*. Asia and the Pacific. Armonk, NY: M.E. Sharpe.

———. 2005. "Recent Trends in China Labour Issues – Signs of Change." *China Perspectives* 57 (February). http://chinaperspectives.revues.org/1115.

Chan, Anita, and Irene Norlund. 1998. "Vietnamese and Chinese Labour Regimes: On the Road to Divergence." *The China Journal* 40 (July): 173–97.

Chan, Anita, and Kaxton Siu. 2012. "Chinese Migrant Workers: Factors Constraining the Emergence of Class Consciousness." In *China's Peasants and Workers: Changing Class Identities*. London: Edward Elgar.

Chan, Anita, and Hong-zen Wang. 2004. "The Impact of the State on Workers' Conditions: Comparing Taiwanese Factories in China and Vietnam." *Pacific Affairs* 77 (4): 629–46.

Chan, Chris King-Chi. 2010. *The Challenge of Labour in China: Strikes and the Changing Labour Regime in Global Factories*. China Policy Series 16. London; New York: Routledge.

Chan, Chris King-Chi, and Pun Ngai. 2009. "The Making of a New Working Class? A Study of Collective Actions of Migrant Workers in South China." *The China Quarterly* 198 (June): 287. doi:10.1017/S0305741009000319.

Chan, Jenny, and Ngai Pun. 2010. "Suicide as Protest for the New Generation of Chinese Migrant Workers: Foxconn, Global Capital, and the State." *The Asia-Pacific Journal* 37 (September). http://japanfocus.org/-Jenny-Chan/3408#sthash.TRsgI2C6.dpuf.

Chan, John. 2011. "Clashes Highlight the Plight of Migrant Workers in China." *World Socialist Web Site*. June 17. http://www.wsws.org/en/articles/2011/06/chin-j17.html.

Chan, Kam Wing. 2009. "The Chinese Hukou System at 50." *Eurasian Geography and Economics* 50 (2): 197–221. doi:10.2747/1539-7216.50.2.197.

———. 2010. "A China Paradox: Migrant Labor Shortage amidst Rural Labor Supply Abundance." *Eurasian Geography and Economics* 51 (4): 513–30. doi:10.2747/1539-7216.51.4.513.

Changzhou Bureau of Statistics. 2014. "Changzhou Statistical Information Network." *Changzhou Statistical Information Network*. Accessed March 5. http://www.cztjj.gov.cn/.

Chen, Dahong. 2007. "Employment of Rural Migrants in 2007 and Labor Demand in the Spring of 2007 [Nongcun Waichu Wugong Renyuan 2006 Nian Jiuye Qingkuang He Qiye 2007 Nian Chunli Yonggong Xuqiu Diaocha Fenxi]." In *Green Book of Population and Labor*. Beijing: Social Science Academic Press.

Chen, Feng. 2000. "Subsistence Crises, Managerial Corruption and Labour Protests in China." *The China Journal* 44 (July): 41–63.

———. 2004a. "Between the State and Labour: The Conflict of Chinese Trade Unions' Double Identity in Market Reform." *The China Quarterly* 176 (February). doi:10.1017/S0305741003000596. http://www.journals.cambridge.org/abstract_S0305741003000596.

———. 2004b. "Legal Mobilization by Trade Unions: The Case of Shanghai." *The China Journal* 52 (July): 27–45.

———. 2013. "Against the State: Labor Protests in China in the 1950s." *Modern China*, September. doi:10.1177/0097700413498201. http://mcx.sagepub.com/cgi/doi/10.1177/0097700413498201.

"Chen Xiwen: Social Development Opportunities and Challenges from the Flow of Migrant Workers [Chen Xiwen: Nongmingong Liudong wei Shehui Fazhang Dailai Jiyu yu Tiaozhan]." 2008. *The Peasant Daily*, September 16.

Cheng, Joseph Y. S., Kinglun Ngok, and Wenjia Zhuang. 2010. "The Survival and Development Space for China's Labor NGOs: Informal Politics and Its Uncertainty." *Asian Survey* 50 (6): 1082–1106. doi:10.1525/as.2010.50.6.1082.

Chengdu Municipal Government. 2010. "Management Approach for Guarding Against Migrant Worker Unpaid Wages in the Construction Industry in Chengdu City [Chengdushi Jianshe Lingyu Fangfan Tuoqian Nongmingong Gongzi Guangli Banfa] 成都市建设领域防范拖欠农民工工资管理办法." http://www.cdbpu.chengdu.gov.cn/wenjian/detail.jsp?id=6bmflhnm1Dc8J2NFS04e&ClassID=07030202090101.

China Development Research Foundation. 2013. *China's New Urbanization Strategy*. Routledge Studies on the Chinese Economy 49. New York: Routledge.

China Internet Network Information Center. 2010. "Statistical Survey Report on the Internet Development in China." http://www1.cnnic.cn/IDR/ReportDownloads/201209/P020120904421102801754.pdf.

"China Issues New Regulations on Labour Dispute Resolution – Seeks to Create Early Warning System." 2011. *China Labour Bulletin*. December 13. http://www.clb.org.hk/en/node/101194.

China Labor News Translations. 2008. "The Emergence of Real Trade Unionism in Wal-Mart Stores." *China Labor News Translations*. May 4. http://www.clntranslations.org/article/30/draft.

China Labor Watch. 2010. "Case Research: Foxconn (Honghai) Science and Technology Group [Anlie Yanjiu: Fushikang (Honghai) Keji Jituan]." China Labor Watch.

China Labour Bulletin. 2005. "Deadly Dust: The Silicosis Epidemic among Guangdong Jewelry Workers and the Defects of China's Occupational Illnesses Prevention and Compensation System." China Labor Bulletin Research Reports. China Labor Bulletin. http://www.clb.org.hk/en/fs/view/downloadables/Deadly_Dust_Dec2005.pdf.

———. 2007. "Speaking Out: The Workers Movement in China: 2005-2006." China Labor Bulletin Research Reports. Hong Kong: China Labor Bulletin.

———. 2009. "Going It Alone: The Workers' Movement in China (2007-2008)." China Labor Bulletin Research Reports. Hong Kong: China Labor Bulletin. http://www.clb.org.hk/en/files/share/File/research_reports/workers_movement_07-08.pdf.

————. 2009. "Protecting Workers' Rights or Serving the Party: The Way Forward for China's Trade Unions." China Labor Bulletin Research Reports. China Labor Bulletin. http://www.clb.org.hk/en/files/share/File/research_reports/acftu_report.pdf.

————. 2010. "The Hard Road: Seeking Justice for Victims of Pneumoconiosis in China." China Labor Bulletin Research Reports. China Labor Bulletin. http://www.clb.org.hk/en/files/share/File/research_reports/Hard_Road.pdf.

————. 2011. "Unity Is Strength: The Workers' Movement in China: 2009-2011." China Labor Bulletin Research Reports. Hong Kong: China Labor Bulletin. http://www.clb.org.hk/en/node/101134.

————. 2013a. "Report Claims Coal Mine Deaths in China Fell by One Third in 2012." *China Labour Bulletin.* January 29. http://www.clb.org.hk/en/node/110204.

————. 2013b. "Time to Pay the Bill: China's Obligation to Victims of Pneumoconiosis." China Labor Bulletin Research Reports. Hong Kong: China Labor Bulletin. http://www.clb.org.hk/en/sites/default/files/File/research_reports/Time%20to%20Pay%20the%20Bill.pdf.

"China Pays Internet Users to Flood Web Forums with pro-Government Propaganda." 2011. *News.com.au.* May 16. http://www.news.com.au/technology/chinese-government-pays-internet-users-to-troll-comment-forums-with-pro-government-propaganda/story-e6frfro0-1226056659550.

"China Says It Saw a Drop in Mining Deaths in 2013." 2014. *Associated Press*, January 6. http://www.chinamining.org/News/2014-01-06/1388990236d65412.html.

"China's Constitutional Framework." 2014. *Congressional-Executive Commission on China.* Accessed February 16. http://www.cecc.gov/resources/legal-provisions/china's-constitutional-framework.

"China's Pneumoconiosis Victims Take Drastic Steps in Their Search for Compensation." http://www.clb.org.hk/en/node/100533.

"Chinese Police Crack Down on Guangdong Protesters." 2012. *Voice of America.* June 28. http://www.voanews.com/content/china-guangdong-crackdown/1275545.html.

"Chinese Police Restore Order to Restive Town." 2011. *The Wall Street Journal.* June 15. http://online.wsj.com/news/articles/SB10001424052702304665904576385420593195718?mg=reno64-wsj&url=http%3A%2F%2Fonline.wsj.com%2Farticle%2FSB100014240527023046659045763854205 93195718.html.

Civil Rights and Livelihood Watch. 2007. "Succession of Pearl River Delta Labor Rights Activists Attacked By Thugs [Zhusanjiao Laogong Weiquan Renshi Lianxu Zao Baotu Xiji]." http://www.msguancha.com/Article/ShowArticle.asp?ArticleID=826.

Cohen, Noam. 2009. "Twitter on the Barricades - Six Lessons Learned." *The New York Times.* June 20. http://www.nytimes.com/2009/06/21/weekinreview/21cohenweb.html?_r=1&.

Congressional Executive Commission on China. 2008. "Annual Report 2008". United States One Hundred Tenth Congress. http://www.gpo.gov/fdsys/pkg/CHRG-110hhrg45233/pdf/CHRG-110hhrg45233.pdf.

Crothall, Geoffrey. 2010. "SCMP: Bargaining Power." *China Labor Bulletin.* June 2. http://www.clb.org.hk/en/node/100775.

Dagongzhe. 2007. *Workers Winning Step by Step [Dagong Bubuwei Yin].* Shenzhen: Dagongzhe.

Demick, Barbara. 2009a. "140 Slain as Chinese Riot Police, Muslims Clash in Northwestern City." *L.A. Times,* July 6.

————. 2009b. "Chinese Riot Police, Muslims Clash in Northwestern City." *Los Angeles Times.* July 6. http://articles.latimes.com/2009/jul/06/world/fg-china-protest6.

Deng, Guosheng. 2010. "The Hidden Rules Governing China's Unregistered NGOs: Management and Consequences." *The China Review* 10 (1).

Deng, Yanhua, and Kevin J. O'Brien. 2013. "Relational Repression in China: Using Social Ties to Demobilize Protesters." *The China Quarterly* 215 (July): 533–52. doi:10.1017/S0305741013000714.

Department of Rural Social Economy Surveys, National Bureau of Statistics. 2008. *China Rural Household Survey Statistical Yearbook 2007.* Beijing: China Statistics Press.

Devnath, Arun. 2013. "Bangladesh Labor Protests on Wages Shut 100 Garment Factories." *Bloomberg News*. November 12. http://www.bloomberg.com/news/2013-11-12/bangladesh-labor-protests-on-wages-shut-100-garment-factories.html.

Deyo, Frederic C. 1989. *Beneath the Miracle: Labor Subordination in the New Asian Industrialism*. Berkeley: University of California Press.

Diamant, Neil, Stanley B. Lubman, and Kevin J. O'Brien, ed. 2010. *Engaging the Law in China: State, Society, and Possibilities for Justice*. Stanford: Stanford University Press.

Dickson, Bruce J. 2000. "Cooptation and Corporatism in China: The Logic of Party Adaptation." *Political Science Quarterly* 115 (4): 517–40. doi:10.2307/2657608.

———. 2003. *Red Capitalists in China: The Party, Private Entrepreneurs, and Prospects for Political Change*. Cambridge Modern China Series. Cambridge, UK; New York: Cambridge University Press.

———. 2008. *Wealth into Power: The Communist Party's Embrace of China's Private Sector*. Cambridge; New York: Cambridge University Press.

Dong, Baohua, and Runqing Dong. 2007. *Case Analysis on Latest PRC Labor Contract Law*. Beijing: China Law Press.

Dong, Ruifang. 2009. "Early Warning Group Events." *Outlook*. http://lw.xinhuanet.com/htm/content_4254.htm.

EastWestNorthSouth, trans. 2010. "With a Whimper and Not a Bang." *Beijing Times*, July 13. http://www.zonaeuropa.com/201007b.brief.htm#003.

Edin, Maria. 1998. "Why Do Chinese Local Cadres Promote Growth? Institutional Incentives and Constraints of Local Cadres." *Forum for Development Studies* 25 (1): 97–127. doi:10.1080/08039410.1998.9666077.

Elfstrom, Manfred. 2014. "China Strikes - Mapping Labor Unrest across China." *China Strikes*. Accessed February 25. https://chinastrikes.crowdmap.com/main.

Eli Friedman. 2012. "Getting Through the Hard Times Together? Chinese Workers and Unions Respond to the Economic Crisis." *Journal of Industrial Relations* 54 (4): 459–75. doi:10.1177/0022185612448762.

Emerson, John Philip. 2009. "Urban School-Leavers and Unemployment in China." *The China Quarterly* 93 (February): 1. doi:10.1017/S0305741000016143.

"End Begging for Wages, Editorials." 2011. *China Daily*. December 8. http://usa.chinadaily.com.cn/opinion/2011-12/08/content_14230430.htm.

"Ethnic Tensions Spark Brawl at China Factory." 2009. *Reuters*. June 26. http://www.reuters.com/article/2009/06/27/idUSHKG364598.

Fabre, Guilhem, and Victor G Rodwin. 2011. "Public Health and Medical Care for the World's Factory: China's Pearl River Delta Region." *BMC Medicine* 9 (1): 110. doi:10.1186/1741-7015-9-110.

Feng, Tu, and Hanxin Lu. 2008. "Garment Boss Killed: Confrontation with Worker Possible Cause [Yiyin Zhengduo Gongren Zhiyi Laoban Bei Sha]." *Southern Metropolitan Daily*, April 3.

Fifth Session of the Seventh National People's Congress. 1992. "Trade Union Law of the People's Republic of China." http://www.lehmanlaw.com/resource-centre/laws-and-regulations/labor/trade-union-law-of-the-peoples-republic-of-china-1992.html.

Foster, Peter. 2009. "Chinese Worker Blows Himself up over Unpaid Wage Claim." *The Telegraph*. April 3. http://www.telegraph.co.uk/news/worldnews/asia/china/5100613/Chinese-worker-blows-himself-up-over-unpaid-wage-claim.html.

Friedman, Eli. "China in Revolt." *The Jacobin*.

Fu, He. 2007. "Who Did Dagongzhe Offend? [Dagongzhe Zhongxin Dezuile Shui?] 打工者中心得罪了谁?" *Nanjng Daily*. November 28. http://nd.oeeee.com/H/html/2007-11/28/content_322157.htm.

Gallagher, Mary E. 2007a. *Contagious Capitalism Globalization and the Politics of Labor in China*. Princeton, NJ; Woodstock: Princeton University Press. http://site.ebrary.com/id/10477105.

———. 2007b. "Hope For Protection and Hopeless Choices." In *Grassroots Political Reform in Contemporary China*. Cambridge: Harvard University Press.

Gallagher, Mary E., and Junlu Jiang. 2002. "Guest Editors' Introduction." *Chinese Law & Government* 35 (6): 3–15. doi:10.2753/CLG0009-460935063.

Gates, H. 1979. "Dependency and the Part-Time Proletariat in Taiwan." *Modern China* 5 (3): 381–407. doi:10.1177/009770047900500305.

Geary, Dick. 1984. *European Labour Protest 1848-1939*. London: Methuen.

General Office of the State Council. 2003. "Notice of the General Office of the State Council on Settlement of Delinquent Construction Project Costs in the Construction Business [Guanyu Qieshi Jiejue Jianshe Lingyu Tuoqian Gongchengkuan Wenti de Tongzhi] 国办关于切实解决建设领域拖欠工程款问题的通知." http://news.xinhuanet.com/zhengfu/2003-12/15/content_1231226.htm.

George, Omana. 2007. "Khambhat Exchange." *Asia Monitor Resource Centre*. September 28. http://www.amrc.org.hk/alu_special/ohs/state_and_corporate_neglect_of_occupational_health_and_safety_in_taiwan.

Gilboy, George J., and Eric Heginbotham. 2004. "The Latin Americanization of China?" *Current History* 103 (674): 256.

Givan, Rebecca Kolins, Kenneth M. Roberts, and Sarah Anne Soule, ed. 2010. *The Diffusion of Social Movements: Actors, Mechanisms, and Political Effects*. Cambridge; New York: Cambridge University Press.

———. 2011. "The Dimensions of Diffusion." In *The Diffusion of Social Movements: Actors, Mechanisms, and Political Effects*. Cambridge: Cambridge University Press.

Golub, Steven. 2006. "The Legal Empowerment Alternative." In *Promoting the Rule of Law Abroad*. Washington, DC: Carnegie Endowment for International Peace.

Granovetter, Mark. 1973. "The Strength of Weak Ties." *American Journal of Sociology* 78 (6): 1360. doi:10.1086/225469.

———. 1983. "The Strength of Weak Ties: A Network Theory Revisited." *Sociological Theory* 1: 201. doi:10.2307/202051.

Guangzhou Municipal Statistics Bureau. 2008. *Guangzhou Statistical Yearbook*. Beijing: China Statistics Press.

Gurr, Ted Robert. 1970. *Why Men Rebel*. Boulder, CO.: Paradigm Pub.

Halegua, Aaron. 2008. "Getting Paid: Processing the Labor Disputes of China's Migrant Workers." *Berkeley Journal of International Law* 26 (254).

Han, Dongfang. 2008. "The Prospects for Legal Enforcement of Labor Rights in China Today: A Glass Half Full." Congressional Testimony. http://www.clb.org.hk/en/files/File/HDF%20testimony%20for%20CECC%20hearing%20June%202008(1).pdf.

Harney, Alexandra. 2004. "Going Home: Chinese Migrant Workers Shun Long Factory Hours and Low Pay." *Financial Times*, November 3. http://www.ft.com/cms/s/0/d6ead458-2d4a-11d9-8b8d-00000e2511c8.html#axzz2PoUpr3bB.

He, Huifeng. 2008. "No Rest for Busiest Judges on Mainland." *South China Morning Post*, December.

Hirschman, Albert O. 2004. *Exit, Voice, and Loyalty: Responses to Decline in Firms, Organizations, and States*. Cambridge, MA: Harvard University Press.

Ho, Sam P. S. 1994. *Rural China in Transition: Non-Agricultural Development in Rural Jiangsu, 1978-1990*. Studies on Contemporary China. Oxford; New York: Clarendon Press ; Oxford University Press.

Ho, Virginia Harper. 2003. *Labor Dispute Resolution in China: Implications for Labor Rights and Legal Reform*. China Research Monograph 59. Berkeley, Calif: Institute of East Asian Studies, University of California - Berkeley.

Hong Kong Liaison Office (IHLO). 2010. "Imprisoned Labour Rights Activists in China". International Trade Union Federation – Global Union Federation (ITUC/GUF).

Hook, Leslie. 2011. "Beijing Raises Spending on Internal Security." *Financial Times*, March 6. http://www.ft.com/intl/cms/s/0/f70936b0-4811-11e0-b323-00144feab49a.html#axzz1ZdoAdFdF.

Howell, Jude A, ed. 2004. *Governance in China*. Lanham, MD: Rowman & Littlefield Publishers.

———. 2008. "Civil Society and Migrants in China." In *Labour Migration and Social Development in Contemporary China*. New York: Routledge.

————. 2009. "All-China Federation of Trades Unions beyond Reform? The Slow March of Direct Elections." *The China Quarterly* 196 (January): 845. doi:10.1017/S030574100800115X.

Hsing, You-tien. 2012. *The Great Urban Transformation: Politics of Land and Property in China.* Oxford: Oxford University Press.

Hu, Jian. 2006. "An Analysis of the Organizational Factors in Our Nation's Labor Inspection Protection Regime [Woguo Laodong Baozhang Jiancha Gongneng Queshi de Zuzhi Yinsu Fenxi]." *Contemporary Manager.*

Huang, Ping, and Genevieve Domenach-Chich. 2012. *Urban Migrants and Poverty Reduction in China.* [Reading, England]; [Beijing]: Paths International Ltd.; Social Sciences Academic Press.

Huang, Ping, and Shaohua Zhan. 2005. "Internal Migration in China: Linking It to Development." in vol. 14–16. Lanzhou, China.

Huang, Yan. 2007. "Workers' 'Self Help' Efforts Under Globalisation [Quanqiuhua Beijingxia de Laogong Zijiu] 全球化背景下的劳工自救." *Southern Window*, November 15. http://news.sina.com.cn/c/2007-11-15/122014311592.shtml.

Hui, Cheng. 2009. "Giving Tiaolou the Third Degree: Why Do We Sympathize With Tiaolou Protesters? [Tiaolouxiu de Kaowen: Women Weishenme Tongqing Tiaolouzhe]." *China News Week [Zhongguo Xinwen Zhoukan]* 中国新闻周刊.

Human Rights in China. 2003. "Cautious Welcome: HRIC Response to PRC State Council Decision to Abolish C & R System." *Human Rights in China.* June 22. http://www.renyurenquan.org/ryrq_article.adp?article_id=223.

Hurst, William. 2004. "Understanding Contentious Collective Action by Chinese Laid-off Workers: The Importance of Regional Political Economy." *Studies in Comparative International Development* 39 (2): 94–120. doi:10.1007/BF02686279.

"Implications of the Strike in Honda Auto Parts Manufacturing Co Ltd (CHAM)." 2010. *International Trade Union Federation – Global Union Federation (ITUC/GUF) Hong Kong Liaison Office (IHLO).* July. http://www.ihlo.org/LRC/ACFTU/000710.html.

International Labor Organization. 2007. "Equality at Work: Tackling the Challenges. Global Report under the Follow-up of the ILO Declaration on Fundamental Principles and Rights at Work". Geneva: International Labor Organization. www.ilo.org/wcmsp5/groups/public/---dgreports/---dcomm/---webdev/documents/publication/wcms_082607.pdf.

————. 2010. "Labour and Social Trends in Cambodia 2010." Phnom Penh, Cambodia: National Institute of Statistics.

Jiang, De. 2006. "Nanjing Legal Aid Station Moves into Labor Market [Nanjing Falv Yuanzhuzhan Kaijin Laowu Shichang]." *Legal Daily*, August 9. http://www.jssf.gov.cn/flyz/tbgz/nmg/200610/t20061027_4486.htm.

Jiang, Zemin. 2002. "Build a Well-off Society in an All-Round Way and Create a New Situation in Building Socialism with Chinese Characteristics." http://english.people.com.cn/200211/18/eng20021118_106983.shtml.

Jim, Claire. 2012. "Foxconn China Plant Closed after Clash Involving 2,000." *The Star Online.* September 24. http://www.thestar.com.my/story.aspx/?file=%2f2012%2f9%2f24%2fworldupdates%2f2012-09-24T092210Z_1_BRE88N0B1_RTROPTT_0_UK-HON-HAI&sec=Worldupdates.

Keith, Ronald C. 2001. *Law and Justice in China's New Marketplace.* Houndmills, Basingstoke, Hampshire; New York: Palgrave.

Kelliher, Daniel. 1993. "Keeping Democracy Safe from the Masses: Intellectuals and Elitism in the Chinese Protest Movement." *Comparative Politics* 25 (4): 379. doi:10.2307/422032.

Kennan, John. 1986. "The Economics of Strikes." In *Handbook of Labor Economics.* New York: North-Holland.

Kerr, Clark, John T. Dunlop, Frederick H. Harbison, and Charles A. Myers. 1960. *Industrialism and Industrial Man: The Problems of Labor and Management in Economic Growth.* Cambridge: Harvard University Press.

Knight, John, Quheng Deng, and Shi Li. 2011. "The Puzzle of Migrant Labour Shortage and Rural Labour Surplus in China." *China Economic Review* 22 (4): 585–600. doi:10.1016/j.chieco.2011.01.006.

Korzec, Michel. 1988. "Contract Labor the 'Right to Work' and New Labor Laws in the People's Republic of China." *Comparative Economic Studies* 30 (2): 117–49.

Kuran, Timur. 2011. "Now out of Never: The Element of Surprise in the East European Revolution of 1989." *World Politics* 44 (01): 7–48. doi:10.2307/2010422.

Kurzman, Charles. 1996. "Structural Opportunity and Perceived Opportunity in Social-Movement Theory: The Iranian Revolution of 1979." *American Sociological Review* 61 (1): 153. doi:10.2307/2096411.

Kwok, Kristine. 2004. "Migrant Labour Shuns Back-Breaking Work." *South China Morning Post.* September 10. http://www.scmp.com/article/469829/migrant-labour-shuns-back-breaking-work.

Labor Injury Office of the Nanjing Municipal Human Resource and Social Security Bureau. 2011. "Further Improve the City's Migrant Workers' Compensation Insurance [Jinyibu Wanshan Wo Shi Nongmingong Gongshang Baoxian Zhengce] 进一步完善我市农民工工伤保险政策." *Nanjing Municipal Human Resources and Social Security Bureau.* March 17. http://www.njhrss.gov.cn/38966/38973/38977/201103/t20110317_2189397.html.

"Labor Law Enforcement Recovers 20.08 Billion Yuan in Wages for Workers [Laodong Zhifa Wei Laodongzhe Zhuifa Gongzi Deng Daiyu 200.8 Yiyuan] 劳监执法为劳动者追发工资等待遇200.8亿元." 2013. *Xinhuanet.* May 27. http://news.xinhuanet.com/2013-05/27/c_115927396.htm.

"Labor Law of the People's Republic of China." 2002. *Chinese Law & Government* 35 (6): 16–33. doi:10.2753/CLG0009-4609350616.

"Labour Shortage Bites in the South." 2014. Accessed February 21. http://www.scmp.com/article/469656/labour-shortage-bites-south.

Lam, Willy Wo-Lap. 2006. *Chinese Politics in the Hu Jintao Era New Leaders, New Challenges.* Armonk, NY: M.E. Sharpe. http://public.eblib.com/EBLPublic/PublicView.do?ptiID=302415.

Landry, Pierre, and Yanqi Tong. 2005. "Disputing the Authoritarian State in China." in Annual Meeting of the American Political Science Association, Washington, DC.

Lange, Peter. 1984. "Unions, Workers, and Wage. Regulation: The Rational Bases of Consent." In *Order and Conflict in Contemporary Capitalism.* Oxford: Oxford University Press.

Lardy, Nicholas R. 2012. *Sustaining China's Economic Growth after the Global Financial Crisis.* Washington, DC: Peterson Institute for International Economics.

Lee, Ching Kwan. 1998. *Gender and the South China Miracle: Two Worlds of Factory Women.* Berkeley: University of California Press.

———. 2007. *Against the Law: Labor Protests in China's Rustbelt and Sunbelt.* Berkeley: University of California Press.

Lee, Don. 2004. "Some Owners Deserting Factories in China." *L.A. Times*, September 10.

Lee, Eric, and Benjamin Weinthal. 2014. "Trade Unions: The Revolutionary Social Network at Play in Egypt and Tunisia." *The Guardian.* Accessed February 18. http://www.theguardian.com/commentisfree/2011/feb/10/trade-unions-egypt-tunisia.

Li, Lianjiang. 2004. "Political Trust in Rural China." *Modern China* 30 (2): 228–58. doi:10.1177/0097700403261824.

Li, Peilin. 1996. "Social Network of Rural-Urban Labor Migration in China [Liudong Mingong de Shihui Wangluo He Shihui Diwei]." *Sociological Research.* http://www.unesco.org/most/chlpei.htm.

Li, Xiaofeng. 2005. "Violence at Construction Site, Migrant Workers Demanding Pay Are Thrown into Sewers [Jianzhugongdishang Fasheng Baoli Chongtu Taoxin Mingong Bei Rengjin Choushuigou] 建筑工地上发生暴力冲突 讨薪民工被扔进臭水沟." *Xinhuanet.* May 11. http://news.xinhuanet.com/legal/2005-05/11/content_2943805.htm.

Liao, Leifeng. 2010. "Daily Losses Exceed 200 Million Yuan as Nanhai Honda Strike Takes Heavy Toll [Meitian Chao 2 Yiyuan Sunshi Nanhai Bentian Bagong Yingxiang Juda] 每天超2亿元损失 南海本田罢工影响巨大." *Carschina.com [Qiche Zhongguowang].* May 28. http://www.qi-che.com/yejie/changjiaxinwen/2010052874751.html.

Lieberthal, Kenneth, and Michel Oksenberg. 1988. *Policy Making in China: Leaders, Structures, and Processes.* Princeton, NJ: Princeton University Press.

Liebman, Benjamin. 1999. "Legal Aid and Public Interest Law in China." *Texas International Law Journal* 34: 211–86.

Liu, Huaiqian. 2004. "Thoughts on the Theory That Migrant Workers Are an Integral Part of the Industrial Workforce." *Worker Daily*, October 13.

Liu, Huilong. 2008. "250 Workers Work for 10 Years Without Formal Contract, Stir Up Trouble and Are Dismissed [250 Minggongren Jinchang 10 Nian Meiqian Zhengshi Hetong Shandong Tinggong Beichao]." *Southern Metropolitan Daily*, May 8.

Liu, Kaiming. 2004. *The Price of a Life: China's Industrial Industry Case Research [Shenti de Jiage: Zhongguo Gongshang Suopei Yanjiu]*. Beijing: People's Daily Press.

———. 2005. *A Social Structure of Lost Entitlements*. Shenzhen: Institute of Contemporary Observation.

Liu, Linpin, and Xiangdong Wan. 2007. *Institutional Absence and Labor Shortages*. Beijing: Academy of Social Science Press.

Liu, Sheng. 2004. "The Six Great Difficulties Facing Our Country's Migrant Workers in the Construction Industry [Woguo Jianzhuye Nongmingong Mianlin Liuda Kunnan]." *Beijing Youth Daily*, November.

Liu, Yuzhu. 2000. *The Cultural Situation of Contemporary Chinese Migrant Workers [Dangdai Zhongguo Nongmingong Wenhua Shenghuo Zhuangkuang]*. Social Science Press.

Lo, Vai Io. 1999. *Law and Industrial Relations: China and Japan after World War II*. Studies in Social Policy v. 4. The Hague; Boston: Kluwer Law International.

Lu, Hong, and Shunfeng Song. 2006. "Rural Migrants' Perceptions of Public Safety Protections in Urban China: The Case of Tianjin." *Chinese Economy* 39 (3): 26–41. doi:10.2753/ CES1097-1475390303.

Lubman, Stanley B. 1999. *Bird in a Cage: Legal Reform in China after Mao*. Stanford, CA: Stanford University Press.

Ma, Qiusha. 2009. *Non-Governmental Organizations in Contemporary China Paving the Way to Civil Society?* Routledge.

Marshall, Samantha. 2000. "Vietnam's Urban Migration Spawns Class Questions." *The Wall Street Journal*, February 14.

McAdam, Doug. 1999. *Political Process and the Development of Black Insurgency, 1930–1970*. 2nd ed. Chicago: University of Chicago Press.

McAdam, Doug, John D. McCarthy, and Mayer Zald, eds. 1996. *Comparative Perspectives on Social Movements: Political Opportunities, Mobilizing Structures, and Cultural Framings*. Cambridge Studies in Comparative Politics. Cambridge [England]; New York: Cambridge University Press.

McCarthy, John D., Doug McAdam, and Mayer N. Zald. 1996. "Introduction." In *Comparative Perspectives on Social Movements: Political Opportunities, Mobilizing Structures, and Cultural Framings*. Cambridge [England]; New York: Cambridge University Press.

McCarthy, John D., and Mayer N. Zald. 1977. "Resource Mobilization and Social Movements: A Partial Theory." *American Journal of Sociology* 82 (6): 1212. doi:10.1086/226464.

Meyer, David S. 2004. "Protest and Political Opportunities." *Annual Review of Sociology* 30 (1): 125–45. doi:10.1146/annurev.soc.30.012703.110545.

Michelson, Ethan. 2006. "The Practice of Law as an Obstacle to Justice: Chinese Lawyers at Work." *Law & Society Review* 40 (1): 1–38. doi:10.1111/j.1540-5893.2006.00257.x.

"Migrant Workers Flock to Join China's Trade Unions." 2003. *China.org.cn*. September 21. http://www.china.org.cn/english/MATERIAL/75737.htm.

"Migrant Workers in China." 2008. *China Labor Bulletin*. June 6. http://www.clb.org.hk/en/ node/100259#47.

"Migrant Workers Make Up 70% of Labor Dispute Cases [Laodong Zhengyi Anjian Nongmingong Zhan Qicheng] 劳动争议案件农民工占七成." 2011. *Beijing Youth Daily*, May 17. http://www.bjhd.gov.cn/geren/ldjy/ldsbflfw/201105/t20110517_259045.htm.

"Migrant Workers Riot in East China: Rights Group." 2008. *Agence France Presse*, July 14.

Mikkelsen, Flemming. 1996. "Working-Class Formation in Europe: In Search of a Synthesis." Research Paper 22. International Institute of Social History.

Miller, Tom. 2012. *China's Urban Billion: The Story behind the Biggest Migration in Human History*. Asian Arguments. London; New York: New York: Palgrave Macmillan.

Ministry of Civil Affairs of the People's Republic of China. 2008. "Civil Administration Development Report 2007 [2007 Nian Minzheng Sheye Fazhan Tongji Baogao]." Beijing. http://cws.mca.gov.cn/article/tjkb/.

———. 2012. "2012 Quarterly Statistical Report on the Service Sector [Shihui Fuwuye Tongji Jibao]." 4th Quarter. http://files2.mca.gov.cn/cws/201301/20130128174655179.htm.

Ministry of Construction. 2004. "An Urgent Notice on Stepping up the Resolution of the Issue of Migrant Labor Wages. [Guanyu Jinyibu Jiejue Tuoqian Nongmingong Gongzi Wenti de Jinji Tongzhi]." http://www.hapds.lss.gov.cn/Article/ShowArticle.asp?ArticleID=158.

"Ministry of Human Resources and Social Security: Migrant Worker Wage Arrears Phenomenon Effectively Curbed [Renli Ziyuan Shehui Baozhangbu: Nongmingong Gongzi Tuoqian Xianxiang Dedao Youxiao Ezhi]." 2010. *Xinhuanet.* March 22. http://politics.people.com.cn/GB/1027/14208056.html.

Ministry of Industry and Information Technology. 2011. "2010 National Telecommunications Statistical Report [2010 Nian Qianguo Dianxinye Tongji Gongbao]." http://www.gov.cn/gzdt/2011-01/26/content_1793136.htm.

———. 2014. "Statistical Report on the Situation of China's Internet Development [Zhongguo Hulianwangluo Fazhan Zhuangkuang Tongji Baodao]." http://www.cnnic.net.cn/hlwfzyj/hlwxzbg/hlwtjbg/201401/P020140116395418429515.pdf.

Ministry of Information Industry. 2010. "Regulations on the Management of Internet Electronic Bulletin Services: Passed by the Fourth Ministry Affairs Meeting of the Ministry of Information Industry on October 8, 2000." *Chinese Law & Government* 43 (5): 107–11. doi:10.2753/CLG0009-4609430517.

Ministry of Labor and Social Security. 2006. "Research Questions on Our Country's Labor Dispute Resolution System [Woguo Laodong Zhengyi Chuli Zhidu Gaige Wenti Yanjiu]." *China Labor Social Insurance Daily [Zhongguo Laodong Baozhangbao]*, March.

Ministry of Labor and Social Security, and Ministry of Construction. 2003. "Notice on Resolving Migrant Worker Wage Arrear Issues in the Construction Industry [Guanyu Qieshi Jiejue Jianzhu Qiye Tuoqian Nongmingong Gongzi Wenti de Tongzhi]." http://chinalawlib.com/78745521.html.

———. 2004. "Joint Circular on Provisional Methods for Managing Wage Payment to Peasant Workers in the Construction Sector. [Jianshi Lingyu Nongmingong Gongzi Zhifu Guanli Zanxing Banfa]." http://news.xinhuanet.com/zhengfu/200411/10/content_2199744.htm.

Ministry of Labor and Social Security, and State Statistics Bureau Rural Investigation Team. 2002. "The Situation of the Peasant Labor Force and Migrant Population in 2000 [2000 Nian Zhongguo Nongcun Laodongli Jiuye Ji Liudong Zhuangkuan]." September 2. http://www.chinajob.gov.cn/gb/data/2002-09/02/content_3464.htm.

Minzner, Carl F. 2007. "Are Mass Incidents Increasing or Decreasing in China?" *Chinese Law and Politics Blog.* March 31. http://sinolaw.typepad.com/chinese_law_and_politics_/2007/03/are_mass_incide.html.

———. 2009. "Back and Forth From Beijing." *The New York Times.* May 29. http://www.nytimes.com/2009/05/30/opinion/30iht-edminzner.html?_r=1&.

———. 2011. "China's Turn Against Law." *American Journal of Comparative Law* 59 (4): 935–84. doi:10.5131/AJCL.2011.0006.

Montlake, Simon. 2010. "Vietnam Seeks Gains as China Labor Costs Rise." *Reuters*, September 12.

Mooney, Paul. 2006. "How To Deal With NGOs – Part I, China." *Yale Global.* August 1. http://yaleglobal.yale.edu/content/how-deal-ngos-%E2%80%93-part-i-china.

Mulvenon, James C., and Michael Chase. 2002. *You've Got Dissent!: Chinese Dissident Use of the Internet and Beijing's Counter-Strategies.* Santa Monica, CA: RAND, National Security Research Division Center for Asia Pacific Policy.

Murphy, Rachel, ed. 2008. *Labour Migration and Social Development in Contemporary China.* Comparative Development and Policy in Asia Series 2. Abingdon, Oxon; New York: Routledge.

Nang, Leung Pak, and Pun Ngai. 2009. "The Radicalisation of the New Chinese Working Class: A Case Study of Collective Action in the Gemstone Industry." *Third World Quarterly* 30 (3): 551–65. doi:10.1080/01436590902742321.

Nathan, Andrew J. 2003. "Authoritarian Resilience." *Journal of Democracy* 14 (1): 6–17. doi:10.1353/jod.2003.0019.

National Bureau of Statistics. 2000. *China 2000 Population Census*. Beijing: China Statistics Press.

———. 2010a. *China Labor Statistics Yearbook 2010*. Beijing: China Statistics Press.

———. 2010b. "2009 National Migrant Worker Research Monitor Report."

———. 2012a. "China's Total Population and Structural Changes in 2011." January 20. http://www.stats.gov.cn/english/pressrelease/201201/t20120120_72112.html.

———. 2012b. "2011 Survey Monitor Report of China's Migrant Labor Population [2011 Nian Woguo Nongmingong Diaocha Jiance Baogao]."

———. 2013a. *China Labor Statistical Yearbook 2012*. Beijing: China Statistics Press.

———. 2013b. "2012 National Migrant Worker Research Monitor Report."

National Development and Reform Commission, and Ministry of Finance. 2001. "Joint Notice by the National Development and Reform Commission and the Ministry of Finance on Clearing up Assorted Fees Levied on Incoming and Outgoing Migrant Workers [Guojia Jiwei, Caizhengbu Guanyu Qianmian Qingli Zhengdun Waichu He Wailai Wugong Renyuan Shoufei de Tongzhi]." Beijing.

National People's Congress Standing Committee. 1995. *Labor Law of the People's Republic of China*. http://www.lehmanlaw.com/resource-centre/laws-and-regulations/labor/labor-law-of-the-peoples-republic-of-china-1995.html.

———. 2007. "Labor Contract Law of the People's Republic of China." January 1. http://www.lehmanlaw.com/resource-centre/laws-and-regulations/labor/labor-contract-law-of-the-peoples-republic-of-china.html.

"National Trade Union System of Wage Arrears Helps Migrants Recover 2.2 Billion [Quanguo Gonghui Xitong Qian 7 Yue Wei Nongmingong Zhuihui Tuoqian Gongzi 22Yi] 全国工会系统前7月为农民工追回拖欠工资22亿." 2011. *Xinhuanet*. August 17. http://www.fjsen.com/h/2011-08/17/content_5622420.htm.

Nelson, Joan M. 1991. "Organized Labor, Politics, and Labor Market Flexibility in Developing Countries." *The World Bank Research Observer* 6 (1): 37–56. doi:10.1093/wbro/6.1.37.

———. 1994. *Labor Markets in an Era of Adjustment*. Vol. 1. Issue Papers. Washington, DC: The World Bank.

"New Ministry Resolves 'Split' in Labor Market." 2008. *China Daily*, March 14. http://www.china.org.cn/government/NPC_PCC_sessions2008/2008-03/14/content_12567148.htm.

Ngan, Raymond, and Stephen Ma. 2008. "The Relationship of Mobile Telephony to Job Mobility in China's Pearl River Delta." *Knowledge, Technology & Policy* 21 (2): 55–63. doi:10.1007/s12130-008-9046-8.

Ngok, Kinglun. 2008. "The Changes of Chinese Labor Policy and Labor Legislation in the Context of Market Transition." *International Labor and Working-Class History* 73 (01). doi:10.1017/S0147547908000045.   http://www.journals.cambridge.org/abstract_S0147547908000045.

O'Brien, Kevin J. 2006. *Rightful Resistance in Rural China*. Cambridge Studies in Contentious Politics. Cambridge; New York: Cambridge University Press.

———., ed. 2008. *Popular Protest in China*. Harvard Contemporary China Series 15. Cambridge, MA: Harvard University Press.

———. 2011. "Rightful Resistance." *World Politics* 49 (01): 31–55. doi:10.1353/wp.1996.0022.

O'Brien, Kevin J., and Lianjiang Li. 1999. "Selective Policy Implementation in Rural China." *Comparative Politics* 31 (2).

O'Brien, Kevin J., and Lianjiang Li. 2004. "Suing the Local State: Administrative Litigation in Rural China." *The China Journal* 51 (January).

O'Neil, Patrick H., ed. 1998. *Communicating Democracy: The Media and Political Transitions*. Boulder: Lynne Rienner.

Offe, Claus, and John Keane. 1985. *Disorganized Capitalism: Contemporary Transformations of Work and Politics*. Cambridge, MA.: MIT Press.

Opp, Karl-Dieter, and Christiane Gern. 1993. "Dissident Groups, Personal Networks, and Spontaneous Cooperation: The East German Revolution of 1989." *American Sociological Review* 58 (5): 659–80.

Ossa, Maryjane, and Cristina Corduneanu-Huci. 2003. "Running Uphill: Political Opportunity in Nondemocratic Regimes." *Comparative Sociology* 2 (4): 605–29.

"Owed Wages: Unresolved After Five Years, The Difficulties of a Migrant Worker Chasing Back Wages [Yi Tao Xin She Wunian Nan Juekan Kan Nongmingong Taoxin Suqiao Zhe Nan] 讨薪题五年难解开 看农民工讨薪诉求之难." 2006. *Xinhuanet*. November 30. http://news.xinhuanet.com/fortune/2006-11/30/content_5414540.htm.

Pan, Philip. 2002. "When Workers Organize, China's Party-Run Unions Resist." *The Washington Post*, October 15.

"Peasant Migrants Creates Both Opportunity and Challenges for Society [Nongmingong Liudong Wei Shehui Fazhan Dailai Jiyu Yu Tiaozhan]." 2008. *Peasant Daily Online*. September 16. http://www.agri.gov.cn/llzy/t20080916_1133319.htm.

Peerenboom, R. P. 2002. *China's Long March toward Rule of Law*. Cambridge, UK; New York: Cambridge University Press.

Peng, Yinni. 2008. "Internet Use of Migrant Workers in the Pearl River Delta." *Knowledge, Technology & Policy* 21 (2): 47–54. doi:10.1007/s12130-008-9048-6.

Perry, Elizabeth J. 1994. *Shanghai on Strike: The Politics of Chinese Labor*. Stanford, CA: Stanford Univ. Press.

Perry, Elizabeth J., ed. 1996. *Putting Class in Its Place: Worker Identities in East Asia*. China Research Monograph 48. Berkeley, CA: Institute of East Asian Studies, University of California, Berkeley.

———. 1997. *Proletarian Power: Shanghai in the Cultural Revolution*. Transitions--Asia and Asian America. Boulder, CO: Westview Press.

Perry, Elizabeth J., and Merle Goldman, ed. 2007. *Grassroots Political Reform in Contemporary China*. Harvard Contemporary China Series 14. Cambridge, MA: Harvard University Press.

Pfaff, S. 1996. "Collective Identity and Informal Groups in Revolutionary Mobilization: East Germany in 1989." *Social Forces* 75 (1): 91–117. doi:10.1093/sf/75.1.91.

Piante, Catherine, and Haibo Zhu. 1995. "Life and Death of Zhejiang Village: A Law unto Itself – Peking's Zhejiang Cun." *China Perspectives*, December, 12–15.

Pierson, David. 2010. "China's Factory Workers Finding, and Flexing, Their Muscle." *Los Angeles Times*. June 2. http://articles.latimes.com/2010/jun/02/business/la-fi-china-labor-20100602.

Pike, Fredrick B., and Thomas Stricht. 1974. *The New Corporatism: Social-Political Structures in the Iberian World*. Notre Dame: University of Notre Dame.

Ping, Jianhua. 2008. "How Is Action Possible? (Xingdong Heyi Keneng?)." Sun Yat-sen University.

Piven, Frances Fox, and Richard A. Cloward. 1979. *Poor People's Movements Why They Succeed, How They Fail*. New York: Vintage books. http://ezproxy.library.arizona.edu/login?url=http://lib.myilibrary.com?id=435475.

Pomfret, James. 2009. "Ethnic Tensions Spark Brawl at China Factory-Report." *Reuters*, June 26. http://www.reuters.com/article/latestCrisis/idUSHKG364598.

Poole, Teresa. 1996. "Fatal Fire Reveals Price of China's Boom." *The Independent*. January 3. http://www.independent.co.uk/news/world/fatal-fire-reveals-price-of-chinas-boom-1322170.html.

Posusney, Marsha Pripstein. 1997. *Labor and the State in Egypt: Workers, Unions, and Economic Restructuring*. New York: Columbia University Press.

PRC Ministry of Labor and Social Security, and Ministry of Construction. 2004. "Interim Measures on Wage Payments to Migrant Workers in the Construction Industry, [Jianshi Lingyu Nongmingong Gongzi Zhifu Guanli Zanxing Banfa]." http://news.xinhuanet.com/zhengfu/2004-11/10/content_2199744.htm.

"'Premier Wen Helps Recover My Payment!'" 2003. *People's Daily Online*. November 12. http://english.peopledaily.com.cn/200311/12/eng20031112_128143.shtml.

"Protests in China: The Cauldron Boils." 2005. *The Economist.* September 29. http://www.economist.com/node/4462719.

Qi, Xingfa. 2008. "Migrant Worker Party Recruitment and Employment Recruitment - Issues, Significance and Methods [Nongmingong Rujia Yu Nongmingong Jiudi Rujia—Wenti,Jianyi Yu Lujing]." *Theory and Reform*, no. 2.

Qiu, Quanlin. 2009. "Police Criticized for Targeting Migrants." *China Daily.* December 10. http://www.chinadaily.com.cn/cndy/2009-12/10/content_9151287.htm.

Quan, He. 2007. *Jiangsu Provincial Migrant Worker Research Report [Jiangsusheng Nongmingong Diaoyan Baogao].* Nanjing: Nanjing University Press.

"Recent Worker Actions in China." 2010. *Congressional-Executive Commission on China.* July 2. http://www.cecc.gov/publications/commission-analysis/recent-worker-actions-in-china.

"Requesting Salary Rebuffed: A Nanjing Migrant Worker Has Hand Cut Off [Taoxin Bucheng: Nanjing Yi Nongmingongshou Bei Kanduan]." 2008. *Liberation Daily*, January 1. http://www.jfdaily.com/gb/jfxww/xinwen/node1221/node39948/userobject1ai1920306.html.

Research Office of the Ningxia Central Party Committee Party and Government Office. 2006. "Attaching a High Degree of Importance to the Question of Youth Farmers Joining the Party [Gaodu ZhongshiQingnian Nongmingong Rudang Wenti]." *Communist Party Member Journal.*

Research Office of the State Council. 2006. *Research Report on Chinese Migrant Workers.* Beijing: Yanshi Press.

"Review of China's Internet Regulations." *Rights and Democracy.* http://www.ichrdd.ca/english/commdoc/publications/ globalization/legislationInternetChinaEng.pdf.

Richburg, Keith. 2009. "China's 'Netizens' Holding Officials Accountable." *The Washington Post.* November 9. http://www.washingtonpost.com/wp-dyn/content/article/2009/11/08/AR2009110818166.html.

———. 2011. "In China, Microblogging Sites Become Free-Speech Platform." *The Washington Post.* March 27. http://www.washingtonpost.com/world/in-china-microblogging-sites-become-free-speech-platform/2011/03/22/AFcsxlkB_story.html.

Riskin, Carl, Renwei Zhao, and Shi Li, ed. 2001. *China's Retreat from Equality: Income Distribution and Economic Transition.* Asia and the Pacific. Armonk, N.Y: M.E. Sharpe.

Ru, Xin, Xueyi Lu, and Peilin Li. 2007. *The China Society Yearbook: China's Social Development: Analysis and Forecast.* Leiden: Brill.

"Rumormonger Held over South China Toy Factory Brawl." 2009. *Xinhuanet.* June 29. http://news.xinhuanet.com/english/2009-06/29/content_11616274.htm.

Sarat, Austin, and Stuart A.Scheingold. 2006. *Cause Lawyers and Social Movements.* Stanford, CA: Stanford Law and Politics.

Schmitter, Philippe. 1974. "Still the Century of Corporatism?" In *The New Corporatism: Social-Political Structures in the Iberian World.* South Bend: University of Notre Dame Press.

Schock, Kurt. 2005. *Unarmed Insurrections: People Power Movements in Nondemocracies.* Social Movements, Protest, and Contention v. 22. Minneapolis: University of Minnesota Press.

Scott, James C. 1976. *The Moral Economy of the Peasant: Rebellion and Subsistence in Southeast Asia.* New Haven: Yale University Press.

———. 1985. *Weapons of the Weak: Everyday Forms of Peasant Resistance.* New Haven: Yale University Press.

Shambaugh, David L. 2009. *China's Communist Party: Atrophy and Adaptation.* Washington, DC; Berkeley: Woodrow Wilson Center Press; University of California Press.

Shen, Tan. 1998. "At the Pearl River Delta: The Relations of Women Migrants to Foreign Invested Enterprises and Local Government." In *Annual Meeting of the American Sociological Association.* San Francisco.

Shen, Wei. 2013. "Preparing for China's 'Urban Billion'—Policy Implications and Potential for International Cooperation." *Environmental Practice* 15 (03): 323–38. doi:10.1017/S1466046613000367.

Shi, Fayong, and Yongshun Cai. 2006. "Disaggregating the State: Networks and Collective Resistance in Shanghai." *The China Quarterly* 186 (July): 314. doi:10.1017/S0305741006000178.

Shi, Jiangtao. 2004. "Labour Shortage Bites in the South." *South China Morning Post.* September 9. http://www.scmp.com/article/469656/labour-shortage-bites-south.

Shino, Yuasa. 2007. "AFP: Technology Puts Myanmar Protests in International Eye." *Agence France Presse.* September 25. http://www.google.com/hostednews/afp/article/ALeqM5iJSm8iV7-nOVXRByJScIcrS9CsNA.

Shirky, Clay. 2011. "The Political Power of Social Media: Technology, the Public Sphere, and Political Change." *Foreign Affairs* 90 (1). http://www.foreignaffairs.com/articles/67038/clay-shirky/the-political-power-of-social-media.

Shirouzu, Norihiko. 2010. "Transmission-Factory Strike Shuts down Honda's Chinese Plants." *The Wall Street Journal*, May 27.

Sichuan Migrant Worker Legal Aid Station. 2011. "Research Report on the Shifting of Legal Attorney Fees in Labor Dispute Cases [Laodong Zhengyi Anjian Zhong Lushifei Zhuanyi Zhifu Diaocha Baogao]. Sichuan.

Simon, Karla W. 2013. *Civil Society in China: The Legal Framework from Ancient Times to the New Reform Era.* Oxford; New York: Oxford University Press.

Solinger, Dorothy J. 1999. *Contesting Citizenship in Urban China: Peasant Migrants, the State, and the Logic of the Market.* Studies of the East Asian Institute, Columbia University. Berkeley: University of California Press.

———. 2001. "Why We Cannot Count the 'Unemployed.'" *The China Quarterly* 167 (November). doi:10.1017/S0009443901000377. http://www.journals.cambridge.org/abstract_S0009443901000377.

Spring Wind Labor Dispute Service. 2008. *Worker Protection Handbook [Laodongzhe Weiquan Shouci].* Shenzhen: Spring Wind Labor Dispute Service Office.

Standing Committee of the 10th National People's Congress. 2007. *Law of the People's Republic of China on Mediation and Arbitration of Labor Disputes.* http://tradeinservices.mofcom.gov.cn/en/b/2007-12-29/27880.shtml.

Standing Committee of the National People's Congress. 1999. *Law of the People's Republic of China on Donation for Public Welfare Undertakings.* http://www.asianlii.org/cn/legis/cen/laws/lotprocodfpwu688/.

———. 2012. *Decision of the Standing Committee of the National People's Congress on Amending the Labor Contract Law of the People's Republic of China [Quanguo Renmin Daibiao Dahui Changwu Weiyuanhui Guanyu Xiugai Zhongguo Renmin Laodong Hetongfa de Jueding].*

Standing Committee of the Shenzhen Municipal People's Congress. 2004. *Regulations of the Shenzhen Municipality on the Wage Payment to Employees.* http://www.eduzhai.net/yingyu/615/763/yingyu_247299.html.

Statistics Buereau of the Municipal Government of Shenzhen. 2008. *Shenzhen Statistics Yearbook 2008.* Beijing: China Statistics Press.

State Council of the People's Republic of China. 1981. *State Council Notice on Strict Control Over Rural Labor Entering Cities to Work and Agricultural Population Becoming Nonagricultural Population.*

———. 1997. *Computer Information Network and Internet Security, Protection and Management Regulations.* http://www.lehmanlaw.com/resource-centre/laws-and-regulations/information-technology/computer-information-network-and-internet-security-protection-and-management-regulations-1997.html.

———. 2003a. *Notice on the Issue of Settling Delinquent Construction Project Costs in the Construction Business. [Guowuyuan Bangongding Guanyu Qieshi Jiejue Jianshe Lingyu Tuoqian Gongcheng Wenti de Tongzhi]* 国务院办公厅关于切实解决建设领域拖欠工程款问题的通知. http://www.gov.cn/xxgk/pub/govpublic/mrlm/200803/t20080328_32340.html.

———. 2003b. *Circular on the Improvement of the Services and Management of Migrant Workers [Guowuyuan Bangongting Guanyu Zuohao Nongmingong Jincheng Wugong Jiuye Guanli He Fuwu Gongzuo de Tongzhe].*

————. 2003c. *Circular on the Protection of the Legal Rights of Migrant Workers [Guowuyu-an Bangongting Guanyu Zuohao Nongmin Jincheng Wugong Jiuye Guanli he Fuwu Gong-zuo de Tongzhi]* 国务院办公厅关于做好农民进城务工就业管理和服务工作的通知. http://202.123.110.5/zwgk/2005-08/12/content_21839.htm.

————. 2004. *Regulations for the Management of Foundations (基金会管理条例).* http://www.chinadevelopmentbrief.com/node/301.

————. 2006. *Some Opinions on Resolving the Problems Faced by Migrant Workers [Guow-uyuan Guanyu Jiejue Nongmingong Wenti de Ruogan Yijian]* 国务院关于解决农民工问题的若干意见. http://www.gov.cn/jrzg/2006-03/27/content_237644.htm.

————. 2014. *Regulations for Registration and Management of Social Organisations.* Accessed February 22. http://www.chinadevelopmentbrief.com/node/298.

Statistical Bureau of the Municipal Government of Nanjing. 2008. *Nanjing Statistical Yearbook 2008.* Nanjing: Nanjing Publishing House.

Statistics Bureau of the Municipal Government of Guangzhou. various years. *Guangzhou Statistical Yearbook.* Beijing: China Statistics Press.

Statistics Bureau of the Municipal Government of Shenzhen. 2008. "Shenzhen Bureau of Statistics—Shenzhen Statistics Yearbook 2008." December 1. http://www.sztj.gov.cn/.

————. 2010. "Shenzhen 2009 National Economy and Social Development Statistics Report [Shenzhenshi 2009 Nian Guomin Jingji He Shehui Fazhan Tongji Gongbao] 深圳市2009年国民经济和社会发展统计公报-深圳市统计局." *Shenzhen Statistics.* April 27. http://www.sztj.gov.cn/xxgk/tjsj/tjgb/201004/t20100427_2061608.htm.

Stockmann, D., and Mary E. Gallagher. 2011. "Remote Control: How the Media Sustain Authoritarian Rule in China." *Comparative Political Studies* 44 (4): 436–67. doi:10.1177/0010414010394773.

Students and Scholars Against Corporate Misbehavior. 2009. "Migrant Workers in the Construction Industry: 21st Century 'Indentured Servants' [Jianzhuye Nongmingong: Nianyi Shijide 'Baoshengong]. SACOM Research Report. Hong Kong: SACOM.

Sun, Liping. 2011. "Social Disorganization is Currently a Serious Challenge [Shehui Shixu shi Dangxia de Yanjun Tiaozhanshi]." *Economic Observer*, February. http://www.21ccom.net/plus/wapview.php?aid=30678.

Sun, Zhengjuan. 2004. "Institutional Transfer and the Study of Peasant Workers' Labor Rights and Interests in the City". Nanjing: Nanjing University, Department of Sociology.

Swider, Sarah C. 2008. "Behind Great Walls: Modes of Employment Among Migrant Construction Workers in China's Informal Labor Market". University of Wisconsin-Madison.

Tai, Zixue. 2006. *The Internet in China Cyberspace and Civil Society.* New York: Routledge.

Tanner, Murray Scot. 2004. "China Rethinks Unrest." *The Washington Quarterly* 27 (3): 137–56. doi:10.1162/016366004323090304.

Tao, Jiang, and Baojuan Sun. "Impact and Constraint of Non-Governmental Organizations (NGOs) on Migrant Workers' Rights and Interests Protection in China [Lun Zhongguo Feizhengfu Zuzhi (NGO) Dui Nongmingong Weiquan de Yingxiang Yu Zhiyue]." *China Development* 8 (2).

Tarrow, Sidney G. 2011. *Power in Movement: Social Movements and Contentious Politics.* Rev. & updated 3rd ed. Cambridge Studies in Comparative Politics. Cambridge; New York: Cambridge University Press.

Taylor, Bill, Kai Chang, and Qi Li. 2003. *Industrial Relations in China.* Cheltenham, UK; Northampton, Mass., USA: E. Elgar Pub.

"The Awkward Strides of Little Bird: Subordinate to the Donghuamen Sub-District Justice [Xiaoxiaoniaode Qugangga: Lishu Donghuamen Sifasuo Quezai Quan Beijing Weiquan] 北京：四区劳动部门回应农民工讨薪." 2005. *People's Daily Online.* December 12. http://lady.people.com.cn/GB/1089/3976690.html.

"The Impact of the Real Name System in University BBS's." 2005. *EastWestNorthSouth.* November 11. http://www.zonaeuropa.com/20051201_1.htm.

The Joint Economic Committee, Congress of the United States, ed. 1992. *China's Economic Dilemmas in the 1990s: The Problems of Reforms, Modernization, and Interdependence.* Studies on Contemporary China. Armonk, NY: M.E. Sharpe.

"The Long March: Surveys and Case Studies of Work Injuries in the Pearl River Delta Region." 2007. China Labor Watch. http://www.chinalaborwatch.org/news/new-281.html.

The Politics and Law Committee of Guangdong Province. 2009. "Research Report on the Issue of 'Professional Citizen Representatives' [Guanyu Guangdongsheng 'Zhiye Gongmin Dailiren' Wenti de Diaoyan Baogao]." Government Research Report. Guangdong.

Thompson, E. P. 1964. *The Making of the English Working Class*. New York: Pantheon Books.

Thul, Prak Chan. 2010. "Cambodia Garment Workers Strike, Seek Higher Wages." *Reuters*. September 13. http://www.reuters.com/article/2010/09/13/cambodia-garments-strike-idUSSGE67U09320100913.

Tilly, Charles. 1978. *From Mobilization to Revolution*. New York: Random House.

Tilly, Charles, Louise Tilly, and Richard H Tilly. 1975. *The Rebellious Century, 1830-1930*. Cambridge: Harvard University Press.

Tong, James. 2002. "An Organizational Analysis of the Falun Gong: Structure, Communications, Financing." *The China Quarterly* 171 (September): 636–60. doi:10.1017/S0009443902000402.

"Tong Lihua and His Migrant Worker Legal Aid Workstation [Tong Lihua he Ta Chuangban de Jincheng Wugong Nongmingong Falv Yuanzhu Gongzuozhan] 佟丽华和他创办的进城务工农民法律援助工作站." 2005. *CRI*. May 21. http://gb.cri.cn/1321/2007/05/21/1569@1597310.htm.

"Trade Union Official Says China Is Just One Step Away from the Right to Strike." 2008. *China Labour Bulletin*. June 17. http://www.clb.org.hk/en/node/100263.

"Trade Unions Extend Aid for Migrant Workers in Financial Crisis." 2009. *People's Daily Online*. February 16. http://english.people.com.cn/90001/90776/90882/6593278.html.

Van Ours, Jan C., and Rob F. van de Wijngaert. 1996. "Holdouts and Wage Bargaining in The Netherlands." *Economics Letters* 53 (1): 83–88. doi:10.1016/S0165-1765(96)00884-1.

Walder, Andrew G. 1986. *Communist Neo-Traditionalism: Work and Authority in Chinese Industry*. Berkeley: University of California Press.

Wang, Fei-Ling. 2005. *Organizing through Division and Exclusion China's Hukou System*. Stanford, CA: Stanford University Press.

Wang, Hongqi, and Xuan Gao. 2007. "Painter Demanding Salary Rebuffed, Sets Fire to Factory, Arson Suspect Arrested [Youqigong Taoxin Bucheng Huoshao Changfang Shexian Zonghuo Bei Ju]." *Beijing Times*, July 30.

Wang, Hongyan. 2006. "Improving Basic Rights of Migrant Workers." In *Urban Poverty Reduction Among Migrants*. Beijing: Social Science Academic Press.

Wang, Huazhong. 2011. "Coal mine deaths fall 'but still remain high.'" *China Daily*. February 26. http://www.chinadaily.com.cn/china/2011-02/26/content_12081456.htm.

Wang, Kan. 2009. "Chinese Trade Unions Under Pressure to Guarantee Labor Rights." *International Union Rights Journal* 16 (4).

Wang, Meiyan. 2007. "The Basic Situation of Rural Migrants' Wage Arrears." In *Green Book of Population and Labor*. Beijing: Social Science Academic Press.

Wang, Stephanie. 2009. "Shenzhen Raises Iron Fist to Protests." *Asia Times Online*. December 12. http://www.atimes.com/atimes/China/KL12Ad01.html.

Wang, Zhuoqiong. 2007. "Construction Workers 'Alienated.'" *China Daily*. July 9. http://www.chinadaily.com.cn/china/2007-07/09/content_5421626.htm.

Wasserstrom, Jeffrey N. 1991. *Student Protests in Twentieth-Century China: The View from Shanghai*. Stanford, CA: Stanford University Press.

Wen, Jiabao. 2004. "Report on the Work of the Government Delivered by Premier Wen Jiabao at the Second Session of the Tenth National People's Congress." http://news.xinhuanet.com/english/2004-03/16/content_1368830.htm.

White, Lynn T., ed. 2005. *Legitimacy: Ambiguities of Political Success or Failure in East and Southeast Asia*. Series on Contemporary China vol. 1. Singapore; New Jersey: World Scientific.

Whyte, Martin King. 2010. *Myth of the Social Volcano: Perceptions of Inequality and Distributive Injustice in Contemporary China*. Stanford, CA: Stanford University Press.

"Wife of a Small Factory Owner Stabbed to Death Outside Factory Gates [Xiao Gongchan Laobanniang Changmenkou Bei Tongsi]." 2008. *Nanjing Daily*, January 12.

Wines, Michael. 2011a. "China Creates New Agency to Regulate the Internet." *The New York Times*. May 4. http://www.nytimes.com/2011/05/05/world/asia/05china.html?_r=0.

———. 2011b. "Accounts of Chinese Bloggers on Weibo Suspended, Causing Protests." *The New York Times*. August 26. http://www.nytimes.com/2011/08/27/world/asia/27weibo.html?_r=1&ref=internetcensorship.

Wing Chan, Kam, and Will Buckingham. 2008. "Is China Abolishing the Hukou System?" *The China Quarterly* 195 (September). doi:10.1017/S0305741008000787. http://www.journals.cambridge.org/abstract_S0305741008000787.

Woetzel, Jonathan, Lenny Mendonca, Janamitra Devan, Stefano Negri, Yangmel Hu, Luke Jordan, Xiujun Li, Alexander Maasry, Geoff Tsen, and Flora Yu. 2009. "Preparing for China's Urban Billion." McKinsey Global Institute. http://www.mckinsey.com/insights/urbanization/preparing_for_urban_billion_in_china.

Wong, Edward. 2010. "Chinese Export Centers Face Worker Shortages." *The New York Times*. November 29. http://www.nytimes.com/2010/11/30/world/asia/30china.html?_r=2&.

Woo, Margaret Y. K. 2011. *Contemporary Chinese Justice: Civil Dispute Resolution in China*. Cambridge: Cambridge Univ. Press.

Worker Empowerment. 2007. "Research on the Labour Situation of Migrant Workers in the Construction Sector of Shenzhen." Worker Empowerment Newsletter 1.

Wright, Teresa. 2008. "Student Movements in China and Taiwan." In *Popular Protest in China*, 26–53. Cambridge: Harvard University Press.

Wu, Chen, and Caixia Wu. 2011. "Jet Li's One Foundation Turns into Independent Public Fund-Raising Organization." *Xinhuanet*. January 12. http://news.xinhuanet.com/english2010/china/2011-01/12/c_13687548.htm.

Xi, Jieying. 2007. *The New Generation: Research Report on Current Youth Migrant Workers [Xinshengdai Dangdai Zhongguo Qingnian Nongmingong Yanjiu Baogao]*. Beijing: China Youth Press.

Xiang, Biao. 2005. *Transcending Boundaries: Zhejiangcun: The Story of a Migrant Village in Beijing*. China Studies v. 5. Leiden ; Boston: Brill.

Xie, Chuanjiao. 2009. "Courts to Help Govts Reduce Protests." *China Daily*. June 9. http://www.chinadaily.com.cn/china/2009-06/09/content_8262039.htm.

Xinhua. 2004a. "China to Facilitate Free Flow of Migrant Workers." *China Daily*. April 30. http://www.chinadaily.com.cn/english/doc/2004-04/30/content_327721.htm.

———. 2004b. "Labor Shortage Emerges in Guangdong." *China Daily*. August 8. http://www.chinadaily.com.cn/english/doc/2004-08/08/content_363159.htm.

———. 2006. "Migrant Workers in Risky Industries Must Receive Safety Training." *China.org.cn*. September 30. http://www.china.org.cn/english/GS-e/182817.htm.

———. 2007. "China's Trade Union Reaches out to More Migrant Workers." *Chinagate.com.cn*. March 17. http://chinagate.cn/english/reduction/50450.htm.

———. 2008. "Labor Dispute Turned Violent in Guangdong Toy Factory." *China Daily*. November 26. http://www.chinadaily.com.cn/china/2008-11/26/content_7242413.htm.

———. 2013. "China's Mobile Phone Users Hit 1.22 Billion." *China Daily*. November 21. http://www.chinadaily.com.cn/china/2013-11/21/content_17122259.htm.

Xu, Bo. 2011. "National Bureau of Statistics: 2010 Internal Migrant Labor Population Reaches 242 Million [Tongjiju: 2010 Nian Nei de Nongmingong Zongshu Dai 2.42 Wanren] 统计局：2010年内地农民工总数达2.42亿人." *Xinhuanet*. February 12. http://news.ifeng.com/mainland/detail_2011_02/12/4641191_0.shtml.

Xu, Zhoujun, and Chunwei Zhang. 2008. "Who Pays the Bill for Migrant Workers' Health? [Shui Wei Wailaigong Jiankang Maidan?]." *Southern Weekend*, April.

Yang, Mincong, and Liyuan Yang. 2010. "Investigation of the Scale of Migrant Workers in Contemporary China [Dangdai Zhongguo Nongmingong Liudong Guimo Kaocha]." Beijing: Chinese Academy of Social Sciences. http://www.sociology2010.cass.cn/upload/2010/11/d20101118114842226.pdf.

Yang, Qunhong. 2007. "Boldly Innovating the Management Mode of Migrating Party Members Among Farmer Workers—The Investigation and Thinking about 'Golden Bridge Project' Carried out in Xinyang, Henan [Dadan Chuangxin Nongmingong Liudong Dangyuan de Guanli Fangshi]." *Zhongzhou Xuekan*.

Young, Jason. 2013. *China's Hukou System: Markets, Migrants and Institutional Change.* Basingstoke, Hampshire: Palgrave Macmillan.

Yu, Jianrong. 2008. "Mass Incidents and the Construction of a Harmonious Society [Quntixing Shijian He Hexie Shehui Jianshe]." http://wenku.baidu.com/view/df8c291f650e52ea551898cb.html.

"Yuandian Worker Service Blog." *Yuandian Worker Service Blog.* http://blog.sina.com.cn/yuandianfuwu.

Zeng, Qinghong. 2011. "Regulate the Right to Economic Strike so as to Create Harmonious Labor Relations." Translated by China Labor News Translations. *China Labor News Translations.* March 7. http://www.clntranslations.org/article/62/strike+law.

Zhan, Shaohua, and Jialing Han. "China's Migrant Labor NGOs: Experiences and Challenges." Chinese Academy of Social Sciences. www.sociology.cass.net.cn.

Zhang, Jianfeng. 2012. "Village in Beijing Suburb Destroyed by Floods." *CCTV.* July 23. http://english.cntv.cn/program/newsupdate/20120723/100141.shtml.

Zhang, Jie. 2011. "Weibo, the Chinese Twitter, Does Not Challenge Communist Party at the Elections." *The Washington Post.* November 28. http://www.washingtonpost.com/blogs/blogpost/post/weibo-the-chinese-twitter-does-not-challenge-communist-party-at-the-elections/2011/11/23/gIQAvn6v4N_blog.html.

Zhang, Junqin. 2007. "Debate over the Pros and Cons of Citizens' Agents." Translated by Chinese Labor News Translations. *Outlook*, October 30.

Zhang, Li. 2001. *Strangers in the City: Reconfigurations of Space, Power, and Social Networks within China's Floating Population.* Stanford, CA: Stanford University Press.

Zhang, Liang. 2002. *The Tiananmen Papers.* New York: Public Affairs.

Zhao, Changbao, and Zhigang Wu. 2007. "An Analysis of the Issue of Migrant Worker Wages [Nongmingong Gongzuo Shouru Wenti Fenxi]." In *Green Book of Population and Labor.* Beijing: Social Science Academic Press.

Zhao, Jianyi, Yean Zhou, and Zifeng Song. 2007. "An Assessment of Labor Rights in China's Transition Period [Zhongguo Zhuanxing Shiqi Laodongquan de Pinggu He Baozhang]." Unirule Institute.

Zhao, Xiaojian. 2004. "Migrant Worker Shortage A Warning of Social Inequality." *Caijing.* December 27. http://english.caijing.com.cn/2004-12-27/110029880.html.

Zheng, Guihong. 2003. "84 Days and Nights in Guangzhou." *China.org.cn.* July 8. http://www.china.org.cn/english/2003/Jul/69295.htm.

Zhong, Zhangbao, and Li Fei. 2008. "NGOs and Rural Migrants Social Support [Feizhengfu Zuzhi Yu Nongmingong Shehui Zhiche]." *Social Work*, no. 9: 41–44.

Zhou, Changhe. 2007. "Shenzhen Migrant Worker Incinerates Himself in Front of Employer After Requesting Wages [Shenzhen yi Dagong Nanzi wei Tao Gongzi Zai Laoban Mianqian Zifen]." *Yunan Daily Online.* November 30. http://www.yndaily.com/htmls/20071130/news_96_240002.html.

Zhou, Xueguang. 1993. "Unorganized Interests and Collective Action in Communist China." *American Sociological Review* 58 (1): 54. doi:10.2307/2096218.

Zhou, Yan, and Xu Bai. 2008. "3 Decades On, China's Migrants Still 'Outside Looking in.'" *Xinhuanet.* December 8. http://news.xinhuanet.com/english/2008-12/08/content_10472326.htm.

Zhou, Zhenghua, and Ziqian Liu. 2010. "Avid Young Reader of Mao Zedong's Poetry from the Post-1980s Generation Leads the Honda Strike [Shudu Mao Zedong Shici de 80 Hou Qingnian Lingdao Bentian Gongren Bagong] 熟读毛泽东诗词的80后青年领导本田工人罢工." *China News Weekly [Zhongguo Xinwen Zhoukan] 中国新闻周刊*, June 2.

Zi, Xuan. 2007. "My experience [Wode Jingli]." *Fellow Worker [Tongxin Gongyou].*

Zuo, Jiping, and Robert D. Benford. 1995. "Mobilization Processes and the 1989 Chinese Democracy Movement." *The Sociological Quarterly* 36 (1): 131–56. doi:10.1111/j.1533-8525.1995.tb02324.x.

Index

ACFTU (All China Federation of Trade Unions), 2, 24, 62, 71–72, 77–79, 178, 183, 186
activists. *See* labor activists
age, 18, 19, 44, 89, 100, 102, 103, 109; and internet usage, 146
All China Federation of Trade Unions. *See* ACFTU
arbitration, 2, 12, 21n1, 23, 31, 42–43, 61, 83, 87, 115, 121, 164
authoritarianism, 3, 7–9, 137
authoritarian states, 3, 8, 10, 14, 53, 73, 94, 123, 138, 152, 177, 183

Bangladesh, 2
behavioral diffusion, 138, 141, 148, 152
Beijing, 2, 16, 17–18, 24, 38, 41, 48, 81, 87, 94–95, 113, 141, 150–151, 164, 166
Beijing Migrant Worker Legal Aid Workstation, 158, 164, 173, 174
Bellin, Eva, 88, 90

Cambodia, 2, 179–180
CCP, 76–77, 156, 184–186
cell phones, 47, 135, 137, 138, 139, 139–140, 141, 147, 149, 151, 152, 170
Changzhou, 18, 86, 105, 122, 128–129, 130, 131–132
Chan, Anita, 5, 30, 59, 88, 113, 120, 178
China Democratic Workers Party, 144

China Labor Bulletin, 36, 38–39, 47, 89, 112, 143, 182
China Labor News Translations, 77
China Labor Watch, 91, 97n5, 160
China Strikes, 47
citizen representatives, 131, 156, 158, 174
coal mining, 36, 37
collective actions, 10, 12, 39, 47, 48, 119, 129–130, 135, 156, 167, 174
collective bargaining, 75, 76, 79–80, 96, 99
Communist Party of Vietnam (CPV), 178
connections, 4, 9, 14, 16–17, 100, 101–102, 120, 123, 124, 128, 129, 149, 157, 161, 162, 165, 167, 171, 179, 181
construction industry, 18, 28, 33–35, 58, 62, 68, 113, 120, 128, 179
courts, 6–7, 8, 24, 31, 42, 75, 83, 84, 86–87, 91, 96, 121, 122, 130–131, 162, 163, 165
CPV (Communist Party of Vietnam), 178

Dagongzhe, 160, 168, 170
Dickson, Bruce, 184, 186
disputes, 12, 17, 34, 37, 38, 39, 49, 75, 77, 94, 96, 104–105, 134, 135n4, 146, 163, 169
Dongguan, 13, 17, 18, 36–37, 47, 63, 89, 93, 162

economic growth, 8, 48, 58, 58–59, 61, 184

About the author

Jeffrey Becker holds a Ph.D. in political science from the George Washington University, and his research on Chinese politics has appeared in *Comparative Political Studies*, the *Journal of Chinese Political Science,* and edited volumes on Chinese politics. He is currently a China analyst in the CNA Corporation's China Studies Division. Before joining CNA, Dr. Becker was the China Program Director and Research Coordinator for the International Labor Rights Forum, an international nonprofit organization based in Washington, D.C.